D0847749

Other Books by
Mark Ribowsky

Praise for *The Big Life of Little Richard*

"We had the great pleasure of performing with Little Richard. He opened the door for Elvis Presley, James Brown, Chuck Berry, and all the greats that came thereafter. This is a must-read for music lovers."

—**Dr. Otis Williams**, founding member of The Temptations

"Little Richard kicked open the doors to a new world of wonder for everyone from Dylan to Hendrix to Led Zeppelin to Prince—to everything we now take for granted when we think of the most extraordinary music of the late 20th century. Mark Ribowsky tells the whole tutti-frutti story in a-wop-bop-a-loo-bop style."

—**Mick Wall**, bestselling author of *When Giants Walked the Earth: A Biography of Led Zeppelin*

"Ribowsky rips it up with raucous prose in this affectionate biography of Little Richard.... Richard, Ribowsky astutely writes, combined gospel with the grittiness of blues and then amped it up with his fiery piano playing and singing. This entertaining, fast-paced biography will thrill fans of Little Richard and early rock and roll."

—*Publishers Weekly*

"Ribowsky cuts through the gossip and mythologizing and delivers a welcome clear-eyed assessment of the larger-than-life character who boasted he was 'King of the Blues—and the Queen, too!'"

—*Goldmine Magazine*

**Praise for *Dreams to Remember: Otis Redding,
Stax Records, and the Transformation of Southern Soul***

"Subtly passionate... What Mark Ribowsky has done here is to describe someone who was, not divine, but as godlike as a human can be."

—*Wall Street Journal*

"A fascinating tale of the artist and his musical era."

—*Washington Post*

"Evokes the fire of Redding and his Memphis label, Stax Records, the cradle of Southern soul.... Ribowsky tells the story with nonstop energy, while always probing for the larger social and musical pictures. He vividly evokes locales...as well as the Stax sound and Redding's art...his insight-fulness and storytelling gift trump all."

—*New York Times Book Review*

"Ribowsky provides colorful descriptions of Macon's cultural history, including how Redding drew considerable inspiration from its other famous son, Little Richard.... Ribowsky—a veteran chronicler of musical and athletic heroes—also combines thorough descriptions of Redding's songs, and global audiences' growing appreciation for soul, with the social changes of the 1960s."

—*Chicago Tribune*

**Praise for *Signed, Sealed, Delivered:
The Soulful Journey of Stevie Wonder***

"Ribowksy's exploration of Wonder's music is first-rate."

—*Publishers Weekly*

"A fluid and lively read, critical and celebratory."

—*Time Out*

Praise for *The Supremes: A Saga of Motown Dreams, Success and Betrayal*

"A powerful biography."

—*Midwest Book Review*

"A dishy, insider look at Berry Gordy's making of the Supremes.... Ribowsky nicely intersperses some hindsight reflections by the main players.... In this engaging, vivacious account, Ribowksy energetically and thoroughly underscores the Supremes' significance as one of the first crossover successes."

—*Publishers Weekly*

"[Ribowsky] unearths the incredible, real-life drama of Motown's biggest female stars...An extensively researched history of one of the most successful female musical groups of all time."

—*African American Family Magazine*

"A narrative so vivid that you would believe [Ribowsky] was there to witness it firsthand.... Ribowsky succeeds in constructing a definitive account of the group from its humble and seedy origins to its anticlimactic demise."

—*Elmore Magazine*

Praise for *Hank: The Short Life and Long Country Road of Hank Williams*

"A timely biography...Ribowsky has taken on a truly harrowing life...[and] spends a significant amount of time on the music."

—*New York Times Book Review*

"A compassionate yet clear-eyed study of the iconic country star.... It's to [Ribowsky's] credit that he gets as close to Williams as any writer could."

—*Washington Post*

"A new biography that exhumes the strange case of the poet and the peckerwood...[and] offers a feast of juicy anecdotes and sharp analysis that should satisfy devotees and attract newcomers to the fold."

—*Wall Street Journal*

Black Moses

Black Moses

The Hot-Buttered Life
and Soul of
Issac Hayes

Mark Ribowsky

PERMUTED
PRESS

A PERMUTED PRESS BOOK

Black Moses:
The Hot-Buttered Life and Soul of Issac Hayes
©2022 by Mark Ribowsky
All Rights Reserved

ISBN: 978-1-64293-886-9
ISBN (eBook): 978-1-64293-887-6

Cover art by Tiffani Shea
Cover photo by Anthony Barboza/Getty Images
Interior design and composition by Greg Johnson, Textbook Perfect

PERMUTED
PRESS
Permuted Press, LLC
New York • Nashville
permutedpress.com

Published in the United States of America
1 2 3 4 5 6 7 8 9 10

Contents

Introduction:
A Renegade Mentality

"I love women. I'm a romantic. A natural romantic. And I'm very honest with my music. It shows vulnerability, a lot of sensitivity, and that's what women like. They like to see a man show his vulnerabilities. And they like to be seduced. I call it 'eargasms.' Guys would come up to me with his wife and three kids, and he'd point to the kids and say to me, 'Mr. Hayes, this is all your fault.' Guys would say, 'Hey, I ain't got to do nothin' to get a woman, all I gotta do is put you on the stereo.' Listen, James [Brown] may have been the 'Godfather of Soul,' but I was really the godfather of the country."

—ISAAC HAYES, 1973

This work came to mind and to life as the reaction to a personal bugaboo—the amnesia within the post-millennial generation about where its music came from, misplacing the beating heart that unleashed soul music, and transporting it to the feverish tandem rise of modern hip-hop and rap. Authenticity aside, to those of us who were young when it all began, current soul is the type of interchangeable, disposable idiom that creates a new king of the realm seemingly each week. To be sure, back when soul was new and fresh, it seemed timeless. It was a given that the lions who roared the loudest could last as long as their talent and cachet carried them. And none seemed to be more leonine than Isaac Hayes, the guy who put the words "soul man" into the cultural lexicon five-and-a-half decades ago and had the stones—and the earned status—to cast himself as "Black Moses." Hayes grabbed soul by the heart and below, putting into it all the bold elements that would factor into rap and hip hop yet never seemed to reach too high. Wherever he reached was just right.

As a chronicler of pop culture figures, including the incomparable Otis Redding, at whose 1965 session Hayes made his entry as a Stax Records fill-in piano player, the chronicle of Black Moses in his time took a while for me to get to. It shouldn't have. But Hayes in his post-Moses days was something of a lost soul man. As if with an audible sigh, in 2019, Vanderbilt professor Emily Lordi authored an article in the *New Yorker*, "How Isaac Hayes Changed Soul Music," noting that "Hayes' legacy remains elusive. Even now, over a decade after the singer's death, there is still no biography written of him. Younger fans might remember him chiefly as the voice of Chef on *South Park*, while older ones might picture Hayes in his prime as the voice of the hypermasculine *Shaft*, or the sultry Casanova who seduced fans with songs about heartache and fathered fourteen children [actually eleven, four outside of marriage]." As the professor acknowledged, "There was more to Hayes than humor and sex."

Hayes, who was a professor only of the art of the heart of soul, once self-defined: "I had a renegade mentality. I always dared to go where other people said: 'You can't go there.' But at one [point] I looked around and all I was hearing was me, and people trying to be me. And I started to worry about it." A less direct, but just as significant hominy of his went: "If you enjoy the fragrance of a rose, you must accept the thorns which it bears."

That was his way of saying that the life of a soul man—*the* Soul Man—wasn't as easy to live as it was to write songs about. Hayes's only literary efforts were two culinary books, one of which was called *Cooking with Heart and Soul*, and several kids' books. So there was room for a biography, framed by the mighty winds of his times, documenting how he was both influenced by and molded to their literal, aural, and visual identities, though one might expect this story to be written by someone, well, darker than a white, Jewish fellow from a suburb of New York who grew up listening to '60s Top 40 radio. But like all great musical powerhouses, Hayes had a wallop of a multi-racial punch, and for a wide audience, he provided enlightened lessons that made it possible for anyone with a soul to dig.

Indeed, this reality traces Hayes's art and life, and why its formative phase primordially had to take place at Stax, the legendarily maverick Memphis record label for which he co-wrote and co-produced Sam & Dave's immortal 1966 rendition of "Soul Man," the protagonist of which was really Hayes, who could brag perhaps better than anyone else: "I learned how to love before I could eat." That was just one of his obsessions, good lovin' running neck and neck with self-improvement and inclusion, which is why the line in "Soul Man" most have misunderstood—"I was educated at Woodstock"—was *not* an eerie premonition of Yasgur's farm three years later but rather a reference to a segregated school in Jim Crow-era Memphis. Hayes, who dropped out of school but returned and graduated at twenty, foresaw Black youth at those desks. Because when Sam Moore famously shouted "Play it, Steve!" to the white guitarist Steve Cropper on "Soul Man," it was the command of a new order, one that James Brown would soon after unveil with "Say it Loud—I'm Black and I'm Proud!" and that Hayes would forever define when he sang of "this cat Shaft" being the best thing a man could be in 1971—a "bad mutha."

AN IMPORTANT SUBTEXT of this book is the inverted logic that Isaac Hayes made Stax but Stax bankrupted him. The white-owned yet Black-guided soul label rose from dirt to pay dirt on the music of many soul men, but in the end it was two men, Hayes and the company's vice-president and scoutmaster Al Bell, around whom the era rose and fell, though their talent no doubt blinded them to the over-ambition and mismanagement that left them both bankrupt and Bell charged with fraud. In 1973, Hayes was the top act in all of showbiz, and Stax was the second-largest Black label behind Motown; a year later, the company went under in a blaze of mind-numbing fecklessness. Within a few years, the historical landmark that is the old theater with the big "STAX" and "Souls-ville USA" lettering was sold for exactly one dollar, then razed. Allegorically, it was a fittingly cruel end, but for over a decade, Stax was the beehive and the bramble bush of soul men everywhere. And, of them all, Hayes was the most arduously famous, a remarkably dedicated soul man—and a *real* "bad mutha."

Hayes first hit the scene composing pop/soul/funk fit for the mid-'60s, then in the next decade he *was* soul, outfitting himself in what he determined was the funkiest of "black" wares—dashikis, robes, tunics, and chain-link vests. Stax drummer Willie Hall once noted that "Isaac was just cool as shit." And he was until the day he died in 2008, at sixty-five, while riding an exercise bike in his Memphis mansion, killed by a second stroke, but in his open coffin still the picture of cool. After all, coolness was his way of transmuting Blackness. The symbols are all over his legacy. When he went solo as a singer in 1969, his second album, *Hot Buttered Soul*, the first album by a Black artist to go double Platinum, situated him on the cover from the top down, the shaved top of his head above aviator shades, not yet famous for his array of solid gold chains around a bare chest framed by mink boas and gold pants, or sometimes almost nothing at all. Because when he needed to make a statement about himself, it was what he had inside his head that made him so hot and bothered.

In his head was where he foresaw a whole new Blackness, first in the frenetic rhythms of Sam & Dave, then his own, which fruited all that mattered about John Shaft, who was cool for his amorality, the transplanting into Black skin of a sardonic white detective. Shaft was the type of man who could say his only love was his mother and that only his woman understood him, yet during the movie nonchalantly banged two other women; one white, one Black. His turf was Harlem, but he lived in a spacious flat in cool, white Greenwich Village. "Can you dig it?" he asked. And the women of the chorale naughtily replied, "We can dig it."

This was a *very* high hurdle for any composer in 1971, which is why it took until 2014 for the *Shaft* album to be honored by the Library of Congress as "culturally, historically, or aesthetically significant." Because it might have failed miserably. After all, *Shaft* is a pretty awful movie. But Hayes made the character seem, if not exactly plausible, at least too cool to care that he really *was* a private dick. Hayes was able to do this by making white-penis-envy a tool of Black attitude. As the British critic Barney Hoskyns noted, "the black superstar" had become "a symbol of almost mythological sexuality, reaching a kind of apotheosis with the mass worship of Isaac Hayes." Suddenly, cool anti-heroes stoked the Blaxploitation movie trend, moving coolness to the forefront of the culture. And Hayes, a lifetime member of the NAACP, knew the reality that this evolution could only have been primed in the arts.

ALTHOUGH SOME THROUGH the years wrote more into him than there was—one critic imparting that his work "telegraphed a militant black nationalism"—there was nothing "militant" in the *Stax* songbook or Hayes's later, more individually rooted, music. Some of his later compositions, "Out of the Ghetto" in 1977 and "If We Ever Needed Peace" the following year, were disco love songs set in the ghetto, the first about trying to help a "foxy lady" out of the ghetto, and the second a plea that "the sunlight of peace has got to shine through." Both were cosmic miles behind the gritty textures of Elvis's "In the Ghetto." Yet Hayes was translucently ideological for erecting a sort of sexual politics in pop music, and one had to be prepared to listen to his songs all the way through to bravely enter his world. His range was such that he could have performed a set consisting of "Hyperbolicsyllabicsesquedalymistic," "Do Your Thing," "Theme From Shaft," and "Chocolate Salty Balls (P.S. I Love You)," and make them all compatible with each other and him. No one could ever be as cool on stage, not even Miles Davis who shared a gig with him in Philadelphia's Spectrum in 1970, a once-in-a-lifetime concert at only $6.50 a ticket! Ah, 1970.

More generally, Hayes broke molds in ways The Beatles had. There were only four titles on the ground-shaking *Hot Buttered Soul*, including two pop faves turned inside out to reveal their soul, but those four songs ran forty-five minutes and twenty-four seconds, with all the atmospheric swirl of assured bravado and doubt. He was a visionary who could be called a renegade even though his work was correctly called "beautifully executed lounge music." As with *Shaft*, Hayes made his rhythms into a sex organ, every note as if out of a blaring or whimpering horn or a tickling piano and organ, the *wok-a-woka* feedback of an electric guitar and *shish-shish* repetition of a hi-hat cymbal, elements that would form the meridians in soul, funk, and the more impure creature of disco.

One critic posited that Hayes was "a student of Ellington and Gershwin [who] got his biggest kicks from using all the tonal colors in an orchestral palette to paint vivid pictures of the human conditions." Another called him a "race man cut from conventional cloth." His voice was untrained and needed not be otherwise. It was a natural sex machine, a writhing, grinding come-on, rarely rising above a whisper. The message was heard in his near-nineteen-minute renovation of Jimmy Webb's "By the Time I Get to Phoenix" on *Hot Buttered Soul*. He also threw in fifteen minutes of rap, making himself heard that the root of the guy's flight from a lover in the song was the woman's fault, a familiar cover for Hayes until he turned to some self-critique on the astonishing 1972 album *Black Moses*, the themes in which were a kind of self-therapy for the failure of his then-second of four marriages. The nine-and-a-half-minute mega-portmanteau "Hyperbolicsyllabicsesquedalymistic" on *Hot Buttered Soul* was meant not as a soul freak flag but a sly indictment of he and his soul brothers' street-corner jive. Few heard it as such; they only heard the acoustics of soul, because no one could miss that.

AN ORPHANED CHILD of the Jim Crow South, Hayes was surely a restless figure of rugged Black individualism at a time when one was deeply needed, as music was starting to bathe common causes. The *Shaft* franchise made millions in profits, sold in large part by Hayes' musical score in the original that won him an Oscar, the first by a Black composer, two Grammys, and bred unending attempts by other soul producers to recreate it. At the Oscars, his Black psychedelic commandeering of the stage as dancers swiveled and thrust their body parts to the *Shaft* tune left mouths agape. He was that dramatic, that potent, that daring, and directors naturally cast him in movies in the Blaxploitation genre he had helped construct, including Duccio Tessari's *Three Tough Guys* and Jonathan Kaplan's *Truck Turner*.

It was not on the screen but on the turntable that he will always live. The same year as *Shaft*, he emerged with Biblical self-anointment on the *Black Moses* double album, which one may reasonably call the Magna Carta of soul, based on the oldest war of mankind—the tangled battleground of love. To Hayes, of course, that ground was shaped by men like him; as he would put it, "Black men could finally stand up and be men because here's Black Moses; he's the epitome of Black masculinity. Chains that once represented bondage and slavery now can be a sign of power and strength and sexuality and virility." Political power, then, meant sexual power.

Few Black entertainers but him could have used slavery as a counterpoint. And if you needed help understanding that: his overriding message in song wasn't political, it was that life's real metaphor was under the sheets—the lesson being, *Brutha, love is redemption, and don't you forget it.*

The difference between Hayes and his amalgams was the difference between Barry White's "What Am I Gonna Do with You" and Hayes's "What are you gonna do with *me?*" or between George Clinton's "We need the funk, we gotta have that funk" and Hayes's "You got that funk if you just listen." Sometimes, it came wrapped in semiotics only he understood, for example, in "Hyperbolicsyllabicsesquedalymistic":

> *My gastronomical stupensity is really satisfied when you're loving me.*

No, it wasn't English, but it was soul, the language of the street, the mind, in his native tongue. Though it was deeply influential as a genesis of rapping—and would be sung as a duet between Hayes and Public Enemy's scabrous Chuck D on the much later, 1995 album *Branded*, his last one—what rap had become wasn't how he'd foreseen it. And *stupensity* was not his to have for long. In human terms, he was a beloved man but a terrible husband and aberrant father. His spending was emphatically excessive and self-destructive. We can stipulate that Hayes knew he had deep flaws and was so confused by them that they deepened his music. As one critic noted, Hayes "mix[ed] discordantly cruel emotions" and suggested that all people should "listen once a year" to *Hot Buttered Soul* because "the next time you need to be saved or hurt, know that Hayes will be there, waiting."

HAYES ONCE SAID of his work, "I don't plan it, I just rap, man. 'Cause if you go over it too many times, it just gets mechanical." At the time, "rap" was not what it is now. It was meant simply to speak or sing as if in normal conversation. Pulling the words from his head, not a music sheet, his message was always to find love among the ruins of life. This was fertile ground for the likes of Gamble and Huff and Barry White as well, not to mention the greatest funk acts of the '70s like P-Funk, Earth, Wind & Fire, the Commodores, Rufus, Rick James, Prince, and even Quentin Tarantino movies. In 1972, at his acme, Hayes was the linchpin of soul, the dominant image of the Wattstax summer festival in Los Angeles, Black music's first mass convocation, on the seventh anniversary of the Watts riots. This, the "Black Woodstock," held in the middle of Richard Nixon's reign weaponizing white racism, was also a feature film and two double albums and the pivotal core of his Black Moses incarnation, when he could only have been described the way his musicians did; echoing Willie Hall's encomium, his guitarist Skip Pitts said that Hayes was "the shit and that's the truth." No musician ever thought he *wasn't*.

But Hayes always lived on the periphery or within a storm, and being the dual essence of Nat Turner, Moses, and John Shaft caused some white and Black music critics to bite at his pretense and ease, these voices calling him a "Sunset Strip African" or "the ultimate degradation of black music." Sadly, Hayes came to wonder if those sorts of imprecations were true, when so many contemporaries took to following his lead rather than making their own waves. His own were so dynamic that in 2017 the *New York Times* noted that "the music that Hayes recorded from 1969 through 1971 has since supplied the hooks, beats and textures for more than 500 songs by other artists," and that parts of his drastic revision of Dionne Warwick's "Walk on By" have been sampled in no less than *eighty-nine* songs. But Hayes himself could not sample a smooth life. He had a lifelong drinking problem, was a serial adulterer, and spent like a hundred drunken sailors. By 1974, he had publicly renounced the id of Black Moses, replacing his license plates with "ISAAC," whom he never could find.

Yet, the Black Moses persona remained his stamp, even as the soul culture never learned who he really was. He cannot be cataloged by the simple laws of nature or any musical format; *especially* rap, the misogyny of which he loathed—he was clearly capable of uttering guttural phrases like "I'm Isaac Hayes, bitch!" or "Lick my dick and balls," but only in his kick-ass movies, not on records. On those, his pleading romanticism is at once separate from postmodern rap, and more blank verse than rap, though we can't even guess how many standard rappers have gone full Black Moses: the shaven head, the shades, the beard, the bling, the strut, and the "gangsta" mode. As Lordi noted, Isaac Hayes's ephemera spills into "hip-hop fashion trends that explode and exploit America's rags-to-riches mythos. We can even hear Hayes in the quieter aesthetic of conceptual artists like Solange and Sampha. These singers seem to have internalized one of Hayes's key lessons, which was...you don't have to raise your voice to call an army. Sometimes you just have to stretch out your arms."

Now, if only they knew *why* their art can do all those things. "The art itself is suffering," Hayes said as he dissected postmodern soul when he was an elder. "These kids don't even know who their predecessors were. They don't know whose shoulders they're standing on." Thus, the crime.

LIKE MR. SHAFT, Mr. Hayes was a complicated man. During his decade of being either too Black or not Black enough, depending on the critic, he wasn't welcome on mainstream TV shows that instead turned to "safer" soul men, most profitably his analog, Barry White. Hayes believed it was because he wore the role of the Black ball-buster he had created for John Shaft. "I looked militant," he said and had "created some turbulence." Perhaps those chains around his neck weren't quite as cathartic as he hoped they'd be; to some, it meant he was, well, uppity. In truth, he was a nonviolent shaman and if Shaft was the "renegade" in him, his other personae—Soul Man, Black Moses—were more the essence of Nat King Cole.

His own shoulders were the broadest in music. But they never could hold up the monstrous debt he laid on them, which by the end of the '70s had cost him his wealth, his mansions in Memphis and LA, his diamond-dotted duds, his gold-and-peacock-blue El Dorado, his Mercedes, his Jaguars, limos, six motorcycles, and nearly his sanity. He isolated for long, troubled periods, bivouacking in semi-seclusion bouncing from LA to Atlanta, even to Spain for a year, then back to Memphis, resurfacing in the '80s to tour with Dionne Warwick and write another Grammy-winning hit, "Deja Vu," for her. He took acting roles, almost all in the mold of the menacing but reassuring character he defined with *Shaft*, signed with big record companies, and released records now and then adapting to the current flow but keeping the faith of soul, proclaiming, "The King is back!"

His range of credits was quite rife, even being named an honorary king of the Ada region of Ghana where he met the woman who would be his fourth and last wife and mother of his last child. But what exalted him again was the new culture of animated, dirty-mouth satire: *South Park*, the fictional town rife with fables seen through the clueless eyes of eight-year-old boys. The character he agreed to voice—Chef, the bulbous, bearded Plato and soul music shaman, the only Black character to have been a regular in the cast—boiled up another comeback, which overlapped with his induction into both the Songwriters and Rock & Roll Halls of Fame. He got a lot out of Chef and a novelty hit of eminent cultural heft, "Chocolate Salty Balls (P.S. I Love You)," referring to Chef's most relished edible. Chef was adorable and amoral. He was, ergo, Isaac Hayes.

But he still didn't have spiritual peace, which he tried to find in the pocket-picking prophesies of Scientology, which had actually made him a king through its combo of missionary work and prose-lytizing in Ghana. But it also dragged him into a contretemps with the controversy-hungry producers of *South Park* who couldn't help turning his Scientology dalliance into an Emmy-winning episode spoofing the cult, which led to a highly embarrassing change of heart by Ike about what was acceptable parody and his quitting after nine seasons, forced to do so by his "church" masters. Chef was last seen being brutally killed then revived as a cyborg hurtled into the distant universe in eternal exile—for Hayes, it was actually a credible allegory of his own fate.

Naturally, upon his death, there was a laying on of hands by the men and women of soul who eulogized him. He was said to have left $12 million, but that would seem as fanciful as the plot of *Shaft*. His hilltop mansion in Memphis was $1.1 million in default, and just like the mansion he had lived in back in the '70s, it was opened to the public in an estate sale; after it was sold, the house mysteriously burned to the ground.

His music, of course, lived on; to date, around 12 million of his records have been sold—the theme from *Shaft* alone being on the million-times-played list—and heard fairly endlessly. But despite him being one of the world's wealthiest Black men in his prime, his son Isaac Hayes III, a music producer and voice actor, still tries to find lost revenue in the dusty Stax account ledgers that might be owed to his father. That bespeaks a larger story, of a Black man who lived high but was like so many of his cohorts, a victim of a soulless industry and his own delusions of success.

And yet the main thrust of the story is more innervating—the soul of the Soul Man and the music that made the white American ethos a reflection of the culture it has spent hundreds of years trying to deny, disenfranchise, even crush. The undercurrent of soul music is that it was in itself a powerful carrier of political and social change. Thus these pages magnify and amplify the magic Hayes wrought inside a studio and on stage, influenced by previous soul men who had not quite found the right timing. One suspects

Hayes knew he had only a limited time to get it all done, which would explain why he tried to do so much, perhaps too much, so soon. And it's why his story looms as tragic as it is triumphant—but only until an Isaac Hayes song happens to play. At that moment, all is triumphant.

1

An African Tradition

When Isaac Lee Hayes, Jr. checked in on August 20, 1942, America was not yet a year into the pith of World War II, in which Black soldiers had to fight with segregated troops, and soul was something only spoken about in church or around the dinner table in prayers for deliverance. His parents, Isaac Lee Hayes Sr. and Eula Wade Hayes, who had married eight years before in Fayette County, Tennessee when they were both just fifteen, needed just such entreaties to the Lord. They lived in Covington for long months under the molten Southern sun, entombed in a near life-less expanse of rolling fields, where Black sharecroppers, as had the slaves they had descended from, worked to exhaustion picking cotton. Isaac Hayes Sr. was better off than most residents there, owning a small farm. As his son would recall years later, "I was born on that farm. There was no doctor, just a midwife. The first thing I remember was that there were about 400 chickens on the farm."

Hayes displayed an early yen for banging on a table like it was a drum and tinkering with the keys of a toy piano. Singing was something he inherited from Eula. "Church," he once said, "was right across the road from the house and my mother. I was told she was one of the best singers around in those parts." He also liked to sing nursery rhymes with his half-sister Willette, born two years before him, and even at three he was a perfectionist, apt to stop the organist when the wrong note sounded, waving his arms "no," and starting all over again. "I had a feel for the dramatic," he once acknowledged, a trait he would never lose.

Isaac Sr. was a common church-going man with little sense of responsibility, and Eula was a small woman with severe mental health issues who needed to be institutionalized in a hospital ward in Hardeman County, Tennessee. There, she suffered a physical and mental breakdown, and on January 17, 1944, with Ike only a year-and-a-half old, died in the hospital of causes unknown, whereupon Ike Sr. apparently saw no reason to stick around for his children. Giving them to Eula's parents, Willie Wade and his wife, Rushia, to raise, Ike Sr. up and left, resettling in Jackson where he began a new life and fatherhood with another woman, making no contact with his original children, not to reconnect with Ike Jr. until 1972, establishing a distant relationship with him for the rest of Ike Sr.'s days until he died in 1980.

In Isaac Jr.'s youth, Jim Crow was everybody's neighbor in the South. In fact, Covington had made some grim news in 1937 when a Black man named Albert Gooden, accused of killing a Tipton County deputy sheriff on the outskirts of town, was taken from the sheriff by a mob shouting, "to hell with the law," then shot thirty times and burned, a crime no one ever paid for. In these parts, men like Isaac Hayes Sr. had to walk with one eye looking behind them. So did Willie, who worked in those cotton fields until Ike was five before deciding things would be better in the big town—Memphis—thirty miles southwest. Times were hard there too, but as Ike would remember decades later, Black families shared a common bond to insulate themselves from Jim Crow.

"The community there worked together to raise the children," he said. "Everyone on the street knew everyone. If I did something wrong, I got a beating from my neighbor. And when I got home I got another. That's the way it was with all the kids, and we stayed out of trouble that way. That was an African tradition that was passed down." Then, when Jim Crow finally began to be legally torn away, he noticed that Black families seemed to lose that collective kinship: "In came integration and it was lost," an ironic reality he would try and rectify through the great unifying umbra of music.

THINGS WERE JUST as hardscrabble in Memphis where Willie sometimes took Ike into the fields to help out. But there was the salve of music. He began school and regularly attended church where he sang and played piano, teaching himself to play sax and flute as well. Oddly, he never heard the blues when he was a toddler. Through most of the '40s, no blues or jazz records were played on the radio in west Tennessee, and the Wades' living room radio by default would play country music like Hank Williams's "Move It On Over," "I'm a Long Gone Daddy," and "My Bucket's Got a Hole In it" or Roy Acuff's "Blue Eyes Crying in the Rain" and "Tennessee Waltz." The break from hillbilly fare came when some of the stations played gospel songs on Sunday morning, which had an impact on the growing young man. It was through gospel that soul music-to-be emerged. The Wades would take Ike to local churches where touring gospel groups stopped as they made their way across the church circuit. One of the longest-surviving of those groups, the Golden Gate Quartet out of Norfolk, Virginia, could also be heard, barely, on some low-powered stations like WIS in Columbia, South Carolina or WBT in Charlotte, North Carolina singing on jubilee roundup tunes like "Hush, Somebody's Calling My Name" and "Golden Gate Gospel Tour," on which they vamped their own chugging train sounds.

Isaac could detect the blues pulse coming through both the church and hillbilly music. One of the regular programs on WBT was hosted by Arthur "Guitar Boogie" Smith and the Crackerjacks, who sang of the heartaches of life and love, themes passed on by plaintive blues guitar legends such as Robert Johnson and updated with five-string bluegrass banjo pickin'. The biggest country star, at least until he drank himself to death, Hank Williams, adopted the distinct high-pitched yodeling style copied from a white street-corner blues man in Macon, Georgia, Emmitt Miller, whose group was the Georgia Crackers.

But for Ike, there were no Black blues men, or Black men of any kind, heard on the radio until '47 when WDIA started up in Memphis. Its owners were white, and mostly played country but also had some rhythm and blues selections, determined by white program directors, thus becoming the first station in the country to even play such a thing. It was a very good idea. WDIA sent out a signal of only 250 watts of power, yet in Memphis, the growing Black population was glued to their radios to hear the sound of blues and jazz and Black-based comedy programs. That led the station, which was dubbed "the mother station of the Negroes," to hire the first Black disk jockey in 1948, newspaper columnist Nat D. Williams, for a show called *Tan Town Jubilee*.

The audience grew so much that it junked white stuff altogether, going all Black, making it the top-rated station in town; WDIA's power increased to a then-ear-splitting 50,000 watts, which fed similar needs for Black music across state lines, especially when the air waves cleared out at night. In 1951, a sharecropper's son, Rufus Thomas, was given a show called *Hoot and Holler*. He had been a student of Nat Williams when the latter taught history at a Memphis high school, and had since become a Black music celebrity, a tent-show blues singer and dancer, who had recorded songs for the Memphis label Sun Records. Thomas would rhythmically chant things on air like "I'm young, I'm loose, I'm full of juice. I got the juice, so what's the use." The Black-oriented format bloomed in '56 when the first Black-owned station, WLOK, began furnishing airtime to other cool jockeys like Dick "Cane" Cole and Hunky Dory. WLOK only ran on 1,000 watts, but for Isaac Hayes it came in loud and clear. It was a revelation to hear voices that sounded like his own. The first time he heard Nat Williams, he said to himself, "Wow, a black man on the radio!"

The result spread the blues to every crevice of Black society, within which the Wades owned what Ike called a "juke joint" downtown, proudly recalling that anybody who walked in the door there could "sing as good as B.B. King, Sonny Boy William-son, Lightnin' Hopkins, Muddy Waters or Howlin' Wolf. They could do that!" As for his own singing, Ike was still harmonizing in church choirs with Willette, but his secondhand family was break-ing apart. Willie's failure to earn enough forced him and Rushia to give up the kids. Willette was sent to one family while Ike went to a friend of the Wades. Then, when Ike was eleven, Willie passed, and Rushia, needing the comfort of family, took back the two kids. The juke-joint was gone, and Rushia was on welfare. They lived in a one-room apartment above a church in a web of poverty. Unable to pay the utility bills, when the sun set, they lived in the dark. Ike chopped down an outhouse for firewood. They begged a neighbor for water. One very cold winter, Willette nearly died from hunger and the flu.

All this had a traumatic impact on Ike, who as an early teen developed a wanderlust, finding space for himself wherever he could, one time, he recalled, "with this guy who was an alcoholic. He got arrested and I didn't have anywhere to stay, so I slept in junk cars at a garage." He often said that all he really wanted back then was "a warm bed to sleep in and a nice square meal and some decent clothes to wear." Memories of those dead-end days never left the recesses of his thoughts, "I didn't have anybody to talk to," he said decades later. "Even now, I get lonely, just thinking about it."

Growing tall and lean, all arms and legs, he was tarantula-like, and had that unforgettable face—gaunt and thin, with a low hair-line, his wide nose spread across it, his eyes hard and staring. He was no bully, but his baleful-looking countenance kept the hoods from messing with him. Already wise beyond his years, Ike wanted to be a doctor, and studied books on biology, boasting decades later, "I can name every bone in your body." But he had already come to see music as his way out of hell.

He had the advantage of knowing what the blues were, having sung with local blues men while picking cotton in the fields, on the street corners, and on back porches in the neighborhood. He also could see downtown the blues singers who had made it, stepping out in their sharp threads and hats, with arm candy hanging on them, smoking Cuban cigars, and slugging rounds of scotch at the bars. If he imagined really hard, he could see himself in those men—if only he could afford clothes, shoes without holes, and maybe indoor plumbing. He also had a restless libido and got a rush at school assemblies from the way the girls reacted to his performing. Some of his schoolmates called him the "Swing Crooner" when he oozed out his songs or when he dropped to his knees like James Brown. As he remembered, "they just freaked...the whole house came down."

What was missing in this planned metamorphosis were the clothes, the connections, the bread. He knew he wouldn't get them if he had to go to school every day. Feeling "humiliated" by his hobo-like existence, after finishing the eighth grade, which he'd had to repeat, Ike dropped out to work various jobs: short-order cook, usher at the Savoy Theater, shoe-shine boy, even going back to the cotton fields. He didn't tell Rushia he had left school, knowing she would hound him to go back, so he floated about most days, seeking any paying job that could buy him a pair of shoes. But wherever he stepped, music stepped with him. Opportunities to sing and play in bands seemed to pop up most anywhere he was, even if they were mostly small time. He was precocious, to be sure, and if he was too young to be taken seriously, he was blessed to be even a small part of an ever-mounting ambit of music—the streets that delivered to America its soul.

2

Give Me Memphis, Tennessee

Next to New Orleans, Memphis was the most bustling corner of the blues-busting, lamp-lit South. Sitting metaphorically across the state from the white country stars' faux-gilded aerie in Nashville, Memphis had been a prime corridor for the "other side" of country; blues men who fled the stifling racial confines of the Delta and headed north up the Mississippi River. In the early 1900s, the action began to run heavy along McLemore and Beale Streets, in shimmying lines of two-story storefronts that ran through downtown. A hub of Black businesses, barbecue shacks, and barber shops, it was the spigot for musicians and singers to create what was the soundtrack of the city.

Here, Black-owned clubs had been wrought by the redoubtable W. C. Handy, the epochal "Father of the Blues" who toured the innards of the South playing the trumpet and ingesting the spirit and mechanics of the blues which he brought to Memphis, where he wrote blues standards such as "The Memphis Blues" and "Beale Street Blues." Handy's songs, he said, came from "Negro roustabouts," or the "primitive southern Negro" who had emphasized "the third and seventh tone of the scale, slurring between major and minor." These notes, christened as the "blues notes," became the model for the three-stanza format; the lyrics making "a statement, repeat[ing] the statement in the second line, and then telling in the third line why the statement was made."

In time, music men were adhering to the format, flocking to McLemore and Beale, including Louis Armstrong. Another was Rufus Thomas, who had made his debut at the Elks Club on Beale and, while on the radio, became a major emcee of talent at the Palace Theater, also on Beale, where winners included B.B. King, Bobby "Blue" Bland, and Johnny Ace. In the 1940s, B.B. and his partner Lucille—his trusty slide guitar, its bluesy riffs fashioned by his hand sliding up and down the neck—settled into a near-permanent gig at the Sixteenth Avenue Grill, while also hosting his own blues radio show on WDIA. The soul train constantly turned with the likes of Albert King, Memphis Minnie, and Rosco Gordon drawing more riders. In the 1950s, the rock 'n' roll amendments of the blues improvised the formulas even more, going eight-to-the-bar and breaking into twelve bars, spicing the soup with sixths and seventh notes, and embellishing the sound with wild vocal swings.

For the teenage Isaac Hayes, the McLemore/Beale corridor—even as it, and the city as a whole, degenerated into a high-crime district—had become a magic carpet. Throughout the '50s, he played one-night stands, cutting his teeth with bands, and sometimes alone on the stage. He fronted a group called the Teen Tones, who stitched a "T" on their red sweaters, competing at several of Rufus Thomas's amateur talent shows at the Palace Theater, taking home a dollar each, which was good for a hot dog and a Coke at the Harlem House diner. According to Hayes, the Teen Tones were enlisted to sing backup at a recording session by a singer with the pseudonym of Johnny Rebel, though no such record seems to exist. He also traveled with an outfit known as the Morning Stars and another called the Ambassadors.

As he entered the 1960s, his natural talent and skills on the alto saxophone were tutored by Lucian Coleman, who had also mentored his older brother, the great Memphis sax man George Coleman, who had played with Louis Armstrong and B.B. King and recorded with the jazz bands of organist Jimmy Smith and pianist Wild Bill Davis. For a time, Ike lived with Lucian, and that connection helped gain him entry, despite being underage, to the clubs he had been hanging around on Beale Street, digging the scene and the dudes flashing on by with their women. At Currie's Club Tropicana, Fred Ford, who blew the sax in numerous bands as Daddy Goodlow, had the doorman wave him in, and he sang Arthur Prysock's ballad "The Very Thought of You," whereupon the club's owner offered him a steady gig there, his first regular paycheck, three nights a week, Monday, Saturday and Sunday.

The house band at Currie's, the Largos, was led by Ben Branch, a sax man himself (and one of the last people Martin Luther King, Jr. would speak with before he was gunned down at the Lorraine Motel in 1968). Branch, who had a music degree from Tennessee State University, had recorded with B.B. King for Bullet Records and had a great deal of pull. He knew virtually every musician in Memphis and, by extension, Ike fell in with some of them on other gigs as a singer or sax player, such as baritone sax man Floyd Newman and his group, and, another member of the Currie band, pianist Sidney Kirk. And Lucian Coleman himself took him out with a band Ike would barely remember, Calvin and the Swing Cats.

"I got with this blues band—Calvin Valentine and the Swing Kings or something like that," he recalled. "We'd leave Memphis every Friday and stay the weekend in Arkansas. We played store porches, man, with people dancin' around, eatin' fish sandwiches, drinkin' wine. And we played out on these plantations where people would come in from the fields on the weekend and they would ball. You had a big barrel of corn liquor, moonshine. You had crap tables in all these places, man. I slept on crap tables sometimes. Some of these places, a cat get shot, man, they just drag him off. Owner says, 'Keep playing!' and you look up and see the ceiling comin' down from the blast of a double barrel. All this for eight bucks a weekend. We played a raw country blues...unheard-of cats that really sing that blues. I paid my dues on all these levels."

He also closed a circle he had left open when one of his guidance counselors at Manassas High, seeing all the time he had missed, came by Rushia Wade's home. Rushia damn near got a rolling pin to use on Ike's head when she learned of his constant truancy, and Ike spoke of his humiliation as the reason for it, saying that he couldn't bear looking like a scarecrow in school. Rushia, taking pity, said she would drop off some used clothing for him to wear if he returned to class. There was also some talk that if he could get his diploma, his talent might well win him a music scholarship. Already eighteen and street-wise, the thought of sitting at a desk in a room of younger kids over the next two years seemed ludicrous. But he did—in truth, Rushia all but ordered him to do it, something he would be thanking her for when he threw her a hundredth birthday party decades later. "I stayed on the right path," he would say. "Guys in the neighborhood would tell me, 'We're proud of you, man.' That choked me up, that they felt I represented them. And that was my grandmother's doing. She kept me on the right path."

He went on learning more about music on that path, taking band classes and starring in the school's talent shows, in which he sang and played on Lucian's sax. There were more bands formed, one named the Missiles. And when Ike graduated in '62 he indeed received scholarship offers from several Black colleges including Jackson State, Tennessee State, Florida A&M, Lane College, and Rust College. But his unrestrained nature messed up that plan. He had knocked up a local girl named Dancy Doretha, and when he graduated he was an incipient father, necessitating that he marry Dancy that year; their daughter Felicia was born later in the year and another daughter, Veronica, was born two years later. Not chucking his own family as his father had, he moved his brood into a flat downtown on Thomas Street and took a job as a meatpacker, slaughtering pigs and cows, until he got into a tiff with his boss over money and quit. Even then, though, the great distraction of his life was music. And if he was barely on the lowest level of Memphis's music scene, his timing was perfect.

IN THE EARLY '60s, as a new, young president bespoke liberal causes, the culture was starting to catch up with the reality that Black art wasn't a mere sidebar. Entrenched, white record industry men—who had kept their profitable Black acts in near servitude (Black artists could only be nominated for Grammy awards, for example, in the isolated field of "R&B")—now could feel the raw power of soul in their pocketbooks. Soul was a multi-faceted creature: from the acrobatic stage explosions of Jackie Wilson and James Brown to the Latin-influenced, stringed songs of the Drifters to the piping hot pop of Chuck Jackson's "I Don't Wanna Cry" to the plaintive torch songs like Garnet Mimms's "Cry Baby" and the Corsairs' indelible confession of doomed adultery, "Smoky Places."

This mounting veneer would be pivotal, easing the panic of American executives as British pop bands bred on Black American music forced the white pop idols of the American industry into the background. Already, most record companies had moved soul to the forefront. The Cameo-Parkway label in Philadelphia produced Chubby Checker's monumental hit "The Twist" in 1960. The first Black-owned label, Berry Gordy's Motown, bit into Detroit's native blues-rock crowd, with an element of social relevancy—for example, Stevie Wonder's 1963 "Fingertips Part 1" was the country's top pop and soul hit during Martin Luther King, Jr.'s March on Washington, and notably, for its anointment of the word, the song came from an album called *The Jazz Soul of Little Stevie*. Out in Chicago, the Impressions were weaving gospel and social cause with "Grow Closer Together," presaging later anthems like "Amen" and "People Get Ready."

Meanwhile, in Memphis, where rock 'n' roll began in Sam Phillips's Sun Studio in the late '40s, an old movie theater at 926 East McLemore, converted into a recording studio and office for the white-owned label called Stax Records, had re-channeled its original country format to promulgate Southern blues, with one of its earliest signings being Rufus Thomas. The unprepossessing, reedy Stax owner, Jim Stewart, would in time appropriate "Soulsville USA" as its trademark, right under the big uppercase "STAX" on the theater's marquee. This legend, incorporated into Wilson Pickett's 1966 number-one hit recorded there, "634-5789 (Soulsville, U.S.A.)," served as a pointed retort to Motown's more generically-aimed "Hitsville USA." Stewart struck pay dirt in 1962 with "Green Onions," the blissfully groovy, organ-driven instrumental by the house band under the name Booker T. & the M.G.'s, named for the young keyboard man Booker T. Jones. It went to number one on the R&B chart, number three on the pop chart, and earned a Grammy nomination.

Each day now, music wannabes streamed to the theater seeking an audition, including Ike Hayes with the Teen Tones and the Ambassadors, only to be rejected, likely because he was too young. Still, he kept moving onward and upward, if only in inches. He did get into a recording session in '62, not at Stax, but not far off, under the aegis of Lincoln Wayne "Chips" Moman, a self-assured fellow who had once played guitar in Johnny Burnette's band in Los Angeles for Liberty Records and then became Jim Stewart's main adjutant at Stax before his ego demanded he go on his own.

As Ike would remember, "It was right after high school, when word got round that there was a new studio opening on Thomas Street, the same part of Memphis I lived in, owned by Chips Moman who had a label called Youngstown and me and my buddy Sidney Kirk rushed down to audition. We got signed for a single. It was a nice little rock 'n' roll song, but it had a big arrangement with full strings and a lot of voices, which must have left an impression on me. It sold about three copies, which was the end of me on that label."

The song, "Laura, We're on Our Last Go-Round," was a toned-down love plea composed by Memphis songwriter Patty Ferguson. Moman produced three sides at the Kirk session, with "Laura" done in the style of Burnette's hillbilly rock blended with drippy string arrangements. Ike was versatile enough to accommodate him, while injecting a personal touch. His vocal was smooth but slightly rough over a two-one drum beat and the big strings. He also did a slow cover of country crooner Merle Travis's "Sweet Temptation" in a languid blues style. The third song was the most interesting, a cover of Ma Rainey's sexually frank 1925 dirty blues classic "See See Rider," originally about a jilted woman plotting to kill the dude who sneaked out on her, though it was rewritten by soul singer Chuck Willis in 1957 and re-titled as "C.C. Rider," a tale of a self-impressed bounder. This was the version Moman went with, directing Ike's Nat Cole-type vocal tuned to a ragtime harmonica.

Chips put out "Rider" late in '62 as the B-side to "Laura," both under Ike's name and with Moman credited as the former's composer, not Rainey. However, Youngstown had limited resources, and the single flopped. Two years later, after the Rainey family threatened to sue him for his "C.C. Rider" credit theft, Moman elected not to include the song when he sold the other two Hayes recordings to Brunswick Records, where they also failed. Ike's "C.C. Rider" was not to be heard again until it was on the copious 2017 Craft Records box set *Isaac Hayes: The Spirit of Memphis*, perhaps the best omnibus of soul ever put together. For Ike, these diversions passed in the night. He was making stops just about any place including a talent show at WDIA, of which an old photo of the contestants shows him as a rather scrawny guy in the back row. Another was a last-minute invitation by bandleader Jeb Stuart, who needed a piano player for a New Year's Eve 1963 show. Sidney Kirk, who got most of those piano gigs, had gone to a hitch in the Air Force and his sister called Ike telling him to take the gig. There was, however, a small problem.

As Ike said, "I was singin' here and there, pickin' up a little change, just barely survivin', so I said, 'Yeah, man.' I realized I can't play no piano. I could play 'Chopsticks' and maybe 'Heart and Soul.'

But I needed the gig. So it was New Year's Eve and we opened up at this white club called the Southern Club. I didn't know how to play piano. The musicians started comin' in and they were asking me, 'Hey, you know "Twist and Shout"? You know "Stand by Me"?' And I just nodded yes. But I said to myself, 'Goddamn, they're gonna find out, they're gonna fire me.'"

He got to the club early to try and figure it out. He began like any other novice pianist, tickling the keys with two fingers then gradually adding more until he could play a limited melody. He was scared, but "when I got there I found out the other cats couldn't play either. It was New Year's and everybody was drunk, and they were horrible! They didn't care that I didn't know how to play. And everybody [in the audience] was drunk, too, and they thought we were groovy! And the club owner, you know, he was feelin' pretty good. He was so impressed he came over and said, 'You boys were real good,' and he hired us for more shows and that was when we improved fast." That opened another plank for him, one more instrument, one more band, and soon after, Floyd Newman had an opening in his band, which had a steady run at the Plantation Inn. Again, he was on the piano, and better at it. Floyd was taken with him, and suggested he write a song or two.

Ike and Floyd were subsequently hired to help backup bandleader Gene "Bowlegs" Miller's band, which had longtime engagements at Beale Street clubs like the Flamingo, the Tropicana, the Paradise, and the Manhattan. The orchestra leader for the talent shows at WDIA, Miller had played with Ma Rainey (and later worked with the great soul singer and social activist Nina Simone and smooth soul man Peabo Bryson), and his band was often recruited for sessions. Two more came in now, to record gospel singer Spencer Wiggins and soul singer James Carr, both for the small Memphis label Goldwax. The sessions were at the FAME Studio in Muscle Shoals, a former tobacco warehouse in the Alabama woods that Atlantic Records' vice-president Jerry Wexler had helped finance in the late '50s with a loan; though owned by white musicians, the studio had become another prime conveyor of hip soul music. Although FAME had its own house band, Miller took not only his band but also Ike and Floyd as well.

The records didn't stir any interest, but, for Ike, being with Floyd was an entrée. He not only was a fixture on the club scene but was a sometime member of the Stax house band. He had played on the label's first album, and first major hit, in 1961, *Last Night!*, a collection of dance-provoking, horn-stabbing instrumentals jammed by the house band and produced by Chips Moman. It was credited to a fictitious group called the Mar-Keys, and Newman had the only verbal lines in the title song, gutty interjections of "Last night" and "Oh! Yeah!" He also shared a writing credit with the three other musicians on the session, getting nice paychecks from it when the song went top-five on the pop and R&B charts.

And now, Floyd got a chance to cut two sides for Stax. He had no original songs and again asked Ike to see what he could do. Ike brainstormed with the band's drummer, Howard Grimes, another Stax sometimes-player who had drummed for Rufus Thomas on some early Stax sessions (and would later be Al Green's drummer). They combined on a song called "Frog Stomp," a rocking instrumental in the "Last Night"/"Green Onions" mode. Newman thought it worked well enough to use it on his Stax audition. "We went in the studio," Ike would recall. "Man, I was scared stiff. Here I am, in this place I've always dreamed of being where all these greats have been." Jim Stewart dug the song, waving into production a chomping single that he released with another instrumental called "Sassy" on the flip side, both under the name of Floyd Newman (who grabbed the sole writing credit for "Frog Stomp," stiffing Ike and Grimes). Both Floyd's sax and Ike's piano were muted on the final mix, but the record bounced, though it had the bad luck of coming out in December 1963 when the usually fertile Christmastime record market was numbed, as was all American society, following the assassination of John F. Kennedy.

15

A young Stax staffer then, Deanie Parker, recalled, "When I first met Isaac, he had two shirts—one red Ban-Lon and one yellow Ban-Lon—a pair of khaki pants, and one pair of shoes that didn't have laces. He lied his way up into Stax, saying he could play this and that. He was learning all the time [but] he had a symphony in his head."

He also had a tenuous place in the Stax house band, mainly because Booker T. Jones was on leave getting a degree in classical music from a college in Indiana. Like all the Stax crew, save for Cropper, who was also a quasi-executive of the company and something of a Stewart pet, his pay was thin: a standard musician's union ten dollars an hour per session, and sessions were still pretty irregular. Ike considered himself a mere fill-in, a temp. But loose as it was, he was now affiliated with Stax. And brutha, even that was something.

3

Soulsville

The theater that stood as Black America's liveliest wire was razed in 1981, leaving what had been a Camelot of soul to waste away into part of the rotting loam of inner-city Memphis. Later given proper due, the theater was rebuilt from scratch in 2009 on the same drab East McLemore Avenue domain, marked for eternity by a remake of the "STAX" marquee, not as a working studio but as the Stax Museum of American Soul Music. Festooned with photographs of the hardy Stax soul men and women who labored there, there is also a mock-up of the magically invested studio duplicated to the exact specifications of the original, the low ceiling and thick walls draped with cables. In the corridors are guitars and drum skins autographed by the artists and plaques telling tales and fables of the Stax grandeur. Yet they tell you around here that the most enticing and crowded attraction is Isaac Hayes's legendary gold El Dorado, which is fixed on a revolving platform.

Deanie Parker, who became a prominent songwriter and producer within these walls and then president of the museum, duly notes that the car "had to be insured by Lloyd's of London" as she points out its refrigerated bar, television set, twenty-four-carat windshield wipers, and custom crafted wheels. But it also has something else, a scent of can-you-dig-this wonder that can summon a visitor on a metaphoric trip, back to the days when the old theater was no less than the aortic pump of soul's cardiovascular system, which is why Jim Stewart, who had made that heartbeat, and Isaac Hayes himself, a new American coda, for decades after Stax's demise, still found his feet taking him here, almost involuntarily, to walk in the glory and stolen memories.

As of this writing, now in his nineties, Jim Stewart could still relate at length his stewardship of Stax, which began in 1959 when it was called Satellite Records. Stewart's main job at the time was as a clerk for Union Planters Bank, a place that would, with the cruelest irony, help cause the downfall of his soul empire. Stewart was a musician then, a fiddler for a country band, the Canyon Cowboys. He could only afford a rumpled studio in Brunswick, Tennessee for acts he signed, the first one a swamp-rock country band, the Vel-Tones (not the soul group he signed years later, the Veltones), and the future rockabilly star Don Willis, a teenager then who recorded one record there, "Boppin' High School Baby."

In '58, needing more capital, Stewart prevailed on his sister, Estelle Stewart Axton, who mortgaged her home to raise $2,500 for Satellite to buy a two-track tape machine. When Chips Moman found the old theater to house the label, Estelle opened a record store next door, the objective being to sell Satellite's records. She also became co-owner of the label and brought her son Packy into the house band, which veered from country to blues given that Stewart had signed Black singers, an obvious move in Memphis. Indeed, Sam Phillips's Sun Studio had helped to hatch rock 'n' roll with arguably the first records of that idiom in the late '40s and early '50s, the very first being Ike Turner's production of Jackie Brenston's "Rocket 88," a raucous jam of a car as metaphor for sex, its rollicking piano an instant rock staple.

Stewart signed Rufus Thomas and his daughter Carla in 1960, the reward for which was an R&B duet hit, "'Cause I Love You," and Carla's soul breakthrough, the yearning ballad "Gee Whiz (Look At His Eyes)" produced by Moman, a top-ten pop and top-five R&B

hit. Stewart soon phased out the country acts and aimed for a Black audience. He renamed Satellite as Stax (from the first two letters of his sister's surnames)—its logo a hand of long black fingers coolly snapping to a beat. However, the musicians were integrated, the house band on the *Last Night!* sessions the seed of the tight-knit unit that hit pay dirt as Booker T. & the M.G.'s, playing on almost every Stax song in the '60s, the mainstays Steve Cropper and drummer Al Jackson, Jr.

The spindly Cropper was palpably the leader, not only with his six-string Fender Telecaster but as co-writer and co-producer of dozens of hits over the decade. Though, to the consternation of the Black session cats, he was also given more money by Stewart, causing a problem down the road. One more alabaster soul man, trumpet man Wayne Jackson, would be a cog with Floyd Newman and two other sax men. Andrew Love (who played on "Frog Stomp") filled in the brass section later to be memorialized as "the Memphis Horns." Stewart's priority was finding musicians as good as Motown's "Funk Brothers." "We had all played in the clubs, where there were no racial barriers, and where you had to be good," said Jackson. The session men saved many a session—"Green Onions" was strictly a studio creation. While waiting for a tardy singer to show up, Cropper and bass player Lewie Steinberg—a Black man with the most non-Black-sounding name ever—riffed the song, though Steinberg was so unimpressed he suggested it be named "Green Onions" because he thought "it stunk." Stewart wasn't gung-ho either, putting it on the Stax sub-label Volt Records until it exploded whereupon Stewart slapped the Stax label on it. Volt, however, would really flourish, when Stewart put Otis Redding on it and left him on it through his soul mission to the uppermost reaches of '60s soul.

THIS IS WHERE Isaac Hayes entered the picture, as a stand-in while Booker T. Jones was away in Indiana studying. At the time, the big play at Stax already was Otis Redding, son of a Macon, Georgia preacher who despised soul music until his son, a huge, muscular, affable man could reach all the way into his soul for the emotions that drove mesmerizing performances and won over Stewart in a 1962 audition by belting "These Arms of Mine," his first Stax single, issued on Volt. It went top twenty in R&B and number eighty-five in pop, setting off a chain of deep-soul classics such as "Pain in My Heart" in '64. Redding's quick rise within Southern soul was a major factor in the seemingly beneficial arrangement Jim Stewart made with big time Atlantic Records in May 1965.

Not merely a distribution deal, which would have been plenty on its own, it gave Atlantic much reign over the lesser label, specifically by its ruling elitists: the goateed and cerebral Turkish-born co-founder and president Ahmet Ertegun and his right-hand man and VP, Jerry Wexler, a bespectacled, beatnik-bearded hipster and former music writer who had coined the term "rhythm and blues." They were peerless hit makers and the contract assured proprietary rights over Stax artists and records; although there was a little clause stuck in that few in Memphis knew what to make of, or to give much attention to, stating that Atlantic owned "without any limitations or restrictions whatever...the entire right, title and interest in...such masters of recordings." What all this gibberish meant was that any and all Stax recordings were to be in their purview, forever. Wexler would later claim, unconvincingly, that even he didn't know such language was even there. But Wexler was there, for a good many recording sessions by top Atlantic acts, including all of Otis's sessions, as was Atlantic's top sound engineer, Tom Dowd, who installed a spanking new, four-output, two-track stereo Ampex recorder in the Stax studio, though Stewart feared this new technology would wreck the monaural sense of oneness of his records and insisted Dowd cut a mono track along with the stereo one. He would keep releasing primarily mono tracks as singles.

Redding's first album would be released on the Atlantic sub-label, Atco Records, and its singles on Volt. All the Stax records would bear a new logo designed by Atlantic: a stack of records with two spinning off the top of the pile. This was fine with Stewart, whose share of royalties on Atlantic records was like finding gold in a bag on the sidewalk. As a fine point, some rock archivists have pinpointed Isaac Hayes's first Stax sessions during the recording of Redding's first two albums, 1964's *Pain in My Heart* and 1965's *The Great Otis Redding Sings Soul Ballads* (which went back on the Volt label), specifically on "Security" for the former and "Come to Me" on the latter. However, the minutely-detailed Atlantic session sheets reveal that Hayes was not on either one, the pianist being a back-in-the-fold Booker T. Jones, and there is no mention of Ike on any Redding session in '64 until a December 17 session for the Barracudas' cutting of "Yank Me (Doodle)" and "Free for All." In '65, Ike does show up on Otis's July 9 session when he cut two versions of "Respect," as well as "A Change is Gonna Come," "I've Been Loving You Too Long," and his barely recognizable free-form cover of The Rolling Stones' "(I Can't Get No) Satisfaction."

Material recorded that day would appear on no less than eleven Redding albums, and Ike had found himself sandwiched between eight other session men including Cropper, Jackson, Booker T. on a second piano, a new bass player, the sawed-off, rubber-faced Donald "Duck" Dunn, who become the second white musician in the group, having replaced Lewie Steinberg when the latter's drinking got out of hand, and a full brass section that included Bowlegs Miller. As Ike recalled of the pressure-packed vibe in the room, while Stewart was the nominal producer and Cropper always added his advice, the cynosure was always "The Big O."

"This cat would go behind a mike and compose as we went," Ike said. "We'd get a groove on, rhythm section and horns too, and he'd stand there and the lyrics and melody would pop outta his mouth. Talk about being scared. But it was a very loose vibe. We worked up the arrangements around the piano and the drums. In those days, we recorded to one track, so everybody had to really get the parts down. There were very few written parts. A lot of room played for spontaneity." And, apparently, he made his presence known on the incredible "Respect," an open demand for good lovin' and an implied one for Black respect (three years before Aretha Franklin immortalized it as a gritty feminist chant), propelling the marching-band-like beat and banging the pulp out of the piano keys in time with the horns.

Unlike most labels, Stax courted a "live" club feel, all the instruments and vocals done at once. Sharpness was sacrificed for the fat slap of notes against the thick walls, voices co-mingling with instruments. Mistakes or flat notes went uncorrected and most records required only a few takes before Stewart was satisfied. At Motown, by contrast, there were multiple tracks and overdubs of background vocals and strings—two components almost never used on a Stax/Volt recording (an incidental fact being that the "hey, hey, hey" backing vocal of "Respect" was by Earl Sims not, as history has often misreported, William Bell or Eddie Floyd)—the singers and small-room rhythm saturating the sound. It was the difference between over- and under-producing, each working for the specific sonorous aims of the companies.

The Stax studio was unwittingly helpful to its purpose. It was a forty-seven-by-twenty-seven room in the back corner of the old theater, thick curtains covering the windows absorbing some of the sharper edges of the sound. The ceiling was high, twenty-five feet, and the floor sloped, which for reasons no one could explain seemed to swirl notes into a tight ball. With everyone playing and the lead vocal in effect, the acoustics were big around the edges, focused in the middle. Not even prearranged notes always held. On Otis's first recording, Cropper asked him what note he wanted the band to play. "Don't matter," he replied, and as time went on the band would often let him begin and simply adapted. Even the tile floor of the bathroom was useful. There was a reverb effect in there that pinged the vocal, and Stewart ran a mike and speaker into the john to catch it.

It was, in every way, live, though Cropper, Stewart, and Dowd would overdub it to sharpen and separate some of the instrumentation and move the vocals forward in the mix. But Al Jackson, Jr. noted in the '60s, "We cut our drums flat. I don't use any muffling or anything, I just play the way I feel, using the butt end of my left stick" for that classic piston-like Stax beat. Motown's records, he went on, were "made from the switchboard and ours are natural. They use echo and we don't. Flat, no echo. The Telefunken mikes are set up to get the natural sound of the drums, and we don't cover it up with conga, bongos, tambourines and all that creative rhythm." Still, Booker T. thought the quality of the music recorded there was not the highest level of technical proficiency. Rather, it was the aural portrait they all could paint and hit a nerve with.

"To be honest," he said, "I don't think our songs and music are great, I think they're mediocre. We work very hard to create a mood. When people listen to Stax records, they're able to feel it. None of us are extraordinary musicians. We concentrate on letting people know how we felt when we were playing." They weren't the only ones to think that way. Up in Detroit, the "other" soul factory had a grudging respect for their Memphis cousins; the Temptation's Otis Williams, for example, even now praises Stax, especially Otis Redding, who covered "My Girl," but the old sense of native superiority is still there.

"Stax definitely had that Southern feel," he said. "When you hear a Stax record, you think 'the South.' I was born in Texarkana, man. I grew up with those blues. But Motown had a much broader appeal. Not that we didn't get into the horns, too. Motown was trying to copy Stax to an extent. Stax laid it on full force, it was very exciting, but it wasn't geared to a crossover market like us." As it was, no one at Stax would have disagreed. Their mission statement would be that they recorded neither Black nor white, only whatever it was that someone in the room thought would work. And sometimes it wasn't an easy sell. It would take another year, until March 1965, for Redding's second album, *The Great Otis Redding Sings Soul Ballads*, to drop in the then-rare stereo format, which Motown was still resisting.

In the meantime, Isaac Hayes was growing as well, again aided by Booker T.'s periodic absence, this time when his girlfriend in Indiana became pregnant and he remained with her until she gave birth. That left Ike in place, and making more mental notes, which Booker T. noticed when he got back in early '65. He remembered Ike then as "a phantom" who would "quietly appear, standing behind me when I played. If I didn't look to the side, I didn't know he was there." In time, Booker T. would be hearing "my triad placements and chord voicing" all over again, on songs produced by the very impressionable newcomer.

BEFORE THAT HAPPENED, however, a lack of steady work at Stax kept Ike clubbing. He formed another band, a trio he loftily called Sir Isaac Hayes and the Doo Dads. On August 1, 1964, the Black columnist Ted Watson (aka the "Midnight Man") of the Black newspaper *The Pittsburgh Courier*, found some space between blurbs about jazz diva Ruth Brown appearing at Chicago's Sutherland Club and Kenny Mitchell, formerly of the Rhythm Kings, at Earl's New Cocktail Lounge and also at a Windy City Club, to note that "Jeb Stuart, the Memphis songster...is appearing at the Thai Club in Memphis along with the Jebettes [and] Sir Isaac Hayes and the Doo Dads." Even as the lowest supporting act, it was a big gig for the Doo Dads, and Ike talked his way into a record date of his own at Stax. He oversaw the production of two sides, "Blue Groove," a slow and sexy blues instrumental with Ike on piano engaging in a call-response groove with bandmates George Hudson's tremulous trumpet line and Ed Skinner's jazzy drum and "The Big Dipper," an up-tempo dance jam, both tunes co-written with Skinner and Hudson. But Stewart sat on both. He still sized Hayes up strictly as a side man, who had made key strides inside the studio. As did Booker T., who saw him as "a man of amazing aptitude, skill, and patience," but also one who "took over my piano seat by looking over my shoulder," despite Booker T.'s renown on the keys. Not offended by giving his seat up to an unknown with talent, Booker T. said, "I started moving to organ when Isaac was around [and] we became a keyboard team."

Jim Stewart went further than that: on the advice of another young hand at Stax, David Porter, a compact, impish man just a year older than Ike and a familiar face at the company since he was hired as the first staff writer in 1961. Before that, he had earned some recognition as a teenager while at Booker T. Washington High School. The ninth of twelve children and the brother of a Pentecostal minister, he was also a performer in sundry groups with names like the Marquettes, sometimes competing against and hanging out with Ike. Alternating gospel and soul singing, he landed gigs with backup chorales and somehow got to record low-grade records under the names Little David and Kenny Cain for labels like Hi, Golden Eagle, and Savoy. He rarely missed talking about singing at an Elvis Presley Christmas party at Graceland.

As with Ike, his eye was on the converted theater on East McLemore. In high school, he got into the same situation as Ike had; getting a girl pregnant, marrying her, and needing to pay for the child, so he took a job at a grocery store across the street from Satellite Records. He was bold enough to march into Chips Moman's office in the theater to offer the sage advice that the company needed to record soul music. Moman was taken with Porter's moxie and offered him a job as a songwriter. Porter split his time between Satellite and classes he took at Le Moyne College, which he soon left to concentrate on music, though he kept a side job selling insurance in case the music thing didn't work out.

Porter was akin to Stewart's version of Smokey Robinson, a young general factotum for a young company: sweeping up, singing, writing, producing, and being a conduit for similar young talent around town. At his audition, when Porter sang what he calls a "terrible" soul version of "The Old Gray Mare," he brought with him a piano-playing friend from Booker T. Washington High, the green Booker T. Jones, who was then added to the company's house band. Porter also had a harmony singer with him, William Bell, who soon became the first male solo act signed by Stax. (Another of his friends was his neighbor, Maurice White, who might have come aboard as well but moved to Chicago, paying dues as a session drummer before moving to LA and creating the priceless soul franchise Earth, Wind & Fire.)

Porter did little to keep the newly rechristened Stax from hitting a rut. Besides "Green Onions" and Redding's string of R&B hits, the label's only other hits were meager ones, essentially Rufus Thomas's "Walking the Dog." The M.G.'s were strapped into copycat songs such as "Jelly Bread" and "Mo' Onions," and keeping alive the Mar-Keys brand, such empty vinyl calories like "The Dribble." Rufus's follow-up efforts included the pale copycat "Somebody Stole My Dog." And Stax even made a mercifully brief diversion to the seemingly aberrant idiom of soul beach music with the Mad Lads's "Surf Jerk." Stewart also gave the longtime blues-hall novelty Gorgeous George a shot, with a triviality called "Biggest Fool in Town." With Stax under pressure from Atlantic's rulers, Jim Stewart knew he had to find an upward path. As it happened, Porter, who still was unsure he wouldn't be better off selling insurance, came to him with a solution: to team up with the other kid who always seemed to be found in the studio—Isaac Hayes—and get deeper into the soul wilderness writing and producing songs. Stewart readily assented, though such a teaming of talent was a first at Stax. However, Ike wasn't sure the chemistry was right.

"The partnership," he once said, "began as serious rivals. The day I came into Stax [Porter] introduced himself, as if I didn't know who he was," meaning that he believed Porter was playing a mind game on him. Ike played his own game, keeping a distance from him, but when Porter sought him out again, he was more humble. "He came straight out and said, 'You play music, I'm pretty much a lyric man, why don't we team up and try something?' We wrote a bunch of shit at first, and then we wrote some tunes for David [as a singer] which didn't do too badly locally."

The songs written for Porter were "Can't See You When I Want To" and "Win You Over," on which Porter's high-pitch voice sounds like Robert Parker's and on the former prefacing Percy Sledge's "When a Man Loves a Woman" with refrains of love's pain: "I'm gonna keep on loving you / Even though I can't see you when I want to, oh oh." This was the A-side of a single, and "Win You Over," a dance riff with Porter imitating James Brown, on the flip. It was released in January 1965, each tune credited to Porter and "Ed Lee," a pseudonym Ike used to elude a previously signed writing agreement with one of the labels he had recorded for. (Although any song written under the Stax roof meant the publishing rights, the real money-making aspect of any record, were taken from the writers and subsumed by East/Memphis Publishing, Jim Stewart's company.)

The record, distributed by Atlantic, stiffed, but "Can't See" would leave a mark. During the '70s, working off Hayes's soul masterpieces, Porter would enter the market again as a singer; he re-cut the song, which was produced by Ike as a six-minute emotional plea coated in strings and female backup singers. In real time, the original tune also established the duo as a prime Stax asset, and they set out to write more songs in the same style—rough and macho but with a breaking heart ready to fight for requital. Indeed, the more bluesy hue was calculated to add more of the fire Redding had put into the label's signature sound but with a more urban-style scrabbling.

They moved further upward and turned in a nifty torch-song called "How Do You Quit (Someone You Love)" for Carla Thomas, which made her reach deep in irrational love, pining for the return of "my baby" who "had another woman in his arms holding her tight." Released in February 1965, backed with Thomas's own "The Puppet," and produced with mounting intensity and clever starts and stops, it hit number thirty-nine, the first pop charting for Hayes/Porter, with Ike now using his real name on the credits. Hayes also wrote the A-side of a Mar-Keys instrumental single in March, "Banana Juice," playing the organ on the song; and, with Porter, a couple of other low-level R&B runners, the Astors' "Candy" and "In the Twilight Zone," the Premiers' "Make It Me," and the Mad Lads' "Patch My Heart."

None of them moved the needle much, but Stewart was satisfied Hayes/Porter could move the notch further. What they needed was a hardcore soul act to carry their work to its fulfillment. And as soul was rising all around, a fuse was lit that would make things hotter at 926 East McLemore.

By mid-'65, Atlantic's Ahmet Ertegun and Jerry Wexler were so blown away by the sound and depth of the Stax songs that they sought to dip their own label's talent in the Memphis shop. At the time, Wexler was discontented that the lavish productions Atlantic footed in New York had lost their edge. Doing their work in a far less distracting atmosphere, the Stax crew always showed up on time and their work was always superb. And so Wexler looked around his stable for acts to take to Memphis, all but bribing Stewart to allow this by agreeing to pay all studio costs and extend to Stax half the publishing rights on any Atlantic song that was cut there, as well as 15 percent of any profits racked up by the songs. For Stewart it was a godsend, or so he believed.

The first outsider was the cobra-like Wilson Pickett, who was called "Wicked" Wilson for a reason beyond music. He wasn't only gruff on his records, but foul mouthed, ungracious, and uncompromising all other times. He was especially perturbed that he had to reduce himself to the rubes in Memphis. Yet, following limited success with his first two records, the first single he cut at Stax was

"In the Midnight Hour," co-written and co-produced by Pickett and Cropper and engineered by Tom Dowd, and one of the greatest soul songs of all time, a sexually torrid riff geared to the Black-created dance the Jerk. It soared to number one in R&B and twenty-one in pop over the summer, was the title of his first album, and was on at least a dozen Pickett and Stax album sets thereafter. The swift success of Pickett combined with the Stax persona led Wexler to try the same thing with another act Atlantic needed to break, Sam & Dave, a veteran pair of spry soul men—Sam Moore was already thirty, Dave Prater twenty-eight. Formed in 1961 in Miami, Moore's birthplace, after singing in club bands for a decade, Prater with his older brother in the gospel group the Sensational Hummingbirds, they had brief stints with two labels before. In '64, Wexler inked them to Atlantic, with Moore serving as the Sam Cooke/Solomon Burke-style soul comforter, Prater more amoral as "the preacher turned hellfire," as Wexler put it.

However, while they meshed on stage, prancing, alternating lead vocals and combining meshed harmonies—the slender, puckish Sam Cooke-lookalike Moore's tenor screaming against the beefier Prater's raw, sandpaper-like baritone—offstage they loathed each other and brooded about having to share space. But they too craved a song and production outlet to get them chart-bound and gladly went to Memphis on a midnight ride with Wexler in the early spring of '65 seeking a magic ring. The start-up involved only Porter, not Hayes, the duo cutting his "A Place Nobody Can Find" and a Porter/Cropper song, "Goodnight Baby," on March 19. Both were cool blues featuring Prater on lead before the tight dual harmonies, but Prater's less melodic voice couldn't push the record, released on Stax, onto the charts.

This sent Wexler looking for a funkier beat, and Stewart's solution was to reconstitute Hayes/Porter. They penned "I Take What I Want" and "Sweet Home," the former co-written with Teenie Hodges, a young guitarist who lurked around the studio and who Porter put into the band for the session to play the main guitar line as a way of getting Teenie some cred. (Hodges would parlay it in the '70s as a mainstay in Al Green's band, during which he co-wrote "Take Me to the River" and "Love and Happiness.") On "I Take What I Want," a hip-shaking blues rocker, Sam & Dave sang mainly as a duet, each breaking for frenetic solos, but still not the formula that would suit them and the record didn't chart. Meanwhile, in early September, Wexler furnished Wilson Pickett with two Hayes/Porter numbers; "It's All Over" and "Danger Zone." Hayes/Porter produced them with Dowd on the board and Ike on the piano. And though Pickett was again a bastard to be with, the results were impressive. "It's All Over" was a deceptively simple gospel blues number, with Ike's piano triplets, driving guitar, horn accents and the pleading female chorale—that part added to the tape from afar, in New York, when Wexler sent Atlantic's girl group Patti LaBelle and the Bluebelles into a studio to sing it. Pickett's style was like a squirt of hot sauce. "Danger Zone" was a polar opposite, a bouncy Otis Redding kind of R&B, ending appropriately with a call of "Lord have mercy!" Both tunes would go out on a single "It's All Over," hitting number four in R&B and fifty-three in pop, soon to be on Pickett's second album, and, over the years, on four more.

For Wexler, this flash of success wasn't yet attained by Sam & Dave, who on October 25 recorded two more Hayes/Porter songs, "You Don't Know Like I Know" and "Blame Me (Don't Blame My Heart)." The first grew from Porter wanting to do a "Motown" record. Ike composed the melody, which he said "came right from the church, from a gospel tune. 'You don't know like I do what the Lord has done for me.' I thought, *Well, if the Lord can make you feel good and do things for you, why can't a woman do the same?*" His palette had heavily echoed horns and vocals and Al Jackson hammering away at his snare with rock-steady fourth notes, causing Sam & Dave's intensity to boil with each line. "Blame Me" was a languid gospel ballad, and again, on both songs they sang mostly in unison, which worked fine given the two men's instinctive way of feeding off each other, one sometimes grabbing the other's words. It was as if they were playing can-you-top-this, even with the orchestra, the horn-drenched fade becoming a wild, ear-shattering cacophony. Still, Hayes and Porter came to believe they needed to isolate each man's voice more. When the single "You Don't Know" ran up the R&B chart to number seven and ninety in pop, it was gratifying. But they knew there was gold waiting for Sam & Dave with another slight adjustment.

ON DECEMBER 20, Wilson Pickett came in and recorded three more tunes there that he, Cropper, and Eddie Floyd collaborated on, including "634-5789 (Soulsville, USA)," a rhythmic romp made sexy by Pickett's growls to "Call on me, baby" for lovin' and huggin'. The Bluebelles again added the chorale in New York and the record went to number one in R&B, thirteen in pop. Clearly, Stax and Atlantic had gotten quite a run out of the ten months of collaborations with Pickett and Sam & Dave, which established the primacy of Southern soul. But there were storm clouds gathering. Pickett was just too damn wicked for the Stax musicians, who detested him and believed the Atlantic incursion was crimping the Stax roster. Stewart, who suspected that Pickett was blitzed on booze and drugs, broke it to Wexler that Pickett was no longer permitted in the studio. Stewart would even use language rare for him, saying in future interviews that his boys called Pickett "that asshole."

After a similar bad-blood incident with Atlantic's Don Covay, who had also recorded hits at Stax such as "See Saw" and "Sookie Sookie" but ragged the musicians endlessly, Stewart had to stand up for his people. Although it would surely cost his company future profits, he banned outside artists from Stax. Wexler had a ready standby, rerouting Pickett, Covay, and a new Atlantic acquisition named Aretha Franklin, whom he was about to take to Memphis, to the FAME Studio in Muscle Shoals. Wexler, who felt to his core that he had been responsible for Stax becoming big league, vowed he would never return to Memphis. (Within a year, he would not return to Muscle Shoals, either, after a tiff with studio boss Rick Hall over Aretha's husband and manager being allowed to run sessions.)

But as self-important as Wexler was, he was still not through with Stax. Needing to keep Sam & Dave on the prime track he had found at Stax, he backed down a bit and made a side deal with Stewart, which also kept Tom Dowd coming to Memphis for Otis Redding's sessions. The problem for Jim Stewart was that Sam & Dave's writers, Hayes and Porter, had been stewing for some time about being treated like poor cousins by Stewart. And as the new year of 1967 beckoned, Jim found himself without them. Although he didn't realize it, getting them back would be the difference between the life and death of soul.

4

OK, What's Next?

Isaac Hayes had, in those providential months, let semi-fame go to his head, and further into his loins. As if living out the misogyny Wilson Pickett boasted of in song, Ike's blatant disregard for Dancy and his two daughters caused him to leave her and run around with a new woman seemingly every waking day. One of them, Emily Ruth Watson, he called his "fiancée" after Dancy filed for a divorce. Booker T. Jones recalled that Ike was "as crazy as I was in those days, we were wearing long coats and boots and couldn't get our fill of women. At the time Isaac was divorcing his first wife, living with his fiancée, and going with about six women that I knew of, and I know he didn't tell me everything. Two of the women he was going with were roommates."

The divorce was settled with Ike ceding parental rights, and he married Emily on November 24, 1965. She would then give birth to three children named Eric, Melanie Mia, and Nicole, not that they made him any better of a husband; he simply went about philandering his way through Memphis, which he only seemed to interrupt to write and produce. Only Porter had a contract with Stax at a paltry fifty dollars a week, of which he gave half to Ike, whose only other income now was from infrequent royalties and the twenty-five bucks he'd be paid for sessions.

It wasn't only that Stewart was cheap; he himself was actually being shorted by Atlantic, whose contractual commitment to cede Stax an unspecified override—some would say kickback—on each record had, contrary to Stewart's expectations, amounted to very little. Even so, he was able to make a major move late in '65 when he hired Alvertis "Al" Bell, a very cool former disc jockey at WLOK where he had called himself "your six-feet-four bundle of joy, 212 pounds of Mrs. Bell's baby boy." Bell, who as a college kid had been a confidant of Martin Luther King, Jr., had worked for a time at Motown and been a freelance record promoter when Stewart made him head of national promotions. Bell rigged up a pipeline of Black radio stations, and Stax artists had to attend his weekly blackboard chalk talks on promotional strategy. He also sent them on the road with the house band and pushed to put the musicians under contract.

Bell's hip lingo and long-legged strut around the office gave the place an air of hip insouciance. Compared to the laconic Stewart, Bell would wrap his arm around people's shoulders, and jib and jab with them. When he became close to the artists, he took his cool into the studio and co-wrote songs with the staff writers. As his authority expanded, some in the Stax silo would call him "God." Bell, who in his eighties would thoroughly reflect on the best and then worst of times at Stax, giggled about his ascension.

"No, I was not God," he said. "As a young man I was a divinity student, got a degree in theology. I studied God. I was not God. Nor was I the coolest guy at Stax. Isaac Hayes was the coolest. Actually, he was the coolest guy I've ever known. It wasn't his look. It was his mind. The brother was a genius. His problem was that he didn't know himself, who he was. He would speak quite movingly of his father leaving him, his mother's death, feeling completely alone, wanting to love and be loved but not knowing how or where to find it. These were things Isaac would later sing about. But back in the sixties, he went from record to record like he did woman to woman, not knowing what or who was next. It worked as far as the music went because Ike put all he had into every song, every session. He was a true genius, he had it in his head and wouldn't settle for less than that. But he was lost outside the studio. He tried to be a loving husband and father but it was like his records—he'd always be thinkin', *Okay, what's next?* He never could just kick back, enjoy the present. With Isaac, today was always [not good enough for] tomorrow."

To Ike, Bell represented something more important than a business and creative asset. Ike, as had a good number of the Black staffers at Stax, had been taken aback by Stewart's largess with Steve Cropper, who stood as the unofficial liege of the studio and was paid a higher salary—"Jim's boy" was Ike's pejorative term for the lanky guitarist. Under the surface, this was an innate Black-white issue, which was partly why Stewart had hired Bell, to make Stax "Blacker;" the irony being that when given the leeway to hire his own staff, Bell brought in a tireless traveling pitchman to radio stations, Eddie Braddock, who was white but swore—and proved—he had free access at any radio station in the country. Stewart's approval of Bell's upward thrust was both out of admiration for his alter ego but also an acknowledgment that his employees needed to be more invested personally in Stax.

But this only went on to a certain point. There even seemed to be a quiet revolt going on at 926 East McLemore. Stewart was being blamed for not developing a new order of Black artists while "outsiders" Wilson Pickett and Sam & Dave became the faces of the label and, to Stax originals like Rufus Washington, moving Hayes and Porter up the ladder came at the expense of what Rufus called "the pioneer people" who were being left behind. Having it up to here with Porter's corpulent ego, Rufus confronted him one day, saying, "You around here bragging all the time. Every time I turn around, I hear you bragging what a helluva songwriter you are. I told him, 'Until you write a hit song for Rufus Thomas, you ain't shit.' And he never did." This was only technically true. While they were not meaningful hits, Hayes/Porter did write for Rufus and, of course, for his daughter Carla; one being "Willy Nilly," another a duet with Carla, "When You Move You Lose." Still, these sort of complaints were legion at Stax. Jerry Wexler, having sniffed a noxious fume of petty jealousies and backbiting at Stax, described it as "Memphis intrigue...imaginary and paranoid."

Al Bell had also brought in Eddie Floyd, who had founded the Detroit-based Falcons in the '50s, as a writer and singer whose 1966 smash "Knock on Wood" was co-written with Steve Cropper. He reserved Hayes/Porter mainly for Sam & Dave, which implemented a strategy employed by Motown in pairing Eddie and Brian Holland with Lamont Dozier as The Supremes and Four Tops' near-exclusive writers/producers. Acts who would have killed to have Hayes/Porter working with them were pretty much out of luck.

Moreover, Stax was beginning to show cracks in the "family" facade. Stewart and Estelle were at odds after her son Packy left Stax to record for Pure Soul Records, and Estelle, behind Jim's back, had the Stax house band back Packy up on some of his sessions, which had Jim steaming when one of the songs became a hit for Pure Soul. Estelle, who had seen her role diminished when Bell arrived, left Jim to deal with the undercurrent of disaffection and to finally take charge of the business. The problem was Stewart was a skinflint, explaining why Porter had kept selling insurance and Ike periodically went back to the meatpacking plant when things got slow. By early '66, they were itchy enough to saunter down the street to see Chips Moman, who had walked on Jim and opened American Sound Studio, to record not only for his own Youngstown label, which had a top-five hit in '65 with The Gentrys' Beatles-esque "Keep on Dancing" and other acts, sometimes including Wilson Pickett.

Moman, who had put together his own house band that included guitarist Reggie Young, bassist Tommy Cogbill, and drummer Gene Chrisman, was clearly trying to dethrone Stax. He made lucrative co-royalty deals with other labels, and the studio spun out other hits like The Box Tops' "Cry Like a Baby," Neil Diamond's "Sweet Caroline," B.J. Thomas's "Raindrops Keep Fallin' on My Head," and Elvis Presley's then-daring "In the Ghetto" and "Suspicious Minds." Now, Hayes and Porter had a proposition for Moman: starting a sub-label with Moman and his business partner, Harold Atkins. Within days the new label, Genie Records, was up and running with Hayes/Porter writing and producing the emotionally wrought "Lady of Stone" and "Sweetie Pie" for crooner Homer Banks.

Stewart on his part had never thought that Hayes and Porter, whose contract at Stax was a handshake agreement, were the backbone of his operation. Neither had he considered the racial implications of treating Cropper as his "boy," extending to Cropper a contract that, unlike the rest of the musicians and writers, gave him a comfortable salary of $125 per week and a share of publishing rights on songs he wrote. Now, pushed by Estelle to take Hayes and Porter back, Stewart had to accede to Estelle, to whom he owed a lot. He gave them the same contract Cropper had: $125 a week along with publishing shares and total authority in the studio. In return, Hayes/Porter agreed to dissolve Genie Records, but only if Stewart agreed to also take in Homer Banks as a Stax staff songwriter. Stewart may have winced having to bend this much, but, looking back, it took Stax to the promised land of soul.

HAYES AND PORTER, for all their symbiosis, were as seemingly mismatched as Sam & Dave. As time passed, they migrated further apart in appearance. While Porter remained elfin and cuddly, Hayes had begun building his thin physique with regular weightlifting and, for effect as a soul man on the make, shaved his head and took to wearing wraparound shades in proto-"gangsta" style. Hayes could look both fly and sinister, but Porter was much more business-oriented and capable of anger. As for Hayes, when he once said, "I confront things," he meant confronting not people but the challenges of music.

He and Porter spent endless hours together in writing sessions down the street at the Lorraine Hotel, where Stewart had a permanent room for his writers to work in isolation. Hayes and Porter worked the artists they wrote for as if they were pieces of a greater puzzle, shaping their vocals to emerging melodies, rehearsing them over and over so that they *could* get it done in one or two live takes when the mikes were turned on. Ike admitted in interviews that he was not much of a lyricist due to the fact that he was "too lazy" to write cohesive verses, thus someone like Porter was a godsend, leaving Ike to concentrate on the art of the blues. He could go about assimilating the ingredients that W. C. Handy had built into the form—the B7 chord, the major 6th note, and Django Reinhardt's three-note jazz chords on the guitar.

Ike's sudden hunches on chord or tempo changes were seldom wrong. Steve Cropper had to chart all the changes so he could draw up a chord sheet, which was itself only temporary. Organized chaos was the best way to describe it, though Al Bell's description of Ike as a genius was shared by all who inhabited Stax. As was Porter, whose lyrical inspirations emanated from lines from philosophy books to comic books, which he would then tailor into poetry. The two of them clearly had the perfect alchemy of a great songwriting team in the rock era on the same turf as Carole King-Gerry Goffin, Doc Pomus-Mort Shuman, Boudleaux and Felice Bryant, and, oh yes, Lennon-McCartney.

Like Sam & Dave, they were working off mutual but different waves, merging synergy and biorhythms. Porter could intuitively read Hayes's bold chord changes, working off melodic surges that only he could hear, as the cue for bolder words and dramatic breaks. Either Hayes or Porter could come up with an entirely fresh chorus or hook just from a few idle words bandied around during the writing process or even in the studio. They both revered pop music as well as soul's growing demands. This was why they could get a rise from Mable John, a soul diva who had left a stint at Motown and was practically ignored until they wrote "Your Good Thing (Is

About to End)," a winking, racy, torch song with horn-and-piano crashing and John's dewy "Yeah...yeah...YEAH" fade out. Backed by another Hayes/Porter song, "It's Catching," "Your Good Thing (Is About to End)" went to number six on the R&B chart early in '66 and was later covered by Lou Rawls and Etta James.

Ike's rhythmic perspectives were clearly the fulcrum of the songs. That he could create those nifty chord changes and winsome dance grooves led Stewart to release Ike's suddenly inviting The Do-Dads records, "Blue Groove" and "The Big Dipper," as a Volt single late in '65; though, with Atlantic refusing to distribute anything from Stax other than the Sam & Dave records, they didn't sell much (and were not heard again until the box sets *The Complete Stax Singles 1959-1969, Volume 5* and *The Spirit of Memphis*). Ike and Porter kept on delivering songs that Stewart shuttled to various Stax acts, including Rufus Thomas. They also wrote and produced material for Stax newbies, such as the spindly Johnnie Taylor's "I Had a Dream" and "I Got to Love Somebody's Baby," both slow, sensuous jams with Ike's bluesy piano flavoring the honking horns. Both were fine songs that got little traction, a far cry from Taylor's coming fame which was sparked by his rendering of Homer Banks's playfully leering "Who's Making Love," a number one R&B hit and number five pop smash. They also did a solid for Al Bell, who brought soul diva Ruby Johnson to Stax; her recording of their "I'll Run Your Hurt Away" went to number thirty-one on the pop chart. And, with Booker T., they co-wrote William Bell's funky "Never Like This Before," which made the R&B top thirty.

Although all were quality records, there was, nonetheless, a sense of diminishing returns to Hayes and Porter's work together, given that Stewart lost money financing their records. Indeed, Porter recalled that not for one day did he believe he and Ike would keep their jobs for long and only Estelle's fealty was preventing it. But how long could *that* last?

HAVING TO ABIDE by Hayes/Porter had also made Sam & Dave skittish. As Sam would relate, "Fifty percent of what they presented to me at Stax I didn't like." Hayes and Porter had to bend to the pair's sometimes unnatural timbres, which, at times, were radically different from what Hayes had asked for. On the dual melodies that Hayes and Porter called "abstract harmony parts," Dave especially would deviate. But, as Porter once said, "what Sam & Dave did often worked and we wouldn't say anything." The next clutch of songs from Hayes/Porter were recorded on March 8, 1966. The first one was "Hold On, I'm Comin'," a tightly wound call and response with a series of repeating lines and tempos. This is when Sam was first given the opening verse, trilling over a riveting horn and drum rhythm, telling a lover to "lean on me when times are bad / When... you're down, in a river of trouble and about to drown." To make it more grabbing, Hayes directed the band to play in a key higher than he normally sang, the sort of thing that Sam admitted, "I would get angry, but that's what I would do"—exactly what Hayes and Porter said about *them*.

As Hayes and Porter told of the song's genesis, during a writing session, the latter had taken a bathroom break that went on for a while. Impatiently, Hayes would remember many times, he called out to Porter to finish up. "Hold on, man, I'm comin'!" was the reply from behind the door. As soon as Porter said it, Hayes knew he had a title, and his brain began growing a song. Stumbling out of the john, "still trying to get his pants up," Hayes noted, Porter was knitting it into a guy's vow of being "your cover." Within fifteen minutes, it had a hook and a clock-steady rhythm track to be biffed with mellow horns and a slower bridge for Sam to hand off the lead for Dave to repeat similar vows then back to Sam's cheeky windup. As always, both the singers and Hayes/Porter made allowances to each other's whims. Sam & Dave rolled with it all the way through the usual wild fade out histrionics. Cropper's guitar diddled some funky sauce, and, getting funkier, Hayes had Booker T. play a tangy tambourine line over Duck Dunn's bass and Al Jackson's hypnotic drum, which was altered only for a closing shuffle.

This was what both Stax and Atlantic were waiting for, a soul confection of elemental soul and rock. Backed by "I Got Everything I Need," co-written by Cropper, Eddie Floyd, and Al Bell, it lit up the charts, almost immediately prompting an instrumental cover by jazz drummer and bandleader Art Blakey. However, in the early run of the record, program directors started fretting that the title could be construed as a reference to "coming" in the sexual sense— not at all Hayes or Porter's intention. As if it really mattered, given that rock 'n' roll itself was originally slang for sex among musicians and had already seen songs about one-eyed cats peepin' in a seafood store, backdoor men, and a woman named Good Golly Miss Molly who sure liked to ball.

Even so, in no position to joust with radio stations, Stewart changed the title to "Hold On, I'm A-Coming," though how that was supposed to change anything was unclear. (Stewart left the original title on album cuts, and soon, it was restored on the single.) By summer, Sam & Dave—and Hayes and Porter—had their first number one R&B hit, and it bled over to number twenty-one on the pop chart. In mid-stream, Atlantic began releasing new batches of the record on its own label. Hayes would overstate a bit, saying later that "Hold On" was "the first one of ours we ever heard played on the radio. That was such a feeling, I wanted to run out into the street and tell people, 'Listen, I wrote that!'" and that "it was the 'Dynamic Duo' that took our writing to a whole 'nother level, and after that, we wrote for pretty much everybody on the label."

The song also garnered a Grammy nomination for Best Rhythm & Blues Group Performance—the Grammys were still half a decade from including soul music in the "regular" categories dominated by white mainstream acts; the Record of the Year being Frank Sinatra's "Strangers in the Night" and Song of the Year being The Beatles' "Michelle." Sam & Dave, Hayes, and Porter got tickets and plane fare to the show in Los Angeles, but lost to Ramsey

Lewis's instrumental "Hold It Right There," an album track that was never released as a single. Still, they had in their pockets Stax's first Grammy nomination. As a result, Stewart allowed Al Bell to take on more responsibility. Stax began to pump up its single and album production and hired graphic artist Ronnie Stoots to design album covers while Bell wrote liner notes for the albums, taking both functions from Atlantic.

Stax was on the move, and though Dave Prater was no happier being reduced by Sam Moore on their records, the act was becoming as popular on the road as Otis Redding. On an important, two-month Stax road show, the Big O would nearly ruin his throat having to keep pace at the same level as the Dynamic Duo on stage—to the point Otis complained to the promoter, "These motherfuckers are killing me" and demanded that Sam & Dave close the first half of the show and he the second.

However, the lack of direct competition lessened his usual fire. Doing an about face, Otis demanded, "Put those motherfuckers right in front of me. They're making me work harder." But he had a condition that would apply when the tour was over:

"Don't you ever book me with Sam & Dave again. I don't ever want to see those motherfuckers again."

By '66, Otis and Sam & Dave were stretching Southern soul's popularity to new levels in the soul war between North and South—a tidy metaphor for the very different paths taken by Motown and Stax, who were joined in mutual profit. By then, Stax had been solidified by Bell's PR, distribution, and managerial moves; there were even rumors that The Beatles would record covers of Stax songs at the old theater. Though while the Fab Four's manager Brian Epstein indeed checked out the studio, Stewart was leery of letting a circus atmosphere becloud the smaller-time "family" vibe there, and it never came close to happening. In Detroit, Berry Gordy had all but made "soul" a euphemism for tony, white-glove music sung by Black performers and geared to stages in Las Vegas casinos and high-society clubs—both of which were still seemingly off-limits to the more hardcore Stax acts.

That same year, James Brown, the self-appointed "Godfather of Soul," stirred the flames (literally, his backup band being the Fabulous Flames) with "Out of Sight," its staccato horn blasts as if an overture of soul fusion; as Brown noted, with it came "all kinds of rhythms at once," prefacing a high-wattage funk era and rock's deeper dive into soul. And Hayes was clearly moving along that locus. Already lightyears ahead of his time, with his shaved head and jet-black aviator shades, Hayes was already lurking as a figure of Black individualism, which for him came with a lack of concern for conventions or wives. He and Porter now dominated the Stax shop, even if their meal ticket Sam & Dave never liked their songs, which at times also got on Stewart's nerves.

"Because we wanted to put some progressive things in there," Ike once said, "Jim'd say, 'Don't put no chords in there.' We'd say, 'But, Jim—' 'No, no, I don't want that.' Naturally, he won. He was the boss."

Yet, in the end, it was Hayes and Porter who would win, by dint of their track record and ways of working with the musicians such that Booker T. could reflect what they wanted in making changes. In general, sessions went without problem. And the last Sam & Dave session of '66 must have been a lulu. It was a giant affair on November 15; they cut no less than twelve songs over a day as Stewart wanted tracks for Sam & Dave's second album, *Double Dynamite*. (The first, released earlier that year, in April, *Hold On, I'm Comin'*, had featured six Hayes/Porter cuts and another written by them and Cropper.) The songs at the session included Hayes/Porter's "When Something Is Wrong with My Baby," "You Got Me Hummin'," "Said I Wasn't Gonna Tell Nobody," "Sweet Pains," and "Use Me." Two others were co-written by Deanie Parker and the Mad Labs' Randle Catron (later to be a Stax vice-president); "Sleep Good Tonight" with Carl Wells and "I Don't Need Nobody (To Tell

Me 'Bout My Baby)" with Booker T. Jones. There was also Jones and Bell's "Just Can't Get Enough," Jones and sax man Gil Caple's "That's the Way It's Gotta Be," Homer Banks's "I Can't Get Enough," and the late blues writer Rudolph Toombs's "Home at Last."

Booker T. recalled that on the romantic torch song "When Something Is Wrong with My Baby," which featured perhaps the most emotional, soul-deep vocals of any Sam & Dave song, he and Ike "switched roles;" Ike moved to organ and Booker to piano, as if knowing instinctively what each should play. Again the band filled in the gaps. Booker T. carried the power of the track with jazzy triplets, saying the song's new wrinkle was "a respite after the first verse, a quieting, where all the elements settled down for the second verse, as if the song's mood and place were established, and now it could relax for this next part.... Sam appeared to take his time. And this is where Duck Dunn played his famous 'falling' bass line, from B-flat to G-flat. With the vocal, Sam sang his heart out, and when the chorus arrived, it came as a relief, and a release, deliverance in the power of love. That feeling was experienced by all involved."

From this bulging cache of remarkable songs and others recorded over the summer, three singles would be issued in the fall and into the new year. "Said I Wasn't Gonna Tell Nobody," backed with the Hayes/Porter/Cropper "If You Got the Loving (I Got the Time)," (recorded in August), was first, the former a funkified country sound with its opening drum and guitar pairing not unlike the Band's "Cripple Creek," and the pair singing in unison with horns muted. The second, "You Got Me Hummin'," backed by "Sleep Good Tonight," had a sharp two-part rock harmony pumped by a Motownish repetition of horns and rhythm and a false stop on the bridge. The third, the aforementioned "When Something Is Wrong with My Baby," backed by "Small Portion of Your Love" (recorded later, on January 13, 1967), simply melted off the vinyl. They all charted well. "Tell Nobody" hit numbers eight in R&B and sixty-four in pop, "Hummin'" hit numbers seven and seventy-seven, and "When Something Is Wrong" hit numbers two and forty-two. When *Double Dynamite* was released on December 10, it also carried added covers of Sam Cooker's "Soothe Me" and James & Bobby Purify's "I'm Your Puppet." It would hit number 7 in R&B, 118 in pop, and "Hold On, I'm Comin'" was still burning, carving a nineteen-week run on the charts.

Flush with success, stars at last who could sell out any house, there was still a bridge to cross: cracking the top twenty on the pop chart. Sam & Dave, to be sure, had kept Stax in the game of new soul, but if soul was going to do more than hover over pop, and rather *become* pop, they needed to transcend all that they and Stax had done. And that task wasn't really theirs; it was all in Hayes and Porter's hands.

5

I'm a Soul Man

1967 was "the Summer of Love" mainly in white rock 'n' roll, a prism established by The Beatles' *Sgt. Pepper's Lonely Hearts Club Band*. Rare was there a soul man involved in these quirky, stoned-out reveries of peace, love-ins, flowers in one's hair and acid in one's veins. The major exceptions being Sly and the Family Stone, Jimi Hendrix, and Otis Redding—the latter two gave mega performances at the kicking open of the rock culture doors at the epochal Monterey Pop Festival in mid-June, during which Hendrix lit his guitar afire before miming sexual release to cool it, and Otis, backed by a Stax touring band, closed with a wham-bam-thank-you-ma'am rendition of full-on soul. Trying to get down with the nearly all-white hipster audience, a slightly perplexed Otis asked, "This is the Love Crowd, right?" The irony was that Otis's volatile performance for the mostly white, well-off crowd at Monterey seemed to spark a brief reversion to hard soul, sending Janis Joplin, for example, on a "cosmic blues" path and Jim Morrison to blow through The Doors' light-my-fire, organ-piped mode and find the blues as in the horns and harmonica backdrop of "Touch Me" and "Roadside Blues." In this perspective, Stax won the game at Monterey, by which time they had just gotten a taste of how much they had affected the world outside, way outside, the borders of Memphis.

In March, egged on by Otis's manager, Phil Walden, Jim Stewart and Al Bell joined British promoter Arthur Howes to package a caravan of Stax's biggest performers for a tour of England, France, and, in a bit of oddball routing, Norway, to see just how far the appeal of Black artists stretched. And stretch it had. England now had a profusion of "fanzines" for soul artists, whereas there was not a single one of those in America; the all-white audiences on the continent knew their songs by heart, singing them as if in harmony. Otis, having already toured England, was the big gun, and he demanded authority, which included gaining entry to the tour for his protégé, non-Stax singer Arthur Conley, for whom Otis had moonlighted to write and produce the smash "Sweet Soul Music."

Conley's inclusion outraged the rest of the troupe, not least of all Sam & Dave, who loomed above the rest of the cast. Carla Thomas, Eddie Floyd, the Mar-Keys, and Booker T. & the M.G.'s., and Hayes and Porter who were also along on the ride—Hayes to conduct the band (and finding as many white women as he could to hook up with) and Porter to coach the singers—were amazed at the reaction to Sam & Dave, who once again riled up Otis's competitive instincts. As Wayne Jackson remembered, "Every night you would feel sorry for Otis. Sam & Dave [took] audiences to heaven and back.... They would have to carry Dave off like he was dead and then they would carry him back like he was resurrected. [And] Otis would be standing there in the corner praying."

From the tapes made of that remarkable tour would come a video (a rare medium then for rockers except for The Beatles) of Otis singing "Fa-Fa-Fa-Fa-Fa-Fa" on the British TV show *Top of the Pops*. The BBC also ran a radio special of Otis's concert in Norway, which was later packaged into a fourteen-song album. Stax would release two live albums of the tour: in July, *The Stax/Volt Revue, Volume One: Live in London* (the last three cuts being Sam & Dave's "I Take What I Want," "When Something Is Wrong With My Baby," and "Hold On, I'm Comin'") and several months later, *The Stax/Volt Revue, Volume Two: Live in Paris* (three Sam &

Dave tracks: "Soothe Me," "You Don't Know Like I Know," and "You Got Me Hummin'"). Neither LP did especially well in America but sold briskly in Europe, where the first album had a fourth Sam & Dave cut.

But the tour wasn't as beatific as it seemed. In fact, it nearly brought Jim Stewart to blows with Otis Redding, which might have cost Stewart his life had it escalated. It happened because Stewart had gone to considerable effort and cost to record the shows, spending a fortune on remote recording equipment. He judged the performances below par, even hectoring Otis about performing *too* live, cutting corners on his songs' intricate melodies. Otis heard him out, then told him to go fuck himself. Stewart's objections to Otis's and other performers' over-the-top renditions, though, did not deter him from releasing the live albums, or live singles of Sam & Dave's "Soothe Me" and "I'm Your Puppet," the first of which went to number 7 in R&B and number 118 in pop, the second to numbers 16 and 56, with "Soothe Me" also making the British pop chart, a first for Sam & Dave. (The 2007 DVD release, *The 1967 Stax/Volt Revue Live in Norway*, included Sam & Dave's "Hold On, I'm Comin'," "You Don't Know Like I Know," "Something Is Wrong with My Baby," and "Soothe Me.")

There were other undercurrents. The musicians' bad vibes with Steve Cropper prompted Stewart to make a concession: demoting Cropper as the Stax A&R man midway through the trip and giving the job to the overly ambitious Al Bell, who was hardly averse to taking the job from Cropper. And once they were all back home, the jealousies involving the perks given Hayes and Porter picked right back up. Porter, in fact, had all but risen to be Jim Stewart's adjutant on business matters. When Homer Banks, who Stewart was persuaded to hire as a songwriter when Hayes and Porter bartered their return to Stax but treated with less than utmost respect, wrote a song with Allen Jones called "Ain't That Loving You (For More Reasons Than One)," Stewart offered him a contract for the song, which was standard procedure for all the writers when he liked a song, but when Banks wanted to delay signing it until he could show the contract to his wife, it fell to Porter to give Banks an ultimatum. "If you don't want to sign, you can leave," he told Banks, meaning he would no longer have a job at the company.

This proved why Stewart clarified, "When David Porter tells you something, it's like I'm telling you." And Banks, who signed quickly and was able to get the song recorded by Johnnie Taylor, was careful to pay continued obeisance to Porter, which led to Porter agreeing to let Banks write another tune with Jones, "I Can't Stand Up for Falling Down," specifically for Sam & Dave, imitating much of the Hayes/Porter formula. Recorded live during the tour of Europe, it was released as the B-side of "Soothe Me." Porter, for his part, gladly accepted the role of Stewart's enforcer, while Ike spent his off-time wondering why Jim Stewart would not let him record a record of his own, on the grounds that his singing voice was "too romantic" for the Stax template. Often, Ike took his case to Al Bell, who initially sat on the request but would in time, almost on a whim, reverse himself, making Stax's biggest killing in the process.

FOR THE TIME being, it was Hayes/Porter, along with Otis Redding, who kept Stax up and running. They seemed impregnable. When Stewart made them salaried employees, they were included with the M.G.'s—Booker T., Cropper, Dunn, and Jackson—into a coterie called the "Big Six," each of whom would share one-sixth of any royalties from Stax hits. Still, the snipping and sniping within Stax continued to erode the myth that the company was somehow a colorblind colony and a respite from the chaos of the world; the most parlous example being the bile of racial poison flowing through the veins of America.

Each year of the '60s saw a race riot detonate from protests over inner-city poverty, unemployment, and lack of educational opportunity as white suburbanites marched in protest against segregation and the ominously mounting war in the paddies of Vietnam—which Ike, then twenty-seven, and most Stax employees avoided because they were too old to be drafted. There was Birmingham in '63, Harlem in '64, Watts in '65, and Chicago in '66. In '67, there were no less than seven conflagrations, the last one in Detroit, each leaving a toll of injury, arrests, and even death. On July 23, the Motor City erupted after cops raided an after-hours bar and arrested eighty people. Within minutes, the city was being engulfed in flames and looting quelled only by the National Guard, which shot it out with some rioters. In all, 4,000 were arrested; forty-three killed.

As Isaac Hayes stared at grainy images on TV of the mayhem and Black men being shot to death by white cops, he began to envision a curative, a way for music to form a counterargument beyond yelling and shooting, one that could idealize the Black identity just as soul music had done as a rider on the civil rights train in the early '60s. He would later say of the riot, "It was said that if you put 'soul' on the door of your business establishment, they wouldn't burn it. The word 'Soul,' it was a galvanizing kind of thing for African Americans, it had an effect of unity, it was said with a lot of pride. So I thought, 'Why not write a tune called 'Soul Man?' And all you had to do was write about your personal experiences, because all African Americans in this country at the time had similar experiences. But [David Porter and I] realized that in addition to being an African American experience, it was a human experience."

For him, the underlying horror was that Blacks were taking out anger with self-defeating violence, one against the other, doing the work of the racists, while having no essential understanding of their own heritage. With integration, he said, "Blacks had been conditioned, wittingly or not, to think, talk, *act* white." Even when he was in a segregated school, he said, "We never had a Black History month.... The overseers of this society purposefully kept it out of [school curricula] and it was done to perpetuate white domination. It wasn't until later [as an adult] that I finally realized that we did have a history beyond the European perspective.... But the back-lash is, now you've got a society of people that have been oppressed for so long, they're striking back. They're killing each other, which is misplaced hostility...For years we were so racially divided, and it's not going to get any better until we really learn about ourselves and other ethnicities learn about us, too. Then there will come some respect.... Now, America has this big eyesore and it has to do something about it because it's spilling over into the burbs."

Years later, he would posit that hip-hop and rap arose from these same interdictions. "A certain administration, which I won't call by name, took the arts out of the schools, and that left the broth-ers out on the street with nothing, so they went to the turntables and started rhyming. Then they had a way to express themselves, and that's the birth of hip-hop." Before those megaphones offered a way out, though, he considered it his responsibility to do something about the problem in his songwriting with a metaphoric song that cut deeply into the maw of Black pride, and seeing those scenes in Detroit, he had its title before a note was written.

Ike and David quickly began fleshing out "Soul Man." But they had only loosely arranged concepts when the session for it was scheduled on August 10. As always with Sam & Dave, it was on a Saturday, when they'd usually get into Memphis, generally inter-ested more in going out on the prowl than into a studio. "They'd want to go out and chase [women]," Ike recalled. "But we would insist that they stay there, because we wanted to get a good feel. And we'd write whole songs in a few minutes. We'd get to throwing ideas around and the songs would be the musical version of it, the two of us goin' back and forth, just stuff we'd make up. That's why we were so good for Sam & Dave, because they liked to have that conversational thing between them."

They recorded two Hayes/Porter numbers that day, "Soul Man" and "May I Baby." When the musicians saw "Soul Man" written on the note sheet, however, they thought it might have been a joke being played on them. Even Sam Moore implored the producers,

"What the hell is a Soul Man?" As Wayne Jackson remembered, "It was the current trick phrase...like, 'What's happening, Soul Man?' And I hate that kind of stuff. I was a full-grown man, and that didn't appeal to me." Jackson and fellow horn man Andrew Love had written a song expressly for Sam & Dave called "The Good Runs the Bad Away," but had no chance. But playing on the "Soul Man" track, he said, "I was embarrassed."

More than a few of the Black musicians felt the same, but it sure felt right when the room grew into the mood Hayes and Porter wanted, which was to turn the expression holy, within, recalled Ike, "a story about one's struggle to rise above his present conditions. It's almost a tune kind of like boasting, 'I'm a soul man.' It's a pride thing." Porter added, "We talked about a way to make that title have some unique and special thing, an idea that talked about education, that talked about humble beginnings, that talked about all of the special things that make you a special man, a soul man."

Hayes and Porter's aim was to bridge funk and pop, as it was becoming clear that soul could not survive as an echo of the blues that the new rock market knew little about. Otis Redding himself had bluntly ventured to say as much in an interview in '67, saying that the "R&B singers who were around ten years ago [have] got to get out of that old bag. Listen to the beat of today and use it on records." He even bandied around the notion of living in mod Europe, the exact path taken a few years later by Jimi Hendrix as he fully rocked away from soul and into acid rock. Seeking to enter the new rock era, Hayes and Porter saw "Soul Man" as a pop signature—white and black—as the subliminal message beneath a boast about success under the sheets.

After much time and trial and error in the studio, the intro had Ike jangling on the piano as Cropper sprinkled in playful blues sixth-notes—"Stretch it out!" Ike had told him, "pull them strings, make it sound like Elmore James." The opening line was Sam's vow of having a truckload of good loving. One can sense in the song a rhyme of self-parody, that a guy who talks the talk often has to walk the walk of shame. The sheen of Black cool rang throughout; most boldly in the harmony hook, "I'm a soul man, I'm a soul man," which separated the stanzas of uneasy self-satisfaction overcoming commonality. Moore's famous appeal—"Play it, Steve!"—happened when Ike called to Sam to "say something" to cement a lag between the lyrics and the melody. Each instrument hit a vibe for the ages. Al Jackson, Jr.'s metronomic snare didn't deviate for even a split-second—Porter calls it a "sanctified" drum line—melding with Duck Dunn's wicked bass. Cropper's slide guitar undertow was ordered up by Ike, telling him to "take it all the way back to the Mississippi steel guitar beginnings." Cropper did, by holding a Zippo cigarette lighter in his left hand that caressed the frets. The song's close— the required Sam & Dave competitive soul stomping—had a real thrust, as if an order to never forget the representin' they had done for two minutes. In the end, it was perfect rock 'n' roll and soul on a clinical level. A match perhaps achieved for the first time.

LITTLE KNOWN NOW is that this was not the first recording titled "Soul Man." Two successful albums by the criminally overlooked jazz pianist Bobby Timmons and his band, *The Soul Man!* and *Soul Food*, were released over a year before on the Prestige label. What's more is there had been a self-titled "soul man" in the early '60s. James McCleese, aka Jimmy Soul, took the name from his church congregation, and his "party" boogie "If You Wanna Be Happy" went to number 1 in pop and sold a million records. And, in truth, based on Timmons's fusions of jazz, blues and funk—and his image on the album cover; bearded, wearing a white A-shirt and pitch-black sunglasses, and braced against a bleak wall—they can be called *more* tuned in to a cool, alienated soul man motif than the funky shouting and piercing strings of Stax and the now-dimming era of Black performers clad in snazzy suits and dancing shoes. In fact, songs using the word "soul" were common in the early '60s, giving the great sax man King Curtis a shot at a single, "Soul Twist,"

with his band the Noble Knights, and Curtis Mayfield's Impressions intoned the canon that "You've got soul and everybody knows that it's all right." Little Eva coined a new dance called the Loco-Motion by singing it had a little bit of rhythm and a lot of soul. These works predated Otis Redding's *Soul Ballads* album. and this niche would also dominate the mid-late-'60s soul record fold in the form of numerous jazzy soul instrumentals, a prominent idiom in the '50s that had led right to "Last Night" and "Green Onions"— like Cliff Nobles's "The Horse," Hugh Masekela's "Grazing in the Grass" and, in a circular irony, Booker T. & the M.G.'s "Hip Hug-Her" (also the title of their 1967 album) and, a year later, "Time Is Tight," cashing in when the Paramount movie studio wanted Booker T. & the M.G.'s to record a soundtrack for the movie *Uptight* and chose the tune from the group's *Soul Limbo* album.

What's more, even as The Beatles' priming of psychedelic rock was just underway, the turf was, inevitably, being populated by a tide of "blue-eyed soul," as Black artists mocked white bands emulating them, some playing that funky music remarkably well, witness the Young Rascals, who already had two massive hits for Atlantic, "Good Lovin'" and "Groovin'," all their records produced by Tom Dowd. There was, too, the Soul Survivors, a Philadelphia group produced by a still-ascendant Kenny Gamble and Leon Huff, who had a massive soul and pop hit that fall, "Expressway to Your Heart." Even non-soul songs could carry a soul tag, such as Neil Young's "Mr. Soul," recorded by his rock group Buffalo Springfield as a bow to Otis Redding, who loosely wore that nickname, and The Yardbirds' "Heart Full of Soul." As well, the Doors tagged the meme in "Soul Kitchen," a song about an L.A. ethnic eatery.

But no other recordings would have half the implicit and explicit reach into the imagination and cathartic association with the Black world that "Soul Man" did. Jim Stewart and Al Bell knew what they had in it and were so picky about tiny details that they had Hayes and Porter cut a second take of the song with the same touches but a lighter, more conventional rock bass line by Duck

54

Dunn than on the first take. Both versions went out as Stax 231 to gauge which sold better, and the original, with the heavier vibe, caught the fever, necessitating its sole run on future distributions, which blasted like greased lightning out of radios and off record players as a proud edict that love and grit were best defined in a blackening white world, loud as a cannon.

The clever hook and flashback verses on "Soul Man," layered with frontal horns and Ike's tinkling jazz runs on the keyboard, took the song on a joy ride up the charts and into the spine of soul music; it was among the most influential three minutes ever recorded, as codified by its selection decades later into the Library of Congress. The chart climb began during the week of September 16 when it hit number forty-six on the R&B chart, sandwiched between King Curtis's incidentally prophetic "Memphis Soul Stew" and The Intruders' "Baby, I'm Lonely," and quietly at number seventy-two on the Hot 100 chart that was topped that week by the countrified pop of Bobbie Gentry's "Ode to Billie Joe." As if by premonition, *Billboard* ran a color picture of Sam & Dave on page one of that issue, reporting that "the Double Dynamite Duo" had "their biggest hit ever with 'Soul Man'," and touted the singers' upcoming tour of Europe.

By the week of October 14, "Soul Man" had eased into the top spot on the R&B chart, bumping Jackie Wilson's "(Your Love Keeps Lifting Me) Higher and Higher." It would stay up there for seven weeks. Only one less than Aretha Franklin's equally immortal cover of "Respect" had earlier in the year, and it was not supplanted until Marvin Gaye's "I Heard It Through the Grapevine" replaced it the week of December 2, meaning that the year's top two soul songs, "Respect" and "Soul Man," traced right to Stax. "Soul Man" also went to number two on the pop chart the week of November 4, kept from the top only by British songbird Lulu's title track from the movie *To Sir, with Love*. Although Wayne Jackson's unchanged verdict even decades later was that "Soul Man" was "another real lesson that corn sells," the song resonated so deeply and significantly that it all but sainted the label, as well as Hayes and Porter, who began getting some major attention in the trade press.

When the record had been released, Porter had made a $20,000 bet with Jim Stewart that the song would hit number one on the pop chart. When it made the top spot on the "lesser" industry rag *Cash Box* pop list, Stewart paid up gladly. It certainly was worth it since the record stayed on the pop chart for nine very lucrative weeks—turning it into the best-selling Stax single up until then—and came in as the nineteenth-highest pop tune for the year; a badge of honor during a time still caught in the lingering backdraft of white pop and white-flavored soul, with the top-ranked mainstream songs that year being Lulu's soothing movie theme, the blue-eyed soul Box Tops' "The Letter," the Association's breezy pop dollop "Windy," and the Monkees' candied The Beatles imitation "I'm a Believer." Amazingly, "Respect" only made it to number thirteen, though it and "Soul Man" today exist in a whole different ether than all the others ahead of them.

The latter's compelling success, and underlying sociological and cultural ferocity, made it necessary to rush another Sam & Dave album out; he logically titled *Soul Men* released in October. Besides the title cut as the opening track, the rest was chaff—beautiful chaff, unreleased previously only because Stewart had a surfeit of Sam & Dave records. Some real heavy hitters on the shelf included two Hayes/Porter songs; one an "I'm Your Puppet" soundalike "May I Baby" and the other a blues rocker called "Don't Knock It." Hayes also co-wrote another track, "Rich Kind of Poverty" (which, rather than social commentary, was an attestation of the love on the poor side of town). The album is, in retrospect, a bonus for Sam & Dave songs rarely heard on the radio (save for "Don't Knock It," which was a flop single early in '68), and for their rendition of Steve Cropper and Stax songwriter Joe Shamwell's "Broke Down Piece of Man," to be later covered by Southside Johnny and the Asbury Jukes. Riding the tiger tail of "Soul Man," the LP rose to number five on the Black Album chart and number sixty-two on the pop album chart. Even over half a century later, all of it would still be ear candy far more compelling than most anything casually called soul music. For Sam Moore, however, the reward was limited.

"I don't believe," he said years later, "the public knows that the writers and the publishers of the songs that are considered classic iconic recordings like our 'Soul Man' get paid, but we the artists and the musicians don't see a penny. As bad or worse, we can't collect the millions and millions of dollars from around the world annually because there's no reciprocity."

As fate had it, that statement was only half true, given that among the victims of industry greed would be the writers and producers at Stax as well. What's more, even in real time, Ike was among a large contingent of Black musicians who complained about the money trail not reaching them even as their work was selling hundreds of thousands of records. And while future penury at Stax was tied to its own mismanagement foibles, in the '60s, the essential contradiction of rock 'n' roll, its original sin for decades, was clearly tied to the inherent Jim Crow-like structures of racial privilege in the industry, even carrying over to white-owned "race music" such as at that created at Stax. The irony was blunt; while Ike was fully in the Stax inner circle, enjoying occasional perks, he still lived in the same small apartment with his wife and daughters. He owed Dancy child support and didn't own a car, depending on Porter to pick him up each day (though God only knew where he would head after work was done because it was rarely back home). Otis Redding, on the other hand, was living high on a farm in the Georgia woods, mocking his image as a country boy on the hit duet with Carla Thomas, "Tramp," by bragging about his fleet of luxury cars and his talents as a lover. Ike could make the same claim on the latter, but for now he was a perpetual rider on other guys' wheels. Porter would pick him up and ferry him to the studio, sometimes also picking up Otis, who'd strum a guitar and sing in the back seat, a scene that would linger in Ike's mind as something as wondrous as money.

Without really knowing it, Ike was priming the pump for a revolutionary liberation of these industry ten-pins. He had co-written one of the best songs of the year, "Soul Man," which would deliver the Grammy for Best Rhythm and Blues Group Performance award they and Sam & Dave had lost the year before, beating out Booker T. & the M.G.'s "Hip Hug-Her," Otis Redding and Carla Thomas's "King & Queen," Marvin Gaye and Tammi Terrell's "Ain't No Mountain High Enough," and Smokey Robinson & the Miracles' "I Second That Emotion." The next year, Redding would posthumously win Best Male Rhythm & Blues Performance for "(Sittin' On) The Dock of the Bay." So Stax was cruising, and all Isaac Hayes had to do was keep it from capsizing. As it happened, however, that wasn't going to be easy.

IKE AND DAVE PORTER were writing almost constantly, adding fuel to the fire—as it was, the still-small company, at least by comparison to Motown, earned around $20 million in 1966 and 1967. A lot of this bounty had come under the watch of Al Bell, whose seeming control of Jim Stewart led to more changes positively affecting the inner sanctum of musicians and writers. They had remained an amazingly close unit, integrated but committed to a purebred form of soul, proving Jerry Wexler's thesis that if one wanted to hear real blues, they had to go to Memphis, a place that most snooty musicians from New York or Nashville regarded as dirty and redneck, where the musicians were stuck on Tobacco Road. Conversely, the Memphis boys resented the Atlantic interlopers as white vipers and users; few were unhappy that Wexler, who was seen as a New York sharpie and who some had actually called an "outside agitator," had left with the abrasive Wilson Pickett.

And yet all the Stax crew felt as if they lived "in a cocoon," as Booker T. put it, meaning in seclusion and at the beck and call of Stewart. With Stax and Southern soul on a roll, Bell understandably worried that Hayes and Porter might be amenable to again walking out on Stax and signing a more lucrative deal with a different label, even though the Big Six agreement worked out to their advantage since they had shared in the wealth generated from Booker T. & the M.G.'s hits they had nothing to do with and were being given credit as producers on their record's labels—an honorific not always extended to Booker T. or Cropper on M.G.'s songs and were treated as nominal musicians only, the labels reading "Produced by the Stax Staff" or having no production credit at all. And as an added perk, Hayes and Porter would see their percentage of the Memphis/East publishing rights increased.

Kept mollified, their next recording was with Carla Thomas, who cut "B-A-B-Y," a cleverly turned slow-and-saucy funk bit. But during the session Carla began to reel at the constant hectoring from behind the glass. She believed the song was too much like "Soul Man" and, unable to hit the right notes, fled from the studio in a huff. In her absence, it fell to Booker T. to get her back, first by tinkering with the song, one that he later said he "put more effort" into than any other song. "I tried everything," he said. "Every rhythm, every tempo, so much trial and error that I got sick of the thing before playing the high piano chords that finally began the song. Carla was done with it. Finished. She didn't want any more of David and Isaac's song."

But, he added, "there was something in this tune." Trying whatever he could, he turned to a sound that had been avoided on the Stax lot. "Maybe a more Motown feel. Motown? At Stax? Nah. Nah. Maybe? Yeah! Why not? Finally, I came up with a Motown-style bass line. [And] it worked! People were dancing in the control room! Carla had a big grin on her face when she was singing." A sidelight of the song is that Porter, whose studio function was working with the vocals, whereas Ike had total command of the musicians, sang a high harmony backup along with Carla's sister Vaneese, going for what he called a "young, hip" feeling. The song's subsequent move to number three in R&B and number fourteen in pop was a very nice return. However, Hayes/Porter were now facing an impossible task, having to equal the near metaphysical outreach of "Soul Man." They were at the point where a hit record, even a fairly high-ranking one like "B-A-B-Y" simply wasn't good enough. That made it necessary for the company brass to find a brand-new focus, with the brightest light falling on Isaac Hayes.

6

Don't Have No Dust on Your Feet

The hip, ever-reaching Alvertis Bell, who deserved much credit for the sale of eight million records in '66 and was in every way the proxy boss man at Stax, considered his mission to never stand pat but to keep maxing out the current roster and soul signature while also finding new horizons for the label. This was a necessity in a fast-changing rock 'n' roll world, requiring him and Jim Stewart to recharge the sound that had built the company's image and following before it went stale. As it was, heavy-weight rock began to rush out of England on the power chords of Cream, the transplanted Jimi Hendrix's unearthly guitar, and The Yardbirds' guttural, rocking versions of Muddy Waters' and Sonny Boy Williamson's classic American R&B. Bell's first solution was to expand the Stax roster to include more soul women, expecting Hayes/Porter to break them out big.

Over '66 and '67, Ike worked long hours tutoring Judy Clay as an updated Carla Thomas, whose only single was the Hayes/ Porter "You Can't Run Away from Your Heart," a scorching Etta James-style ballad about loving a bad dude that failed to bump the charts. Ike also labored to make a foursome called The Charmels into Stax's first girl group, even though that idiom had all but ended save for the Supremes. He chose the members—Eula Jean Rivers, Mary Hunt, Mildred Pratcher, and Barbara McCoy—after scouting the local clubs and put far too much time into grooming them. He and Porter wrote and produced sweetly yearning, soul-specked songs titled "Please Uncle Sam (Send Back My Man)"—a wan copy of the Shirelles's five-year-old "Soldier Boy"—"Something Sweet About My Baby," "As Long as I've Got You," "Baby Come and Get It," "I'll Gladly Take You Back," and "Loving Material." Despite getting no traction, he would continue working with them well into 1968 when their final tune, a cover of The Righteous Brothers' "Lovin' Feeling" also failed.

The last song was part of another Bell directive: to record covers of non-Stax/Volt hits, a rarity when Otis Redding did his wild covers of The Rolling Stones' "Satisfaction," Sam Cooke's "Shake," and The Temptations' "My Girl," but now it became an avenue for releases by Booker T. & the M.G.'s such as "Groovin'," Albert King's version of "Oh, Pretty Woman," and later an album covering every song on the Beatles' *Abbey Road,* named *East McLemore.* Bell also saw an opening to keep profiting from "Soul Man," putting Hayes and Porter to work on a companion song called, naturally, "Soul Girl," for another distaff group, Jeanne & the Darlings, consisting of Jeanne Dolphus, her sister Dee and daughter Paula, and Phefe Harris. Hayes/Porter had written and produced the group's previous songs "How Can You Mistreat the One You Love" and "That Man of Mine" but did little work with "Soul Girl," a shameless dupe of the epic hit with a female twist. Failing on merit—"Soul Girl" to live on only as a collector's favorite—Hayes/Porter had enough and the group was redirected to Homer Banks. To be sure, Bell's bigtime writing/producing team were working like dogs. Bell even tried periodically splitting them as if to double their production. One of Ike's sole-written songs was a Christmas tune, "Winter Snow," for Booker T. & the M.G.'s, while Dave co-wrote "You Can't Get Away from It" for Johnnie Taylor and "Give Everybody Some" for The Bar-Kays. But all this tinkering and wishing and hoping did little for the company which began losing money and kept sinking further into the ranks' open dissension with Jim Stewart. Working overtime as it was, Hayes and Porter now had to turn back to the big guns, Sam & Dave, to accomplish something far harder than "Soul Girl"—equaling the immense *Sturm und Drang* of "Soul Man." But did they have enough left in the tank for a magic trick like that? Just as critical was the question of whether Stax, and all of Black America, would be the same when everything seemed to blow up with one rifle shot.

ON DECEMBER 10, 1967, soul music, as it stood then, died. Late that afternoon, recalling the day Buddy Holly, Ritchie Valens, and the Big Bopper died eight years before, twenty-seven-year-old Otis Redding was on a tour of the frozen Midwest. He was on his way to Madison, Wisconsin when his Beechcraft H18 was over Lake Monona; its engines failed, and it plunged into the near-frozen lake, killing him, the pilot, and four of the five members of The Bar-Kays who were backing him up on the tour. Redding, who had been undergoing a crisis of faith and direction after having polyps removed from his throat making it impossible to hit high notes, left behind as his last recording the eerie "Dock of the Bay." Written during a break in a summer tour in the Bay Area, and at a time when he was being courted by Jerry Wexler to leave Stax and sign with Atlantic, it was a whole new Stax animal, an introspective "folk soul" tune about relieving the loneliness that "won't leave me alone."

Fate determined that Redding would eternally represent the company with "Dock of the Bay," which he wrote after Al Bell had encouraged him to explore new soul horizons yet didn't particularly believe the song was Stax material, or any sort of hit material. Nor did Jerry Wexler, who, after paying respect to Redding at his funeral, turned to rushing out a quickie Redding record. "Dock of the Bay" became that record, though Wexler pushed Steve Cropper to charge up the sparse demo of "Dock of the Bay" with orchestral flourishes, Cropper thought it would be sacrilege to mess with it. He did add some stock bayside sound effects and light horns but kept the peaceful easy feeling, which turned the record into a mournful elegy to the soul man of his era and a chart topper.

At the funeral in Macon, Ike, who went with most everyone else at Stax, was feeling the same sort of alienation Otis had, which for Ike bordered on stupor. He believed that the company had not expanded its roster smartly enough, and he was losing his edge for songs that too often tread similar ground, while his musical horizons were expanding to the sort of soul he could never record at Stax, or so he thought. Indeed, despite Bell's outreach, Stax had no fallback stars beyond Sam & Dave, Eddie Floyd, William Bell, and Johnnie Taylor. With an uncertain road ahead, Sam & Dave came in only weeks later on January 5 and recorded two more Hayes/Porter songs, "I Thank You" and "Wrap It Up." The result can be called '60s soul's last stand.

"I Thank You" was one of the first songs for which Jim Stewart had allowed a real engineer, Ron Capone, to replace him on the sound board, and the sine waves rolled off like bolts. It began with a conjoined wave of clapping, Al Jackson's chugging, thudding snare beat, and Ike's tripping electric organ, doubled by the addition of a slinky clavinet, an instrument Stevie Wonder was using at Motown and a precursor for the later roiling polyphonic synthesizer that would be his '70s signature. Sam's intro came with a preacher's lilt, begging the whole world to keep "old soul's" heart beating.

The hook—testifying that a special woman could have resisted but didn't—was pitch-perfect harmony, buttressed by a male vocal choir, the only such embellishment on a Sam & Dave record. With the horns stabbing instead of rolling and Cropper's mildly distorted guitar, it was definitely more in the rock vein, the horns playing peek-a-boo with Ike's ticklish, Billy Preston-style organ runs. The middle break got funky, the horns easing in at a jazzier tempo, and Sam & Dave's back-and-forth salvos less screechy. The song released in mid-winter with the sprightly blues take "Wrap It Up"—the rhythm track of which had been recorded in Paris during a tour—on the flip side, ran up the charts to number four in R&B, number nine in pop (and be often covered, including by Buddy Miles and Archie Bell & the Drells, and in 1980, it would be the Fabulous Thunderbirds' second top fifty hit). But as its rise on the charts ended, fate again had its say, ripping apart Stax's claim to dominance.

THAT YEAR, 1968, could easily have seen the end of Stax Records. It was also the year that Isaac Hayes was allowed to finally display the odd, gravelly but amorous voice that would become his signature. Ike had asked Stewart once more to let him tool around in the studio to craft his own style as a soul man. He would bid Jim listen to him sing during lulls in recording, and Stewart always responded that he dug Ike's voice but it was too soft and romantic for the Stax template of gut-busting, wallpaper-peeling melodrama. In fact, his body of work then might have been softer had not Jim Stewart sent Marvell Thomas, Rufus's son, to play a second keyboard during recordings. Marvell would begin playing a major seventh on the board and shout to Ike to do the same.

"I don't want that pretty stuff," he'd say. "Gimme some funk!" And Ike complied.

When Al Bell arrived on the scene, he saw the future in Hayes. "As a marketer I'd look at Isaac Hayes and see him banging on the piano and [I] watched his approach, which, in terms of the way he held his hands, was sort of like the kind of stuff I would see those guys playing in the country and western bars, what I would see on television. Isaac looked like one of those guys [but] Black. When he was working up material with Porter, I'd sit around and watch him writing. He was a unique person. He had the bald head and he would come in with a purple shirt on and some pink pants and some lavender socks and some white shoes. There was this little club where I went one time and Isaac was in there playing on the organ and I decided, 'I've gotta record this guy.' I believe we can have us a huge, huge artist."

By then, Ike had gotten off on being a conversation piece around Stax and Memphis. He kept his head shaven, he said, because so few Black men did that, instead using pomades and stiffeners in a bizarre ritual to look like white music stars. With his long beard, Ike thought the contrast with his shorn head made his face more manly, his eyes seeming to stare harder. Out of self-indulgence, he also started hitting the bottle hard, and his voice was ravaged much of the time. And, as it happened, one of those times came just after the new year of 1968 when Bell suddenly hit him up on the idea of cutting a solo album.

"We had a birthday party," Ike remembered, "so we had a few drinks. Duck and I'd drunk about two bottles of hot champagne. And then Al Bell came over and said he wanted me to do an album. At least that's what I thought he said, so I said okay, and went back to the champagne bottle."

But that same day Bell pushed him into the studio. Pleased to be given the shot, but unhappy that he was not allowed any time to plan anything or write new material, a soused Ike pulled in Duck and Al Jackson, Jr. and went into the studio, with not a clue what to record. With Ike on the keyboard, they began jamming as a jazz combo, Ike finding himself playing riffs that reminded him of the blues he'd heard in the clubs on Beale Street, somehow centering on the Muddy Waters rendition of Willie Dickson's "I Just Wanna Make Love to You." As Jackson began a cymbal-fed drum intro, Ike entered with a piano tickle and lit into a coarse, drunken-sounding wail of the well-known blues standard. He sounded like a true victim of love, as if with a cigarette burning in his hand, singing for the four walls in the dead of night, and it eased him without a pause into another blues soul-wringer, B.B. King's "Rock Me Baby," which he got through with the same authentic semi-consciousness.

Obviously, this effect was because he was quite sloshed, but also because, if it sounded nothing like a Stax product, it was because Hayes himself was subconsciously less a Stax product than a blues man, carrying it with him wherever it led, whether or not it made sense in the rock 'n' roll format. He did the same on the languid, six-minute medley of Count Basie's "Going to Chicago Blues" and Erroll Garner's "Misty;" his words slurred but not his blues spirit or his daring to play lounge crooner, at times cranking his voice up to near-yodel levels on "Misty." He filled out the album acing the intricate phrasing of the 1953 love ballad "When I Fall in Love" and both parts of the Hayes/Porter Sam & Dave tune "You Don't Know Like I Know," which ran to eight and half minutes. The album's sole new composition was merely another bout of extemporization—Ike's off-the-cuff piano runs and loud humming in tune with Dunn's bass, much like Erroll Garner's manner of keyboarding on a long, nineteen-minute burst titled "Precious, Precious." Steve Cropper was called in to mix the work, but, to buff up the sound, Bell sent the master tapes to Atlantic's board magician Arif Mardin for mixing.

The Basie-Garner medley was called just that, "Medley: Going to Chicago Blues," and picked to go out as a single. Its six-minute, forty-five-second album length trimmed by two minutes for radio play, and "Precious, Precious" was shortened to a mere two-minutes, forty-five seconds. (A 1995 CD re-release of the album added the full version as a bonus track.) However, neither song nor album, *Presenting Isaac Hayes*, the cover of which was a dashing image of Ike in horn-rimmed glasses and a tux coyly holding a top hat and walking stick—the seeming polar opposite of the soul man—left a mark. This was not a big deal for Bell, who had cautiously put them out on a sub-label, Enterprise Records (named for the star ship from his favorite TV show *Star Trek*). Despite his hunch about Ike as a solo artist, Bell, who listed himself on the album as "Supervisor," could more easily suffer failure on a lesser label. And Ike, too, shrugged it off. The work, he said, was no more than "a fun thing, unrehearsed, completely impromptu" and "I wasn't satisfied with it. I didn't think they were going to release it 'cause at that time I wasn't in full control of my mental and spiritual facilities because I was under the influence of alcohol."

THIS SIDESHOW WAS quickly forgotten, though the album would be cause for Bell to recirculate it in time and a future critic would ret-ro-review the full "Precious, Precious" as "reveal[ing] the extreme sensitivity that exists between music and musician. In fact, so densely packed and involved are some of the passages that it's easy to dismiss that all the sounds are coming from a trio." Ike again went back to writing in the Stax template as its stamp on soul seemed more quaint while all around America paroxysms of separation, polarization, and tribalism were stoked by the war in the jungle and perceived threats to whites in the rise of racial progressive-ness. The newly seated Richard Nixon's successful presidential campaign had been based on flag-bearing and an openly pernicious "Southern Strategy" that made the continued progress of Black Americans the root of all evil. In turn, Black militancy began to radicalize in the intentionally sinister image of the Black Panthers.

To be sure, Memphis had never freed itself of Jim Crow. Racism pervaded the city, making the isolated Beale Street corridors, and specifically Stax Records, regarded as the only "safe" alley for Black life, though not from Black activists looking to hustle racial fear and economic blackmail. Early in '68, Rev. Jesse Jackson, the dashiki-covered, aureate leader of Operation PUSH, made Atlantic Records a target of opportunity, threatening to take Otis Redding and Wilson Pickett from the company's profit byways and set up a picket line outside the building if they didn't kick in finan-cial support—something Jerry Wexler would call a "shakedown." At Stax, glowering hustlers routinely walked the hallways with guns visible, making themselves comfortable. The Panthers and others would remind Jim Stewart that Blacks had made him and his company a lot of money. Now, it was payback time. It's unclear whether Stewart wrote out any checks, but just as important was their intent to have him hire more Blacks, which many Black employees didn't disagree with. But their presence was intimidating and had a deleterious effect on making music when they would hang in the studio with immunity from a petrified Stewart.

Al Bell was mortified at the way young Black men turned on Black mega-performers, even Otis Redding. "You'd think all Black people would have treasured Otis," he said. Instead, "they were yelling 'Uncle Tom' at other brothers. That made me sick." Otis, he said, had resisted attempts to junk Phil Walden and use an "appropriate" Black manager the activists approved of. What the Panthers didn't realize—or worse, perhaps did—was that such intimidation had prevented newer Black record labels from starting up. Seeing this, Otis had proposed to James Brown and Solomon Burke that they create a "union" in order to bond Black entertainers. Brown begged off, saying, "I don't believe in separatism," a hint of his odd Republican leanings to come. Even Otis had conflicted political drives. He had backed a Republican mayoral candidate in Macon, who, after he won, issued "shoot to kill" orders to city cops in the case of rioting and looked the other way when a National Guard tank rolled into a Black elementary school to intimidate would-be criminals.

There were indeed side issues and hesitations that complicated the movement for more moderately inclined Blacks. Some thought the concept of "fighting back" only exacerbated white fears. As it was, there were unwritten but clear barriers on the content of any given song by a Black act; the most prominent of these were Curtis Mayfield's "message" songs with the Impressions cloaked in optimistic gospel language or The Chambers Brothers' amazing "Time Has Come Today" in dizzying colors of "psychedelic soul." A number-one song like Barry McGuire's 1965's "Eve of Destruction" would have been professional suicide for a Black singer. And Bell had no patience for the menacing interlopers. He figured he had to liberate Stax, and their Atlantic overseers, from the grip of the Panthers. He claimed that he contacted a "guy in New York" who "protected Jerry," though who it was and how he did that was unclear. Bell would get in their faces and order them out of the building. He began hiring shady guys with guns in their belts to guard the place, even if that only made the tensions bristle more. But the problem would soon get much worse, and nearly implode Stax.

On April 4, Dr. King, who had survived a knife attack and prison tenures, had come to Memphis to lend support to striking sanitation union workers. The night before, he delivered his "I've Been to the Mountaintop" speech at Mason Temple. Then, he went back to room 306 of the Lorraine Motel, the sanctuary where many Stax staffers would repair to either write songs or just get away from the noxious fumes at the company. King was a devotee of Black music and had wanted to visit with some of the Stax crowd, one of them was Isaac Hayes who had, in the past, joined a King-led march. That day, Stax was afire with excitement. Al Bell was producing a record with Shirley Walton called "Send Peace and Harmony Home," which he had co-written for King. And Ike was supposed to drive to the Lorraine in the beat-up car he had recently bought and pick up a musician who was lodging there. He had hoped to meet King, but Emily needed the car and he had to cancel the plan.

That afternoon, King met with Ben Branch, the sax man who had, years before, hired the young Hayes to be in his band at the Plantation Inn and had recently moved to Chicago to become musical director of Jesse Jackson's Operation Breadbasket. Then, at around 6 p.m., with Jackson, Dr. Ralph Abernathy, and other movement people, as King stepped onto the second-floor balcony, a bang rang out. King crumbled to the ground, a rifle shot entering his right cheek then coursing through his spine. As his retinue knelt down to tend to him, others pointed across the street to a rooming house where the shot came from. Mere steps from the Lorraine, some at Stax would say they heard the deadly shot. An hour later, someone interrupted Bell's session to scream, "They just shot Doctor King, and he's dead!" Shirley Walton broke down. Bell could only utter two words: "My God."

By the time the news broke, Black America was reaching the breaking point in anger in dozens of cities. Though in Boston, James Brown kept things from escalating; when he announced the news during a concert, he stopped cops from clubbing angry Black concertgoers but also castigated a few for storming the stage, shouting, "You ruining everything. You making me ashamed of my color." As the shooter, petty thief and jail escapee James Earl Ray, remained at large—not to be apprehended for three months then sentenced to ninety-nine years to die behind bars in 1998—in Memphis, officials quickly settled the sanitation strike and kept things calm. After the shooting, Ike, Porter, Cropper, and Dunn drove through a teeming crowd on the streets to the Lorraine, not really knowing what they'd do when they got there. But a substantial crowd was already there, preventing entry.

A night later, with a curfew in effect, Hayes was at Stax when Duck Dunn came in to retrieve a bass. They went out to the parking lot, and a police car came screeching over, with cops piling out aiming shotguns at Ike, who they assumed was robbing the white guy. Dunn, who had to explain otherwise, was sickened by the overt racism. Jim and Estelle, fearing the building would be burned down by rioters, emptied the office of finished song tapes, bundled them into a car, and shuttered the place. Blacks who had never spoken in anger walked with their hands bent into fists. Stax seemed to be in the line of fire both for protesters and police, who fired more than a few shots at company personnel in the parking lot. The stench of tear gas wafted in the air all around it. Already in turmoil, it seemed entirely possible that Stax might even close up for good; a victim of the cultural divide that Hayes and Porter had helped bridge through the power of music—soul music, which for some in the Black community began to seem quaint, energy wasted on trying to appeal to whites when creepy white guys were killing Black men. Caught in the middle, Ike felt inconsolable.

"I went blank," he recalled. "I couldn't write for about a year—I was filled with so much bitterness and anguish.... I thought, *What can I do?* Well, I can't do a thing about it."

Actually, he did do something. He had leaned on Stewart to publicly endorse the striking sanitation union, but Stewart refused. Now, during four days of inactivity at Stax, Ike formed an activist group with a Black businessman named Warren Lewis. He called the group the Black Knights, which aligned with the causes of the Black community, including feeding the hungry and housing the poor. At great risk, he spent those days rousting the gangs, getting young Black men off the street and back home, away from danger. He also lobbied the mayor of Memphis, Henry Loeb III, to lift the curfew and allow a concert organized by the Knights, saying that the alternative was that "there's gonna be a blood bath" in town.

He had to make the same argument to the proudly racist chief of police and City Council president. At one point, Loeb clucked that he might agree if Hayes could find "fifteen responsible Black people." But an uneasy detente was made, with Ike standing beside Loeb, a man he detested, promising that there would be no violence initiated by "any member of the community" and Lobe saying that the only violence by cops would be to "control lawlessness," a mighty big loophole. The concert went on at the Mid-South Coliseum, without incident, with Ike commanding the stage to tell the audience, "Today I felt compelled to lead you not in a song, but in a good sense." He would later recall that, all during the night, cops "were trying to provoke Blacks into doing something so they could shoot them like dogs." As it was, while 12,000 tickets were sold, only 3,000 braved the danger to attend. And despite Ike being given an award by the Memphis City Council the next year for outstanding contributions to the community, he figured he had failed since he had pleaded with Loeb in vain to keep the curfew lifted. When the mayor refused, Ike seemed to become more militant. "Y'all got it," he fumed, "somebody's gonna get killed. This thing is still a powder keg. You need to show some good faith or you can forget it!"

That same night, a young boy was run over by a police car and died. Institutional racism did not abate in Memphis.

After a four-day lockdown at Stax, activity resumed with Johnnie Taylor recording "I Ain't Particular" and the appropriate "Where There's Smoke There's Fire." Three days later came another Sam & Dave session, cutting zero Hayes/Porter songs but still produced by them: "That Lucky Old Sun (Just Rolls Around Heaven All Day)," written in 1949 by "Santa Claus Is Coming to Town" lyricist Haven Gillespie and Harry Beasley Smith, and Booker T. Jones and Eddie Floyd's "Still Is the Night." While both had been written before King's death, Ike crafted them as Otis Redding had famously called his "sad songs," almost as dirges—Moore and Prater almost busting a gut on each and Porter's plaintive lyrics on the latter perfectly indicative of the mood around Memphis. Neither went on the market as a single—the latter would be the B-side of a later-recorded Sam & Dave tune written by Homer Banks and Raymond Jackson but produced by Hayes/Porter, "Can't You Feel Another Way (Of Doing It)," which also landed on Sam & Dave's *I Thank You* album in mid-1968. (Like all of Sam & Dave's Stax albums, *I Thank You* was re-released digitally in the 2000s by the classic preservationist Rhino Records in the original monaural format; a prize retro-reviewed as "ambitious, multi-dimensional, and pointedly accents the individual strengths of both singers [and] stands the test of time very well.") In the vapors of suddenly-changed minds about the role of music in the Black community, Sam & Dave—not even a year after "Soul Man," which now had taken on a newly aggressive context—seemed déclassé. And Hayes/Porter, still in a funk about writing new songs, had to ponder that the same might apply to them. At the following Sam & Dave date, on April 25, they produced the Steve Cropper-Eddie Floyd "You Don't Know What You Mean to Me" and Banks's "This Is Your World." The first was a hectic, part-rapped call and response to awareness; the latter was a cop of Curtis Mayfield's emotionally grabbing "People Get Ready," which three years after its release was now the "Soul Man" of a post-Martin Luther

King, Jr. Black worldview. "This is Your World," released as a single, climbed to number twenty in R&B and number forty-eight in pop, which would have been nice two years before.

So the beat went on at Stax, but its future was hanging ever more by a thread. And then, in May, barely a month after King's murder and only six months after Otis Redding's death, the thread was cut.

THAT WAS WHEN the honchos at Atlantic decided that, with Otis gone and discord written all over Stax, it would be better to pull the plug altogether on their Southern "cousins." The backstory to this move had begun the year before, when Atlantic, in a panic over rumors that it was about to be fingered in an FCC investigation into payola "mainly regarding the black acts," as one report put it, was sold to Warner Brothers-Seven Arts for $17.5 million—a figure so low that Ahmet Ertegun lobbied against it but was outvoted by Jerry Wexler and Ahmet's brother and co-founder, Nesuhi Ertegun. Atlantic, which had migrated into white rock bands like the Byrds, Cream, Yes, the Young Rascals, Buffalo Springfield, and soon Led Zeppelin and the Rolling Stones, clearly believed the soul tide had ebbed after Otis Redding's death and needed new branding. Soon, Stax would feel the burn.

Jim Stewart was still technically partners with Atlantic, and, by the terms of the 1965 distribution deal, he had the right to renegotiate if Atlantic was sold. Stewart moved on that but was given the exact same terms of the partnership. Another possibility was the "new" Atlantic buying Stax outright. Not interested in that, Atlantic instead offered a poison pill: a paltry $2 million for Jim and Estelle to split, $5 million less than the company had earned in any given year since the mid-'60s. Knowing that would mean suicide for Stax, the only viable option was the last one Stewart ever thought he would entertain: severing Stax from Atlantic, the very thing the Erteguns and Wexler now wanted. Before making that decision, Stewart and Bell called a staff meeting with Ike, Porter, and Booker T. & the M.G.'s, to discuss what to do, and they all agreed that Atlantic had held them in servitude too long. Concurring with an irate Cropper's judgment that Atlantic had "sold us down the river" for little in return, they said, "Amen."

But when Jim so informed the Atlantic lawyers, the men in expensive suits said that he was perfectly entitled to sever, but oh by the way, Atlantic owned the Stax/Volt catalog of songs they had distributed in perpetuity. For Jim it was the real gut punch. He was told that every song emanating from Stax from the time the agreement had been signed was now the property of Atlantic (actually of Warner, to whom Atlantic had already sold the Stax masters but still oversaw and released the properties). Atlantic would no longer owe Stax a dime in royalties on any of those masters. Still-profit-making songs being heard on the radio and sold in stores were Atlantic's to pocket in overrides from Warner. Worse still, as-yet unreleased masters were also Warner/Atlantic property for the next four years, an interregnum in which Atlantic would exclusively issue four posthumous Otis Redding albums, all moneymakers. Suddenly, Stax's past had ceased to exist. This was all perfectly legal, codified by that suddenly relevant arcane language in the clause dealing with the "entire right, title and interest in...such masters."

When Stewart pressed Wexler about it, the hipper-than-hip sharpie went into cover-your-ass mode, insisting that he never knew the clause existed and that the lawyers must have slipped it in. That was a load of bull, as had been Atlantic's supposed patronage of Stax. When Al Bell combed through the account books, he discovered just how much Atlantic had looted the label. The meed for shared royalties on some of the biggest-selling hits of the '60s came to only around $5,000—not even chump change, and because those overrides were informal and never legally stipulated, Stewart had no legal recourse, nor the right to have the Atlantic account books audited.

Stewart and Bell now knew they had been taken. Bell's take was, "Oh, Wexler knew exactly what he was doing. I know all the dirty laundry, what he was doing." At the beginning of the arrangement, he said, "Atlantic wanted to take over Stax. But then after Otis was gone and we weren't as relevant, they wanted to be rid of us." Wexler's contempt for the Southern rubes was obvious. Indeed, when Stewart rejected the $2 million poison pill and told Wexler he was severing the partnership, Wexler, no doubt still smarting over Wilson Pickett being evicted from Stax, sniffed, "Okay, then we'll take Sam and Dave," who, though still an Atlantic act, had been all but folded into the Stax framework. Steve Cropper's telling of that bitter ending, with far too much candor and too loose a tongue, proved how deeply the regional bigotry had gotten between New York and Memphis.

"When we turned them down," Cropper related, "they just looked at us with their big Jewish eyes and said, 'Okay, we'll take Sam and Dave back.' It was real high school."

Looking back, the Atlantic screw job was the paradigm of low-minded, barely-hidden regional and ethnic contempt and remains one of the record industry's most insidious shanks, still paying off for the company years after the Erteguns and Wexler were dead and buried, such as in the nine-CD box set *The Complete Stax/Volt singles (1959-1968)*, and other projects like the two-CD *Stax 50th* compilation of songs from 1968 on, the four-CD *The Stax Story*, and a horde of Hayes reissues re-released on both vinyl and the SACD format.

The truth was, Atlantic hadn't paid for Stax's services for those six years; they stole them. The one-sided partnership came to an end on May 6, 1968, when Stewart and Estelle officially signed the severance papers, feeling every bit like victims of a crime. Stewart then went looking for some corporate comfort himself but without that priceless catalog, the very history and legacy of his own labor. After negotiations fell through with MCA, MGM, and ABC, Stewart closed a deal with Paramount Pictures, the famous recording and movie and TV giant founded in 1916, which had been bought in '66 by Charles Bluhdorn's Gulf and Western entertainment cartel. The price tag—$4.3 million—included $2.6 million for Stewart's East/Memphis Music publishing company, which was paid in Gulf and Western stock for Stewart and Estelle, $1.3 million each; the balance would also take the form of future Gulf and Western stock. Though at the time the price per share was less than half a dollar, Gulf and Western's pitch was that their corporate raiding, which also landed Dot Records and the Famous Music publishing company, had projected an increase in the price of their stock by over a dollar within a year, given their movie and TV projects in the works. As importantly for Stewart, Paramount had none of Atlantic's rapacious yen to control the music and artists. Stax would solely determine the nature of the product, and records would go out with the Stax logo and a discreet notation that it was "a subsidiary of Paramount."

Stewart believed he had lucked into a dream scenario, but he was no stock market maven, failing to realize that a major corporate player had locked him into a deal that would take his publishing and sales numbers and would be paid from that till at a discount as long as the stock stagnated, which it would as an economic recession dawned on America in the late '60s. This meant Gulf and Western had essentially purchased Stax with Stax's own money and could disburse profits to it as a payback. To anyone who knew about economics—and economic thievery—Stax had again been an easy mark for New York operators; in Memphis, it seemed a real steal, and it was, though not for them.

STAX NOW HAD to do the really hard part: form a brand-new ring of history, another scepter of soul hopefully compatible with present and future tastes and diversions, without benefit of its biggest profit makers, Otis Redding and Sam & Dave. However, there was an odd epilogue to Atlantic's dim-out. Despite Wexler's spiteful threat, he again allowed Sam & Dave to keep recording at Stax, with studio costs paid by Atlantic and the records brought out on the Atlantic label. This was a clear acknowledgment that Atlantic still had no desire to try and maintain the duo's success without the magical Memphis crew. And they would go on being produced by Hayes/Porter, though with other writers' songs added to the mix. At the first session, in July, they cut Homer Banks and Raymond Jackson's "Can't You Find Another Way (Of Doing It)," which went to number nineteen in R&B and number fifty-four in pop. At the next, on September 30, they recorded four songs: Eddie Floyd's "Talk to the Man," Homer Banks and Deanie Parker's "Ain't That a Lot of Love," and two songs hastily written by Hayes/Porter, "If I Didn't Have a Girl Like You" and "Everybody Got to Believe in Somebody."

These new Hayes/Porter-produced cuts were a real departure. The latter, a funky dance groove, was coated with yearning poetry. Ike dimmed the orchestra on the bridge to a full stop then piled it back up. The slow, sinewy "Girl Like You" hit near-operatic levels, Sam & Dave growing near hoarse as their James Brown-like soul pleadings melded into creamy choruses of strings and horns. Both were absolute gems but a single of "Got to Believe" on the A-side only rose to number seventy-three in pop, missing the soul chart altogether. That was the first sign that the game was in the late innings for Sam & Dave. Another session produced by Hayes/Porter went down on October 7, when they recorded a rollicking cover of Redding's "These Arms of Mine"—a Pickett-style soul rocker written by Cropper and Al Bell called "Don't Turn Your Heater On"—as well as two songs by Hayes/Porter, "Love Is After Me" (on which Cropper is also co-credited), and "Don't Waste That Love;" the first an obvious paean to Otis Redding, complete with Sam chanting Redding's signature "Got-ta, got-ta" tag line on the fade out, and the other a gospel-based Wilson Pickett-style soul stirrer. But Bell would not waive any of these into single release.

At a final session, on November 8, they cut just the Hayes/ Porter "Soul Sister, Brown Sugar" and "Get It." With a lot banking on it, the first song was clearly meant to capitalize on the even newer linguistic codes of the streets of Black America—in this case, consciously injecting *two* street slang terms for Black women in the same title, the latter of course to be cadged by the Rolling Stones in 1971. More still were found in Porter's self-consciously double entendre lyrics, such as finding the "icing on the best cake." The horns rang, the guitars riffed, the rhythm rocked with frenetic power and old-time soul. It was the hottest mix of a Sam & Dave record, Hayes and Porter's ultimate clenched fist of behind-the-scenes authority. As well, all the latter Sam & Dave recordings were arranged and orchestrated not by Steve Cropper but by Del Warren, an engineer who happened to be Berry Gordy's nephew-in-law, a classically trained violinist who favored rushed melody lines, breathless harmonies, and new formats like syncopated dance music. "Get It" was by far the loudest Sam & Dave song recorded at Stax, an all-out, breakneck scream-fest prompting the horns to sound as if they would blow out.

Hayes and Porter went along with all of it, but even they couldn't make this formula work. "Soul Sister," released early in '69, backed with another Hayes/Porter tune, "Come On In"—the last Sam & Dave song recorded at Stax, on November 21, its high-water mark at number eighteen in R&B and number forty-one in pop—was a hopeful sign that Stax had found a new paradigm for Sam & Dave. However, the follow-up, another dutiful try at meaningful progression for the pair, the Hayes/Porter "Born Again," a more mellow, and for sure quieter brand of soul, stalled. With "Get It" on the flip, it rose to number twenty-seven in R&B and number ninety-two in pop, confirming to all involved that although Sam & Dave could still wring the living daylights out of any song, the money end of the charts were now falling further away.

Perhaps not coincidentally, good timing had turned against them. These compelling but not quite infectious nuggets were recorded at a time when Black culture had turned more from the heroes of a more optimistic era—all of two years before—when soul was a companion to white attitudes of coolness. But the months had churned by with only more gruesome turns. A month after Martin Luther King's murder, Robert Kennedy was gunned down in a Los Angeles hotel kitchen after winning the Democratic primary, clearing the way for Nixon's election. Suddenly, "Soul Man" was no longer a "what-could-be" but a "what-could-have-been." It seemed almost wistful that James Brown's "Say It Loud—I'm Black and I'm Proud" was the top-selling soul song of the year.

Because Hayes and Porter had been the vanguards of mid-'60s soul, the times seemed to be passing them by. Indeed, when Atlantic picked January of 1969 to release the long-abated *Best of Sam & Dave* album, congregating their lava flow of hit records, it did well but was an overall disappointment, peaking at number twenty-four in R&B and number eighty-seven in pop. Neither did Hayes/Porter write or produce Stax's first post-Atlantic, Paramount-era smash—Johnnie Taylor's coy "Who's Making Love," which was Homer Banks's work, was co-written with Bettye Crutcher and Raymond Jackson, their grooves and cleverly leering lyrics about the ironic flip side of adultery (which might have been an ideal theme for Ike to tackle) perfectly interwoven by new Stax producer Don Davis, whom Al Bell had imported from Motown to apply some of Berry Gordy's more generic pop/soul formula. The record charted a new dance groove of soul with some calling it the beginning of a "new Stax" when it went to number one in R&B for three weeks late in '68 and number five in pop—the only Stax song other than "(Sittin' on) the Dock of the Bay" to hit the top of the soul chart that year.

But Ike and David, the epitome of the "old Stax," still believed they held the golden chalice with Sam & Dave. Far more visible to the public and on the pop charts than Otis Redding had been, they were the only Stax act to be seen on high-rated TV venues such as *The Ed Sullivan Show*, Johnny Carson's *The Tonight Show*, and

The Mike Douglas Show and in important rock clubs like the Fillmore East in Greenwich Village, as well as on major soul reviews at Madison Square Garden and the Apollo Theater. Sam & Dave were money in the bank, and it's doubtful that Stax could have survived this long without them. Even in decline, their *I Thank You* album had peaked at number thirty-eight on the R&B album chart, although not making the pop album list was a hint that they had lost their mass crossover audience. That might have been cause for Stewart and Bell to believe they had done all they could with Sam & Dave beyond the "old" soul sphere, though Jerry Wexler gave it a last shot when he decided to finally break all ties with Stax and indeed "take back" Sam & Dave, with no loopholes left for Stax.

Believing he could rewire them on his own, Wexler shunted them into Atlantic's New York studio, producing songs with Tom Dowd that engaged some of the most celebrated studio cats in the business. Wexler also took them to Muscle Shoals, producing an odd boogie-beat tune with a psychedelic shift, "Ooh Ooh Ooh," co-written by a Muscle Shoals songwriter and Kris Kristofferson's keyboard player Donnie Fritts. The single of it in September 1969 became the first Sam & Dave song not to chart in four years. Still trying, Wexler reached into the Stax leftover bin and produced the Hayes/Porter "Baby Baby, Don't Stop Now" and the Al Bell-Allen Jones "One Part Love-Two Parts Pain." However, he could not replicate the Stax formula and even with a promotional video made for "Baby Baby," it flopped early in 1970, as did "One Part Love." Here, Wexler gave up, later calling his Sam & Dave work "shit-ass recordings" and that "I never really got into their sensibilities as a producer."

He did send them again to Muscle Shoals to work with other producers and one of their songs, "Don't Pull Your Love," got to number thirty-six on the R&B chart (and a few years later was an enormous hit for the country rock band Hamilton, Joe Frank & Reynolds). But Atlantic had enough of the duo and let their contract run out. Sam & Dave moved back to Miami and plied their faded fame into extensive touring and sporadic recording with one album produced by Steve Cropper. They carried on either together or solo, by rote singing the hit songs that Sam Moore in particular detested and said so on stage, until Dave Prater was killed in a car crash in 1988. And as Sam & Dave fell into life as a nostalgia act, the party line about what had befallen them would echo Moore's grudging acceptance that, despite his personal grievances about the songs he and Prater were given, being taken from the tableau of genius and commitment in Memphis was fatal. "We didn't have the same people," he would say, meaning Hayes and Porter. Hayes in particular, he said, was a revelation, his sudden brainstorms on the cloistered studio floor setting off burning flames of energy.

"I believed in whatever he said," Moore raved. "His mouth, to me, was a Bible." And, "Isaac really was the top brain behind what we were doing. He just sat there quietly going about his business and it was quite a while before I was aware just how much he was doing."

Hayes returned the compliment, hazing over the disagreements to say years after that "I miss them. They are two of the nicest guys I've worked with."

An oft-expressed coda around Stax was that "Wexler took Sam & Dave back—and then killed them." That was exaggeration. Hayes/Porter had themselves seemingly lost *their* edge and their final round of songs for Sam & Dave were also missing that certain *something*, perhaps better understood in the context of the times than the studio in the tangled cultural afterlife of "Soul Man." In addition, Sam & Dave's habitual hemming and hawing at sessions confirmed Wexler's later barb that, when it came to working with Sam & Dave, "I always felt that I was talking to a wall of gelatin."

It never got in the way of Hayes's inspired labors with them. But then, the grind of work for him and Porter at Stax had led him to ward off the pressures by often drinking himself into a stupor.

The murder of Martin Luther King, Jr. had sapped his desire to write songs, and in the time since, he seemed to sink deeper into the bottle. Not even being given a shot at a higher rung, with his own albeit short-shrift album, had brought him out of it. The question was, at a crucial juncture of soul and rock, would anything?

7

Fort Stax

In 1969, rock's apotheosis would come on that August weekend when half a million skinny, mostly white teenagers descended on Max Yasgur's 600-acre dairy farm in upstate New York. Within this convocation defining rock's always-revolving identity, soul had an indispensable place but was less like bubbling brown sugar and more like a soothing brownish glaze for emergent Baby Boomers. The producers Ken Gamble and Leon Huff were seeding "romantic soul" in Philadelphia in magical soft soul such as The Intruders' "Cowboys to Girls." Gamble and Huff also allied with other writer-producers on the wrought, high-harmony, string-dipped platforms such as Thom Bell's silky production of The Delfonics' "I'm Sorry," "La-La (Means I Love You)," and "Didn't I (Blow Your Mind This Time)."

As rock 'n' roll reached into political consciousness—witness John Lennon's "Give Peace a Chance" and "Revolution" and The Rolling Stones' "Street Fighting Man"—soul reached within itself for comfort, with The Supremes and The Temptations moving on up to TV specials. Berry Gordy signed an integrated Canadian group, Bobby Taylor & the Vancouvers, whose bassist Tommy Chong (yes, *that* Tommy Chong) co-wrote a highly sensitive racial thistle, "Does Your Mama Know About Me," but the song was hidden on a Motown sub-label. Marvin Gaye's darkly mesmer-izing "I Heard It Through the Grapevine" was originally shelved as too harsh before Berry Gordy gave in, and it became Motown's biggest-ever single. Motown's only real inner city identification now was The Supremes' "ghetto chic" outfits on the Ed Sullivan show while singing the mildly political "Love Child." The Grammy for Song of the Year in '68 and '69 finally went to songs by white writers and sung by Black singers: the Fifth Dimension's "Up, Up and Away" and O. C. Smith's "Little Green Apples."

At Stax, meanwhile, the only label with an ongoing foothold on that "old-time soul," things were just getting back up to speed a year after Martin Luther King, Jr.'s murder, unaware of what road to go down. The company's upper crust had been transformed. Estelle Axton sold her interest in Stax to Jim Stewart for $25,000 a year and Jim himself retreated from the Stax grind, mainly to sit at a desk and worry about how to keep Paramount contented. Stewart all but turned over the management to the never-laid-back Al Bell, promoting him to executive vice president and giving him 20 percent of Stax's stock (with Jim and Estelle each ceding 10 percent of their own shares). For Bell, the threats from Black mili-tants had resumed after King's murder, when gangs again roamed the streets or rode around seeking white targets to stick knives under their chins and demand money. Bell even went to the FBI to set up a sting on a couple of criminal types who had extorted Stax employees.

Looking for muscle, Bell brought in a couple of frightful figures who Wayne Jackson remembered only as "Dino" and "Boom Boom," recalling that they dropped in on the dilapidated shack where the Black Panthers hung and drew Magnums while one warned, "My friend and I now work for Stax Records. If I see your faces [there], I'll kill you."

Dino, whose name was Dino Woodard, was a real riddle; a former Memphis prizefighter who had sparred with Sugar Ray Robinson, he was also a preacher at a local church, though apparently not averse to still using his fists. He had met Boom Boom, aka Johnny Baylor, who had also run with Sugar Ray when Baylor was said to be in the Harlem Mob, before moving into the record business. He had formed a small Harlem label, KoKo Records, producing and managing veteran soul singer Luther Ingram, whom Baylor saw as leverage for more authority, at Stax. Induced by having Ingram record under his ceiling, Bell agreed to distribute KoKo and have Baylor produce Ingram's records at Stax, who would share profits on them. Making himself comfy, the smooth-talking, immaculately dressed Baylor settled in and proceeded to scare the living crap out of everyone around him, sometimes pulling his gun on *them* for no good reason. Others, like Woodard and similar wise guys, made the theater their hangout, which Wayne Jackson now called "Fort Stax."

Baylor even freaked out Ike, who despite his hard fists, kept a wary distance, ducking into a storeroom if he saw Baylor coming down the hallway. At Stax, the question was who was scarier: Boom Boom or the Panthers. And while his influence, which Bell expanded later on, indeed tamed the threats, in time, Bell blew it, not foreseeing the many ways that Baylor's roguish handling of company money would backfire spectacularly.

Bell had enough to worry about as it was, and Ike would figure into an immediate solution: Bell had to plug the gaps in the company's depleted roster. He always treasured Ike, even as he drowned himself in liquor and spent less time at Stax so that he could do the work of his Black Knights social organization, of which he named himself Vice Chairman, dovetailing his vice presidency at Stax. In these roles, Ike believed he needed to soldier the company to the overall Black movement, as Motown had by releasing an album of Martin Luther King, Jr.'s "I Have a Dream" speech after his death. Ironically, though Bell had been an early cohort of King, he had been loath to point Stax in a political direction. As it was, the very few attempts at solidarity by Black performers had failed, such as the "union" proposed by Otis Redding, which actually was implemented after his death in an axis known as the "Soul Clan" and consisting of Wilson Pickett, Solomon Burke, Don Covay, Joe Tex, and Arthur Conley. Intended to foment a Black entertainment empire, it began to frazzle, and, after a joint album for Atlantic, the whole thing was forgotten.

Lobbied by Ike to make Stax movement soldiers for the cause, Bell signed off on socially relevant songs by a real soul family, the Staple Singers, the remarkably engrossing gospel-folk "message" group of father, son, and two daughters who left Epic Records and signed with Stax in '68 after an already significant omnibus of civil rights anthems, one of which, "Freedom Highway," written by the guitar-playing elder Roebuck "Pops" Staples, was played at numerous civil rights events. The center of their melodic gravity, entrancing lead singer Mavis Staples, arguably the most commanding female voice ever in soul, propelled their first albums at Stax, produced by Steve Cropper. Singles such as "Long Walk to D.C.," written by the ubiquitous Homer Banks, continued their rise. As Stax grew more self-serious about its effect on the Black public, Bell had Deanie Parker start up a newsletter called *Stax Fax*, which was sent to a few hundred subscribers of the Stax national fan club; its pages not only pitched the label's records but included articles and think pieces that covered pressing topics in the Black point of view, about the movement, education issues, unemployment, and the mounting campaign to legalize abortion, some of which led irate white readers to send letters back decrying Stax somehow shilling for Communism. Bell also sent out a press release endorsing the aims of Black economic activist James Forman's April 1969 "Black Manifesto" demanding $500 million in reparations from white churches and synagogues for having fomented "black slave labor," though this early reparations appeal was roundly ignored and forgotten.

Still, Ike's mounting profile in such matters was quite real. Only now, in fact, was the public learning who the "Isaac Hayes" written in parentheses under the song titles of those Stax records was. He had been referenced in brief in *Ebony* and *Jet*, but the first real mainstream recognition came when the February 8, 1969 *Saturday Evening Post* devoted a detailed profile to the Memphis music scene. Written by local music journalist Stanley Booth, who was an observer in the studio when Otis Redding had recorded "(Sittin' on) the Dock of the Bay," it was titled *The Rebirth of Blues*. Only part of it dealt with Stax, but it included an intense photograph of Hayes and Porter in the middle of a session: Hayes with his eyes closed, head covered by a fur cap, clad in a red caftan, and a shark's tooth necklace around his neck as he clawed at a piano. In the article, Booth wrote:

> *Nearly every man at Stax dresses in a kind of uniform: narrow cuffless pants, Italian sweaters, shiny, black slip-on shoes. But now, standing in the lobby, there is a tall young Negro man with a shaved head and full beard. He is wearing a Russian-style cap. a white pullover with green stripes, bright green pants, black nylon see-through socks with green ribs, and shiny green lizard shoes. His name is Isaac Hayes. His partner, David Porter dressed less spectacularly in a beige sweater and corduroy pants, is sitting at a desk, thinking about making a phone call.*
>
> *"Come on," says Hayes. "Let's go next door and write. I'm hot."*
> *"I can't go nowhere till I take care of this chick."*
> *"Which chick is this?"*
> *"You know which chick. You think I ought to call her?"*
> *"What the hell do I care? I want to go write."*
> *"Well, she's occupying my mind."*
> *"Let's go, man, let's go. I'm hot."*

The "chick" was a teenage girl in an orange wig who was there auditioning for them and with whom Hayes and Porter began "whirling" around the room singing and dancing. But far more interesting was Booth's notes on how the pair did their production work.

Hayes sits down at the piano and immediately begins to play church chords, slow and earnest. As he plays, he hums, whistles, sings. Porter hums along. He has brought with him a black attaché case. and now he opens it, takes out a ball-point pen and several sheets of white typing paper, and begins writing rapidly. After about three minutes he stops, puts on a pair of shades, throws back his head and sings, "You were raised from your cradle to be loved by only me..."

He begins the next line, then stops. "Don't fit, I'm sorry." He rewrites quickly and starts to sing again. Then Hayes stops playing, turns to Porter, and says, "You know what? That ain't exactly killing me right there. Couldn't we get something going like: "You can run for so long, then you're tired, you can do so and so..."

"Yeah," Porter says. "Got to get the message in."

Booth ended the piece covering a Sam & Dave Revue gig, writing:

It was nearly midnight when, with their coats off, shirts open and wringing with sweat, they got around to the song that seemed to say it all, for soul music's past, present and future...
I'm a Soul Man....

AL BELL, WHO now was essentially running the whole ballgame at Stax, had to keep Memphis soul alive every day, despite having become enmeshed in various gripes around the place. The once-tight tapestry of musicians that had backed almost every Stax recording was splintering. Steve Cropper, who had come to believe he was ostracized by the Black musicians, assumed he was being made into a scapegoat by Bell after Bell had fired him from his A&R job so that he himself could take it. Cropper seemed to exist in a state of perpetual, tight-jawed alienation. Only Estelle had kept him from leaving, kicking in half of her publishing interest to Cropper to keep him there, which only made him seem like more of a special, privileged character to the other musicians who joked behind his back that there were obvious rewards for being "Jim's boy." Bell, for his part, fretted that Cropper would try to sink him as he tried to get Jim to sell his stock and turn the presidency over to him. On the other hand, Cropper felt he was most likely a goner, seeing that Bell had been trying to lure musicians from Muscle Shoals to replace the problem children at Stax. Coarse and politically incorrect, the guitarist was accused by some Black musicians of calling them "niggers," which he vehemently denied and attributed to Bell as the source of the accusations. He would openly label Al Bell as an "asshole."

Bell, who not long before had been the apotheosis of "God," had become the devil to many who thought he was working only for his own enrichment, not theirs. Rumors even cropped up that Bell was cooking the books and that Stax had actually been sold for maybe *$10 million* and Bell and Stewart laundered the money into their own pockets. Bell heard the conspiracy theories and said they were too "preposterous" to address with the rank and file. To him, the stories were "sad reminders that black people had had so much trouble running their own businesses. There was always the notion that those in charge were taking advantage of those under them. That was a problem in black business, and it was something I could do nothing about. I had a company to run, and I had to do it twenty-four hours every damn day."

Nevertheless, Bell didn't downgrade any of Stax's perennial cast, pointing out that one of the most disaffected of all, Booker T. Jones, was also made a vice president at the same financial level as Cropper, Ike Hayes, and Dave Porter. And Bell did indeed release plentiful recordings by the originals like Carla Thomas and Booker T. & the M.G.'s, whose "Soul Limbo" became the first release and title of the first album for the new Stax/Paramount banner. Bell also seemed not to make a move without Hayes and Porter, who, even when they weren't nominal writers/producers of a song, could provide the punch that put it over the top. When

The Bar-Kays recorded "Soul Finger" in '67, it didn't take shape as a party-style dance number until Hayes and Porter had finalized it, with Hayes happening on the title as a riff on the James Bond movie *Goldfinger*.

"Isaac came up with the title 'Soul Finger,'" said Porter. "And I heard the track, went and got twenty-five or thirty kids off the street, directed them like a choir, and brought a couple cases of Cokes in there. When I waved my hand up and down, I asked them to scream, 'Soul Finger!' and they'd just scream. We put that in as the energy on that record. It was the kind of thing where we were doing production at the company for other folks and didn't really realize that's what we were doing. Truth is, we just wanted to be involved, so much that we gave away credits all the time that we deserved. The company was the thing, not our egos or bankrolls."

It was the title and background yelping of it that made the record a crossover hit on Volt. In fact, Hayes's and Porter's fingerprints were all over the lot. Bell had given them even more corporate authority, allowing them to own the publishing on their songs like The Beatles' Apple arrangement under a company called Birdees Music. Almost a cottage industry, they wrote and produced, in Sam & Dave style, Johnnie Taylor's "I Ain't Particular" (number forty-five in R&B), a funkier Marvin-and-Tammi-style duet by William Bell and Judy Clay called "My Baby Specializes" (number forty-five in R&B and later covered by Carla Thomas and Delaney and Bonnie), and three singles by the Soul Children, a dual-gender foursome they had founded. The group, composed of Norman West, former Bar-Kays singer John "Blackfoot" Colbert, Anita Louis, and Shelbra Bennett, had debuted in late 1968 with Hayes and Porter's "Give 'Em Love," a twist-and-shout, horn-greased stomp that went to number forty in R&B, and then in '69 released three more: "I'll Understand," "Tighten Up My Thang," and "The Sweeter He Is." All moved up the R&B chart, with "Sweeter" rising highest to number seven and reaching number fifty-two on the pop chart.

Then, in '69, Hayes and Porter were handed another accomplished family group, the Emotions, a pert gospel-soul harmony group of three sisters, Sheila, Wanda, and Jeanette Hutchinson, whose records were released on Volt. Like the Staple Singers, whose style they emulated, they were already popular in their native Chicago and had a publishing deal with Pervis Staples's publishing company that prevented Jim Stewart from lifting those rights from both groups. Hayes and Porter's first production for them, "So I Can Love You," written by Sheila Hutchinson, was released as a single. Arranged by Hayes, it was a slow grind in deference to Chicago soul, the back beat accented by a snappy and understated guitar line, a gorgeous vibe that went to number three in R&B and number forty-nine in pop, a highly momentous debut that became the title song of *The Soul Children*, which included four songs by Hayes and Porter: "Going On Strike," "Got To Be the Man," "The Best Part of a Love Affair," and "I Like It." Released in the summer, the LP yielded another three mid-level R&B hits: "The Best Part of a Love Affair," "Stealing Love," and "When Tomorrow Comes."

Hayes and Porter were not only keeping Stax profitable; their catalog was like a buffet table for other labels seeking material. Three songs, "60 Minutes of Your Love," "Hooked by Love," and "Lady of Stone," which had been recorded by Homer Banks while at Genie Records, its publishing rights still owned by Hayes and Porter, were licensed by Hayes and Porter to Liberty Records. Another tune, "Check Yourself," written for Ruby Johnson, was recorded by Decca Records singer Debbie Taylor at Willie Mitchell's Royal Studios in Memphis, peaking at number thirty-seven on the R&B chart.

The phlegmatic Ike, who was far more amenable than he looked, rode out the storms perpetually erupting at Stax mainly by drinking himself into his own world. Having failed as a solo act with *Presenting Isaac Hayes* and blaming Bell for rushing him into it, Ike made no further suggestions to make another solo work. But

Bell and Don Davis came up with a plan that was supposed to set a new fire under Stax but would only light a wick named Isaac Hayes.

JUST AFTER THE New Year of 1969, Bell laid the company on the line with a bold dare: decreeing that each of its roster acts record a mélange of songs over the year, which would work out to *twenty-seven* new albums and thirty singles. Bell was justifiably desperate. He believed the company could not survive another year without a jolt of income to rival the hardy return of "Soul Man" and "Who's Making Love." Given the glut of new recordings, Bell had to find more musicians and studios and divide the acts on the company's Stax, Volt, and Enterprise labels—the latter of which had been used sparingly for records by the venerable trumpeter Maynard Ferguson and singer Shirley Walton. Having put *Presenting Isaac Hayes* on Enterprise, Bell would do the same for the new work. What's more, Ike was expected to keep up his superhuman load of writing and producing for other acts, including arranging and producing Dave Porter's entry in the Al Bell album derby, *Gritty, Groovy & Gettin' It*, released early in 1970 with Porter's fabulous soulful redo of "Can't See You When I Want To" but no other Hayes/Porter songs, mainly covering songs from his own favorite influences, Motown and Curtis Mayfield.

Bell permitted Ike to record his album on his own terms, with musicians of his choosing. And, unlike with *Presenting Isaac Hayes*, this time he wasn't blitzed out of his mind enough to lose sight of the possible upside that, as he said, might "let me become successful and powerful enough where I can have a voice to make a difference." But because Bell couldn't spare him the studio cats Ike had worked with for years, he would need to strike the same groove with another triad taken from the post-Otis Redding version of The Bar-Kays: drummer Willie Hall, bassist James Alexander, and guitarist Mike Towles (who also backed on Porter's album). The first priority was to keep it free form and subject to instant variation and individualism. Always sentient about the trends in music, he figured he could "borrow" poppy mainstream tunes and convert them to innate soul. Ike was a fan of Sly Stone's biracial funk band for Sly's touches like applying streetwise tongue as mondegreen titles—"Thank You (Falettinme Be Mice Elf Agin)"—and such lyrical coloration as "Diff'rent strokes for different folks." And Ike was ingesting the soul expansion of pop-soul even by soft soul groups, such as the Friends of Distinction serving up the catchy "Can you dig it?" hook in their hit cover of "Grazing in the Grass."

Even harmless soul patois like this was a step beyond the Stax formula; as an example, it was not Otis Redding but Aretha Franklin who had stuck the streetwise "Take care, TCB" and "Sock it to me" into her cover of "Respect," which Redding detested but had no choice but to repeat when he sang his own song. For Stax, infusing the phraseology of a "soul man" into the language and culture was plenty. But it wasn't enough for Ike, who considered his writing for Stax performers as soul for the masses, though with more bite than what some Black critics called the Black bubblegum of Motown, which bled across the music spectrum in copycat rhythms like Jay and the Techniques' "Apples, Peaches, Pumpkin Pie." Going against the dulling grain, Ike had reverted to jazz and blues on *Presenting Isaac Hayes*. Finding and buffing deep soul within the pop glades would require more slack and thought. The new album would thus be freer form. He would sing not like Sam & Dave, which he freely admitted he could not have done with the softer gleam of his vocal cords, but as the romantic bandit of love, moving from emotion to emotion swathed by strings and chorales, the overall sound not on the ground but in the air.

He came upon this mission as he did almost all of his ideas. He heard on the radio Glen Campbell's quietly emotional "By the Time I Get to Phoenix," songwriter Jimmy Webb's mordant, sentimental rune of a man's sudden and rueful end to a love affair, which Campbell propelled to number two in 1968 on the country chart and high atop the middle-road adult contemporary chart in *Billboard*, resulting in two Grammys. The song was in his head when he toddled to the Tiki Club, as he often did to try out a song idea in front of an audience. The Bar-Kays' trio were playing when he arrived and jumped onstage with them, taking over their set by riffing the song.

"Everybody was talking," he said of the audience. "I thought, 'Damn, I got to get their attention!' And the first chord...I believe was B-flat eleven. I said, 'Hang up on that chord, man. Just keep cycling it.' And I started talking [rapping out lyrics]. And halfway through my talking the conversation [in the house] subsided. People were listening. I thought, 'Damn, I got 'em!'...people were crying and woeing [sic] and involved in it. I did the same thing at a predominantly white club, same response.... So when I had the opportunity, I did it," meaning in the studio, backed by The Bar-Kays trio.

Bell was intrigued by these fanciful notions of highly embellished lyrics and melodies, and made himself the official producer of the album along with Marvell Thomas and Allen Jones. Thomas was brought in because he had not only teamed with Ike on keyboards in the past but also in the Muscle Shoals band when Etta James recorded her amazing cover of Clarence Carter's "Tell Mama," a bone-melting number Ike loved.

Hovering over the project, Bell co-wrote one of the album's two new songs, "Hyperbolicsyllabicsesquedalymistic." The other, "One Woman," was penned by Charles Chalmers, a sax man who played on many of Atlantic's productions at Muscle Shoals, and Memphis songwriter Sandra Rhodes, daughter of country rocker Slim Rhodes. Still, while Ike was satisfied with the new personnel, believing it wise to concentrate on arranging, playing, and singing and leaving the producing to the others, the studio was his; any spontaneous moods and deviations would remain strictly in his hands.

With Stax studio time at a premium, Bell contracted with John Fry's three-studio setup at Ardent Records on National

Street, where Fry had installed much of the same equipment that Tom Dowd had lugged down to Stax's studio, including a state-of-the-art Scully four-track tape machine. Since the acoustics at Ardent were more airy in nature and well suited to leaving space for the symphonic arrangements Ike had in mind, for which strings would be added at a more capacious studio, Bell scheduled Ike's sessions there and hired former bandleader Johnny Allen, who had worked with Don Davis at Motown, to chart the arrangements. Terry Manning, a jack of all trades who was working with the Staple Singers, was made the chief engineer. As the plans progressed, Ike's formative rehearsals made him dead set to swell the two pop covers to whatever length he deemed right, no matter the rules for airplay.

One of these was another pop standard he had an affection for: Burt Bacharach and Hal David's "Walk on By," on which Dionne Warwick's perfect, softly soulful inflections of Bacharach's odd keys and chords swept the record to number one in R&B and number six in pop in 1964. Along with "Phoenix," there could not be any more challenging songs for a revision, given that they were so well known. And Ike went into Ardent not knowing if he had it right. At the time, there seemed to be no end to the potential pitfalls of this dare. No Black or white radio outlet would likely play any long songs in full, and he hated the reality that he would need to trim them to three-minutes as singles. But the white album-oriented FM stations were getting into Sly Stone and the Chambers Brothers' utterly amazing "Time Has Come Today," and that was what he had in mind, wanting to slide *Hot Buttered Soul* into the still-thin ranks of Black "concept" albums that the white bands had made profitable—for that, "Hyperbolicsyllabicsesquedalymistic" would be the weapon. And if the Black stations bought into a short version of a song like "Phoenix," it might even be a sleeper crossover entry.

Bell thought about all these permutations but worried he was boxing out all those markets in going for broke with the album—the name for which he, too, was responsible for, having seen an ad for hot buttered rum while on a flight and conjuring up *Hot Buttered Soul.* Ike liked how the words dripped off his tongue the way the album's songs did. (Amusingly, MOJO typo'd it in 1995 as *Hot Buffered Soul,* which it was definitely *not*). The other side of the coin was that the record might just be high-minded folly. That was the gamble Ike and Bell were taking with such a ridiculously experimental project. As Bell went whole hog into it, he could only hope for the best while preparing for the worst.

8

"Remember The Name— Isaac Hayes"

Peering through history's rear-view mirror, there is something fateful about Isaac Hayes recording *Hot Buttered Soul*, just as The Beatles had taken a break from the contentious *Let It Be* album for what would be their final studio work, the more care-free *Abbey Road*. In retrospect, this yin and yang can be seen as the end of the most incautiously experimental rock era and the commencement of the most incautiously cool soul era, not that Ike or Al Bell expected that sort of revolution from their crazily unique album, which might just as easily have been lost in the eddy of soul recordings far tamer. In fact, Bell had covered his behind by not demanding it break the bank. As Ike recalled, Bell told him, "I don't give a damn if it doesn't sell" and that Bell was "going for the true artistic side, rather than looking for monetary value." Ike himself made the point that the album was "an opportunity to express myself, no holds barred, no restrictions, and that's why I did it," to take "artistic and creative liberties."

And so Ike went in and *expressed*, free to be as romantically obsessed and discursive as he felt, without Marvell Thomas leaning on him shouting, "Gimme some funk!" He already had the funk.

This was Ike's baby, and he led the three Bar-Kays and Marvell Thomas through the paces, completing the whole album in one day over eight hours with all the tracks taking one strenuous take each. "Walk on By" was done as a languid progression initiated by his pulsating organ and a very non-Stax-like fuzzy feedback guitar. Ike's sleepy but intense, low baritone had all the familiar lyrics of the Dionne Warwick hit, interjecting emotional pleas. The tempo slowed, continued at lower or higher keys, and then careened into a six-minute dizzy spell of melody; the last minutes were an instrumental of rhythmic blues, the feedback guitar now an "outta space" *wah-wah* machine, the feral glissandos on organ and piano looping on and on, almost to exhaustion, until the final rim shot.

This mélange was an appetizer for the soul-stirred "By the Time I Get to Phoenix," which recharged the same tonal madness but was a different creature, dominated by an instrument without strings, sticks, or keys, but a whole lot of air—Ike's great unveiling, his rapping, a musical affectation in the Black community that dated back thousands of years to Africans rhythmically speaking while playing rudimentary instruments and rediscovered by slaves and their descendants. Spoken interludes were present on rock 'n' roll records since the '50s—an example being Diana Ross's breathless intonation on The Supremes' "Love Is Here and Now You're Gone"—but the word "rap" was not applied until the early '70s (one of the first to do so was Gamble-Huff, with a blue-eyed soul group, the Jaggerz, in "The Rapper," a *non-rap* song). Incongruously as well, the term "hip-hop" could be heard as early as 1963 from a white Philadelphia group, the Dovells, who in their raucous "You Can't Sit Down" appropriated the gospel song "Sit Down Servant." In truth, Ike knew about rap. As a blues student, he was in fact sampling primal rap as it appeared on songs like B.B. King's "Don't Answer the Door." Additionally, his more mellow raps were a way to create lyrics—his weakest gift as a songwriter, which he ascribed to "laziness" as much as Dave Porter's more magical way with clever lyrics. His unquestioned gift was to turn rap into *long*

side trips within a song, though he was not alone in this affectation. In 1970, Gil Scott-Heron and the Last Poets hit the scene with
heavily incendiary rap content (the latter with such shape-shifters
as "Wake Up, N******") to a blues beat by a Latin-inflected band,
Heron with bassist Ron Carter and drummer Bernard Purdie. Ike's
turf was not political but incendiary sexual/personal confession.
Even years later, he said of *Hot Buttered Soul*, "Some of the lyrics
are kind of raw. I don't want to sound old-fashioned, but they're
raw. [But] when I talked about things that I considered sexy, you
didn't just lay it all out. You left a lot to the imagination. You did
it with better taste. You didn't have to name body parts. Whatever
happened to foreplay? These kids want to jump in and get it over
with, like rabbits. The best part about it is the contemplation and
the foreplay."

That is really what his raps were: foreplay, in his logarithm,
"eargasms." And he certainly moved the rap idiom down the block,
injecting improvised psychological dramas and inner morality
debates into the veins of soul. He began "Phoenix" to the sound
of a repetitive cymbal, filling in Webb's tale of a man splitting a
woman and admitting that "Love can make you or break you." As
his Hammond lent a soap opera/revival feel and The Bar-Kays'
rhythm and Marvell Thomas's piano fills held to that B-flat eleven
chord, he gave a shoutout to Webb for content that he had brought
"down to Soulsville." The rap told of a young man raised in the hills
of Tennessee, who fell in love before the union was felled by money
woes, and when he came home one night, caught his girl cheating.
He then got into a '65 Ford and drove through the wilderness of
night, his mind sweltering with possible suicidal thoughts.

In that spell of angst, he began singing Webb's lyrics, which
made no attempt to say why the tortured guy walked out. Ike supplied the most revelatory nature of the song; as he construed it, it
was all the woman's fault. This convenient route may have been a
way of claiming innocence for his own similar situation since, at
the time, his adultery had become fixed on a twenty-two-year-old

girl he had met named Mignon Harley, a bank teller with whom he had already begun shacking up; thus, it made sense to send up signals that women were the cause of his infidelity. As the rhythm intensified, the band kicked in, drums and organ pounding hard, and Ike's voice met them, pounding at the head and heart until the last poetic lines of aimlessness. Several times it sounded like his self-immolation was ending, but he kept it going for eighteen minutes and fifty-one seconds before a last organ glide took it to silence.

Ike recalled the punishment left on him by this trail of tears; "We were just jamming out. I was raking my hands on the keys and you can hear my fingernails hitting the keys, coming through my vocal mic." One could have only come away from it limp and exhausted, but Ike had delivered a testament to the battlefield of love that would permeate other such tracts of pain and suffering and would wind up being oft sampled; his melodic piano runs in this very track sampled by Public Enemy in "Black Steel in the Hour of Chaos." With good cause, a 1998 retro-review of the album by Uncut's Chris Roberts dissected the song as "a coda of tremendous emotional stature" with "something faith-inducing about voyeuristically observing this gigantic man brought to his knees.... And there's one moment so blatantly autobiographical, and so striking in that Hayes opts for an incongruous falsetto—'You had a good heart, oh, and you abused it'—that you become aware you are hearing the Mount Olympus of soul."

Fulsome as it was, there were two other momentous tracks on the disc, one of them the self-poking taunt of pickup lines in "Hyperbolicsyllabicsesquedalymistic," emerging as a funk paragon framed by Toles's *wah-wah* guitar streaks, Ike's and Marvell's intensifying piano dueling, Alexander's rumbling bass, and Willie Hall's ear-piercing drumming to a wicked dance groove. With Ike's vocal enhanced by a female chorale chanting the nearly non-pronounceable title, his limpid voice was now itself a rhythm instrument, imperfect but dead-on. He finished the work with

"One Woman," a sinewy ballad that, not unlike "Phoenix," related a dense tale of being torn between two lovers—yet another parable of his own existence.

Though Mary Wells had covered this turf at Motown in a funkier, less torturous manner from a feminine viewpoint, it was not as safe as from a man's view—from Isaac Hayes's view—and it opened the soul market for songs of cheaters facing a *Sophie's Choice* of lovers, a pocket that would be filled at Stax by Luther Ingram's "(If Loving You is Wrong) I Don't Want to Be Right," co-written by Homer Banks, and "Me and Mrs. Jones" by Gamble and Huff with Billy Paul, both massive crossover hits. (A lesser such hit, Johnnie Taylor's 1974 "We're Getting Careless with Our Love," produced and co-written by Don Davis, hit number five soul and number thirty-four pop.) Ike's album of concussive confession was completed, James Alexander said, "in two days. [Ike] gave you a creative direction, maybe a line to play, and we kept going." Every vocal passage seemed to extract every drop out of his soul, but only until the next one. The songs were like nothing anyone had ever heard, and they were still not done. Yet to be added were the horns, strings, and background vocals.

For this, the engineers convinced Bell to go to the Motor City's United Sound Systems Studio where they knew the acoustics would send the songs into a metaphysical state. By the end of the dubbing and mixing, two more engineers had been involved, Ed Wolfrum and Russ Terrana, who applied high-tech sound enhance-ments, such as pre-delay reverb, which were the kind of thing that had once been avoided at Stax. The effect was that Ike's meditative vocals sounded transparent, effluvium-like.

Before the crew went to Detroit, Ike had gone back into the studio to overdub a second guitar, bringing in Harold Beane, who tore off amazingly intricate and effusive solos on the album, and amplifying the feel of Toles's. "Ike told me, 'I want to take it out of the box,' so I turned on the fuzz tone and turned up the tremolo," Beane remembered. "Then I took my guitar, and I slid it up and down the microphone stand." A week later, when he heard the final mix, Beane said, "The arranger in Detroit heard [my added guitar part] and he matched that sound with strings."

It was stunning, perfectly balanced, and deep as a well. No one, not even at Motown, would have sniffed at these tracks as merely "Southern soul." But on what planet it was recorded, that was the question.

AL BELL GOT an early indication that he was on to something big when, by sheer accident, one of the background singers took an unfinished tape of "Walk on By" to a Memphis FM radio station, WMPS, to have a copy made for the singers to study. There, a white, twenty-two-year-old DJ named Scott Shannon heard the tape and played the song on the air, numerous times, by request of listeners. Shannon told Ike, "Man, you should put that out as a single." This convinced Bell to reconsider his and Ike's decision not to release any shortened singles. The album came out in June; its cover Christopher Whorf's portrait of Ike's beautifully bald pate right up on the camera lens, his shaded eyes and love beads strung below. The image and sound of the artist were striking, intended to isolate this Black man's brain as the driving force of soul from here on in, the source for not-always fashionable fantasies and truths, the blues for a new world.

It hit the market with a hint of fanfare but in line within the glut of Stax/Volt/Enterprise releases in 1969—forty-five singles and fifteen albums in all, compared to twenty-two singles and ten albums in '68, a big year in itself. Some were from the lingering Stax stable, others by brief Stax drop-ins such as the rock band Delaney & Bonnie, the great bluesman John Lee Hooker, old soul king Billy Eckstine (whose cover of the pop hit "Stormy" was produced at Eckstine's request by Ike), and numerous lesser lights from the blues world. Of them all, though, Bell got his biggest rush from *Hot Buttered Soul* selling unexpectedly well in the big urban markets.

Reviews, however, were mixed. Back then, serious reviews were rare, the normal sort being the pidgin-English in *Billboard* that raved over a song's "rockin' beat." Although the music rags in England buzzed about the LP, with *Blues & Soul* calling it "without doubt, the most significant album of 1969." It did get in the *New York Times*; the review by Lorraine Alterman noted that its "cooler style" of R&B was a "fresh approach to soul music," but that "innovation has turned into gimmick" and he "should not settle for soap opera." *Stereo Review* labeled the album a "Recording of Special Merit," and its review by movie critic Rex Reed began: "Remember the name—Isaac Hayes," whose voice he wrote was "a deep, dark Carlsbad Cavern, out of which soars a black soul capable of weaving an incredible spell of pure musicianship." "Walk on By" was, Reed wrote, "an exciting fugue of soul rock...one of the most entertaining and original things I've heard this year." Reed was transfixed by the repetition in the instrumentation—"I counted twenty-five repeats before the organ took over and spent the last three or four minutes playing variations on the same theme. It is truly a modern jam session that swings, soars, and abruptly meets the drummer, who finally stops it all, after a full twelve minutes of pow."

But he hedged on Ike's raps in "Phoenix," calling it "corny exposition" even as he agreed that they revealed "what love is really all about, what Webb had in mind, and just how deep this song is." Reed concluded, "While I really hate to carp since stylists with flair and originality hit the scene so rarely...if only Isaac Hayes had used a little restraint in *Phoenix*, this would be a perfect album instead of a merely impressive one." It was a mild reservation but the sort that Al Bell had feared might derail the album if others expressed it. And, to be sure, some were oddly stingy. The *Village Voice*'s new music critic, the acerbic, inscrutable Robert Christgau, whose bias toward beatnik-era jazz tended to slight rock and new R&B in his capsule reviews, seemed smitten—"This album is a smash, and it may be so overstated that it has its own validity—a baroque, luscious production job over the non-singing of one half of Sam

& Dave's production-songwriting team"—but then cryptically handed it a "C" rating. Even so, the gathering buzz was that one had to listen to this stuff. Bell did his marketing chores and bought the requisite ads in the trade papers, but Ike was fatalistic about it, noting later that he had only "milked for everything they were worth" from the songs because he didn't expect much given all the other Stax albums that might snow his under. But by doing that much milking, he had nurtured something in *Hot Buttered Soul* that all the hustling and ad dollars couldn't buy: word of mouth.

Similar to the public's selective embrace of Otis Redding's early records, progressive blues and jazz buffs had first caught on to *Hot Buttered Soul*, and then, in the budding era of album-rock in the wake of *Sgt. Pepper*, the progenitor of the "Soul Man" motif seemed to have unleashed a *Black* concept album, with too many variables to define it in one idiom. It soon began spilling across a full spectrum of stations after hitting the charts in June. Truncated versions of "Walk on By" and "By the Time I Get to Phoenix," released together, with "Walk on By" as the chosen A-side, crept up the charts. "Walk on By" went to number thirty on the pop chart and number thirteen on the soul chart. The album continued to fly to number thirty-five on the pop chart in mid-August, number two on the soul chart, and number three on the jazz chart. Then it hit number one on the soul list, the first Stax album to get there other than the three by Otis Redding.

Something big surely was going on. By September, after twenty-four weeks on sale, *Hot Buttered Soul* was, remarkably, number one on the soul album chart for the second week in a row *and* number nine on the pop chart, its peak position, with 5th Dimension's *The Age of Aquarius* and Aretha Franklin's *Aretha's Gold* as the only Black albums on the chart. The album was also high on the new *Billboard* Easy Listening chart, which struck some hard soul enthusiasts as comical. Ultimately breaking off on its own run as a single, "Phoenix" then bolted to number thirty-nine in soul and number thirty-seven in pop. In October, a *Jet* magazine poll called

"Soul Brothers Top 20" had "Phoenix" at number two, behind Aretha's "Share Your Love with Me." "Walk on By" was still hanging at number nine, also becoming an oft-recycled Hayes standard on the soul set, with Diana Ross and The Jackson 5 including his version of the song as a duet on their tour that year.

Nearly a year later, the album would still be charting on the pop chart, at number 126, and still in the top 10 of the jazz chart. *Rolling Stone*, which debuted in early November 1969, didn't weigh in on *Hot Buttered Soul*, but decades later, it would retro-review it as "a landmark album" in which Hayes's "words aren't cued to the rhythm like a modern rapper's, but the contrast between the smoothly spoken and haltingly sung sections adds a delicate tension." In December 1969, this formula took it Gold, selling a million copies, upon which Stax sent out a photo to the trades of promotion man Herb Kole boosting Ike off the ground—no mean feat—in exhilaration. The stranger than fiction LP was, in all respects, a monster, on a glide path to a lifetime achievement of selling three million and going triple Platinum.

THE HAYES BOOM ignited so fast that Bell had to get Ike out on the road. Buying up flashy duds and getting together a five-piece road band with a female chorale, Ike prepared for road gigs. However, through the summer, no invitations came in. It took until September for him to hit the road; that month, *Billboard* reported on his appearance at a Madison Square Garden gospel concert for the Museum of Modern Art, which the magazine said was "warmly received." He was at the piano as he sang, a flashback to Little Richard, playing while singing then standing and shaking to the beat or, on long raps, standing upright and letting his hips slide sensually back and forth. He was also becoming quite comfy with shedding garments to feminine squeals, an updating of his high school assembly days, but now with the real possibility of taking advantage of it.

His sets were short but emphatic, and he had no inclination to sprinkle in any of the Sam & Dave hits, which some of the newer soul fans had no idea he had written. Not that it mattered, since his soliloquies could carry him through an hour. And his stops out on the live circuit beyond the clubs on Beale Street proved how sincere he was about defining himself as a new cog in the rock/soul chassis. One came at San Francisco's famous Winterland Arena, where promoter Bill Graham had, since 1966, been presenting shows headlined by Jefferson Airplane, Grateful Dead, Santana, the Butterfield Blues Band, and Janis Joplin's Big Brother and the Holding Company, as well as hoary blues men Muddy Waters and John Lee Hooker—and Otis Redding, who had made soul a rock property between hours sitting on the dock of the bay.

Ike hit the stage there on November 6, the first of three nights during which he would be down the marquee from the swiftly burgeoning Led Zeppelin, with other obscure acts Roland Kirk and Wolf Gang. Braving some cat calls from the 5,000 in the house wanting Zeppelin to come out, he skimped not a note on the long raps and won most of them over. Graham was impressed and invited him to perform at his cross-country music hall, the Fillmore East in Greenwich Village, on December 12 and 13. Though nowhere near the level of the Motown stars or the lingering Sam & Dave, Ike was no longer a secret, guilty pleasure, but the bookings were still scarce.

While *Hot Buttered Soul* was the second-top-selling soul album in 1969, just behind The Temptations' *Cloud Nine*—that one, too, a dare, with the title song's drug intimations—Ike wouldn't get another gig until March 21, 1970 at Meehan Auditorium in Providence, Rhode Island, and not thereafter until May 3 at Nashville Municipal Auditorium. In the interim, he had ample time to return to the studio in March and record almost exactly the same album—again, as on *Hot Buttered Soul*, with ample short-cutting by programmed keyboards and drums backing four elongated tracks—three of them covers of hits and one new song by Chalmers and

Rhodes, "One Big Unhappy Family." The album's title, suggested to him by Marvell Thomas, was *The Isaac Hayes Movement*, which was Ike's handle for his female chorale and which was intended to roll off the tongue as did the Jimi Hendrix Experience.

There were no nineteen-minute rhapsodies, but Ike didn't scrimp on two covers that lurched nearly twelve minutes each, George Harrison's "Something" and Jerry Butler's "I Stand Accused." He also went back to the Bacharach/David well with "I Just Don't Know What to Do with Myself," which had been recorded by Chuck Jackson and Dusty Springfield, neither with success. Ike's cover doubled over in emotion as he bass-sang, the song reaching seven minutes, "One Big Unhappy Family" almost six, opening as a slow jam with Ike's vocal stirred by strings, building to a more urgent demand.

He directly produced and arranged the songs this time, with The Bar-Kays as the core of the musicians. The tracks were all soul stunners. "Family" a classic downer of cheating parents pretending to be in love for sake of the kids, had Ike lamenting, or perhaps boasting of his own straying, "he's got her thing going and you know I got mine, I got mine." No one could have pulled off those lines better, and on "I Stand Accused" there were a lot more, within a rap that kept reaching for five minutes as he deepened the well of denial, insisting he had sinned only in "the court of love."

Ike drained every ounce he had cutting these sides, smashing any white perspective to The Beatles' song of love's adoration, which Ike stiffened by hammering the song's gentle chord shifts into dramatic, bluesy stops and starts, his restrained, higher-pitched vocal the counterpoint. He even threw in several interludes by improvisational violinist John Blair, his Vi-tar nearly catching on fire. And Bell would pick the two most punishingly self-projected songs as alternate sides of a single, "I Stand Accused" and "I Just Don't Know What to Do with Myself," each cut to radio size. The album, basted and fattened again in Detroit, was released in April, the cover photograph by Joel Brodsky of Ike in zebra skin, looking as if he was climbing from the eye of a psychedelic farrago, his uncovered eyes staring into the camera. And it retraced the paths of *Hot Buttered Soul,* tearing through the same spate of charts. *Movement* would spend seven weeks at the top of the soul album list and ending the year ranked fourth behind The Temptations' *Puzzle People* and The Jackson 5's *ABC* and *Diana Ross Presents The Jackson 5.*

Put into broad context, Ike was still operating on a lower level than the biggest soul acts, and certainly behind the biggest pop acts. Again, there were few reviews. Robert Christgau, this time, snarked, "I admit that his arrangements can be 'interesting'—my my my, a gypsy fiddle on 'Something,'" but slagged the "stately pace" of "four songs per LP" and that "if his voice is best displayed when he talks, why doesn't he do a whole album of raps like the one preceding 'I Stand Accused'? Might be pretty funny." This made exactly zero sense but it did make the point that rapping was the DNA in soul's future, ferried by Ike. However, that year, not a single soul work came near the top of the pop album list that was topped by Simon & Garfunkel's *Bridge Over Troubled Water,* which, interestingly, featured soaring arrangements more like an Isaac Hayes song than any rock format. And soul was still most readily appreciated through the Motown candy dispensary, with The Jackson 5's "I Want You Back" and "The Love You Save," and Stevie Wonder's "Signed, Sealed, Delivered (I'm Yours)," each spending six weeks at number one on the soul chart while Ike's harrowing but enveloping "I Stand Accused" only made it to number twenty-three in soul and number forty-two in pop.

BUT BLACK BUBBLEGUM had a competitor in Black soul from the heart and loins, which now took off in Ike's work and that of the Gamble and Huff clique in Philadelphia. Even at Motown, the forces of new soul were reshaping the drawing board, most notably with "War" and Marvin Gaye's proscription of societal ruin, "What's Going

On"—its genesis being similar to Ike's with "Soul Man," that of a police riot at a student antiwar rally, although Berry Gordy again refused to release a barbed Gaye record until Marvin threatened to quit, whereupon it sold 2 million copies and opened the way for knockout punches like "Mercy Mercy Me (The Ecology)" and "Inner City Blues" that made him "wanna holler" and for Stevie Wonder to find his '70s groove first revealed in his introspective *Where I'm Coming From.* The Temptations' material also grew darker with "Ball of Confusion." But while Marvin would set soul on fire and kill on "Trouble Man," that assignation already applied, affectionately, to the salient soul man in Memphis.

To be sure, the return on Ike's sales raised Stax's bottom line so much that Bell and Stewart were emboldened to throw a goodly amount of cash at Gulf and Western to buy out the two-year-old partnership. And Gulf and Western was ready to listen. Rather than exploding, its stock had deflated when Paramount's movie fare flamed out with a string of big-budget bombs. Thus they took Bell's modest offer of $1 million, ceding all the rights for the songs in the Stax catalog since the deal had been made, a very satisfying twist for Bell and Stewart to be able to pull an "Atlantic" on another corporate porker. But the notion that Stax had taken control of its business affairs was just fiction, not that Bell realized it yet. He believed he could simply ride on the profits and keep spending, and borrowing, without pause.

Bare days after the high-profile buyout, Bell and Stewart took out a $5 million loan from the prestigious classical music label Deutsche Grammophon, under terms that again seemed insanely unfavorable to Stax, whose rulers were bold but still more cock-eyed than money wise. According to the terms, if Stax didn't repay the loan within one year—plus a million dollars in interest—the German label would thereby own 45 percent of Stax's stock. That prospect set into motion an always frantic cycle of borrowing from Peter to pay Paul. It was no way to run a company, and certainly not a pinnacle of Black capitalism. But a look at Stax's books was quite a rush; they had cleared nearly $12 million both in 1971 and 1972, which put them not far from Berry Gordy's Motown as the biggest Black record company in the country. What was not known to non-accountants, though, was that these numbers whittled away when all the debts and IOUs were added up.

Bell and Stewart kept Stax's credit line pumped up with bravado, promises, and bullshit, and the fable persisted with zeal that Stax was as much a business leader as it was a music and cultural beacon. This was especially hyped in the Black press, *Jet* and *Ebony* never far from its next Stax fluffing. To the crowded convoy of Stax creditors, on the other hand, the soul giant was becoming no more than an unmanageable debtor.

9

"You Never Lost The Groove"

Stax did hold up its end paying back Deutsche Grammophon. But it spent heavily on vanity projects through 1971 such as new subsidiary labels, new artists and musicians, reconstruction of the Stax edifice, and community outreach outlays under the banner of the Isaac Hayes Foundation. With so much money going out, Jim Stewart moved back into a lead role for a company he had longed to free himself from, negotiating a loan from Memphis' Union Planters National Bank, Jim and Estelle Stewart's old employer. Al Bell, less and less involved in writing and producing, busied himself trying to secure yet another distribution deal with a big-boy American label.

Of more interest to anyone with an aesthetic rather than an expedient interest in Stax, Ike kept on rolling. *The Isaac Hayes Movement* proved that *Hot Buttered Soul* was not a fluke, and his riffs were being widely incorporated into the highest grades of soul's bloodstream. A 1971 review of James Brown's *Superbad* album noted that Brown's own version of "By the Time I Get to Phoenix," in effect a cover of Ike's, "neither compares with the original version or adds anything new as Isaac Hayes' did." It was nearly impossible *not* to borrow from him. And Bell went digging deeper into the coffers to spend $26,000 for that famous gold

Cadillac El Dorado as a thank-you gift. Ike proceeded to dress the car up in the ultimate shades of '70s soul vanity, transforming the car into a golden tank.

Its interior was something out of the *Playboy* rich-white-guy catalog: red, black velvet, fur, and leather, with radio telephones, a stereo cassette player (a hi-tech item then), closed-circuit security TV, a color TV, a refrigerator, and flashing "go-go" lights. It was immediately identifiable on the streets in Memphis, to the extent that his location could be tracked by wherever it would be parked, usually with a uniformed driver patiently waiting at the wheel in some driveway or another as Ike was with one or another gin-soaked barroom queen in Memphis. Wayne Jackson recalled the car as a gilded landmark of Stax with people always gathering around it in the parking lot, sitting behind a section of metal grating erected to keep the lot from being trespassed after the King assassination. Jackson remembered "the wet bar in the back seat" and that "it took four men to lift the hood, and the hubcaps were worth a fortune." In time, if he felt like roughing it, Ike could hop into his other cars—a Mercedes, two Jaguars, three long limousines—or onto one of his six motorcycles and glide around with the Choppers Motorcycle Club, swathed in denim and leather.

Yet Ike didn't crimp on providing Emily and the kids with a palatial home, anteing up $475,000 for an 8,000-square-foot, fourteen-room three-story mansion on a ten-acre spread in East Memphis, not far from Jim Stewart's own manse and the sort of abode he had only dreamed was possible for Black people in Memphis. With his $7,200 Hammond piano in the living room and a private soundproof studio with an organ and three xylophones, he could record demos. He also could store in the miles of closets his racks of resplendent designer duds he was purchasing in bulk from the upscale Woolf Brothers' clothing store in Memphis, from leather and suede jumpsuits to twined robes, chain-link gold vests and necklaces, sequined tights, and diamond-encrusted socks—most of which he would peel off his body during performances, having assiduously kept in prime condition by building a gym in the basement, right next to his collection of Smith & Wesson guns. Getting up religiously at 6 a.m. to work out, he bulked up from 185 to 215 pounds, eager to "get a muscular body like Charles Atlas," he told a *Jet* writer. He also choked down forty-eight vitamin pills a day.

But more and more he was spending his life chained to hotel rooms—and not only on his rounds of glittery concerts. A fan of the Memphis State Tigers basketball teams, he would charter a private plane to fly to their road games. Nor did he crimp on his concerts, for which he was the uncontested headliner now. He spent big to beef up the outer-space-style clothing for his backup band, the core of which was Marvell Thomas on keyboards, Bobby Manuel on guitar, Allen Jones on bass, and Jerry Norris on drums, as well as the Movement backing trio for harmonies. Rather than going cheap and using a keyboard to fake string sounds or pipe it through an arena's sound system, Ike hired a string section in each city along his travel route. He played big arenas that summer, touching down at Chicago's Auditorium Theater, the Spectrum in Philadelphia for a special July 15 engagement with Miles Davis, Atlanta's Civic Center, New Orleans' Tulane Stadium a day before he doubled back to the Spectrum for a show filled out by Little Esther Phillips and bandleader Mongo Santamaría.

Neither did he hold back in the studio, the hefty expenses for which were, as was the case with all performers, deducted from the royalty checks. That summer, he recorded his second album of 1970, producing, arranging, and playing the keyboards and vibes on the LP's five cuts, four of which were covers of more popular Brill Building-era hits: "The Look of Love," "Our Day Will Come," "You've Lost That Lovin' Feelin'," and Aretha Franklin's "Runnin' Out of Fools." The Bacharach/David "Look of Love" had won an Oscar nomination for Dusty Springfield and been a top five song for Sérgio Mendes & Brasil in '66. "Lovin' Feelin'," The Righteous Brothers' epic rendering of Phil Spector's Wall of Sound, had already been called the "ultimate pop song" (to become the most-played song in rock history). "Our Day Will Come" was a number one pop and soul hit for Ruby and the Romantics. "Runnin' Out of Fools," an early hit for Aretha, helped define her as a soul diva. However, having rewritten the art of the soul cover, he ran the risk of being pinholed as a cover act. Indeed, the album would be titled *To Be Continued...*, a promise of more of the same, though Ike described the work as "big drama-type songs."

Bell trusted him, and allowed Ike to again reach deep, along with the full count of eight Bar-Kays and the contributions of the Memphis Horns and the Memphis Symphony Orchestra. The sole original cut was "Ike's Rap I," another lovelorn rap tuned to a jazz-inflected piano and sound effects of crickets chirping to the tale of woe from a guy about to go into the military promising his girl he'd be back. Though the story was more complex, rife with anger about discrimination and "always messed up situations. Socially, racially."—a hint that the romance he sang of was one of miscegenation, something else he could personally draw upon. On the fifteen-minute expansion of "Lovin' Feelin'," which began with an introductory monologue, he led a five-minute instrumental of varied-tempo riffs, ending with a slowing drum barrage. He would retitle the song by adding "Ike's Mood" as a preamble, intending to do the same with different words on future covers of classic pop tunes he would dress up, enabling him to apply his name to the writing and publishing credits. The last two tracks, "Our Day Will Come" and "Runnin' Out of Fools," were gushy romantic soul, the sound of a quiescent roll in the sheets.

The sessions created another monumental work, but Bell would pick only one song as a single: "Look of Love," which featured a slinky *wah-wah* guitar, crisp horns and strings, and his smooth yet earthy baritone on a nearly twelve-minute soul undulation concluding with him sighing in passion as if in mid-coitus. The album's cover was designed as a mock picture puzzle of five identical Ike images staring upward to the camera, each image angled differently and with pieces missing—the exact metaphor for a man who was actually several men, some of whom he hadn't come to know fully. Much of the rising critical claque reacted in what was to be a predictably opaque manner to his work. In *Rolling Stone,* Vince Aletti labored on Ike "continu[ing] his practice of taking familiar material and expanding it—with introductory spoken monologue, jazz-styled orchestral filler or mere repetition (usually all three)—so that [a song] resembles a drowned and bloated body washed ashore after weeks at sea: pathetic, grossly misshapen, dead."

Yet both Ike and Bell were right. Released in November, *To Be Continued...* tore through the roof, going to number one on the soul and jazz album charts and number eleven on the pop. The cropped "Look of Love," with the flip side "I Just Don't Know What to Do with Myself" (already used as the flip on "Stand Accused"), only rose to number seventy-nine on the pop single chart and missed the soul chart altogether—a disappointment but irrelevant given the overall power of the work as a sinewy soul concept album marking the upward path of new soul in the album-oriented era.

He would remember the effect it had; he said of his rap in "Our Day Will Come" that "I addressed the issue of differences in a relationship—racial and class differences between a rich boy and a girl from the other side of the tracks. A long time later, a white lady walked up to me in the street and told me she was married to a Black man and that the tune had given them heart in the face of a lot of opposition. That was when I knew what I'd wanted to say had worked, which gave me as much personal satisfaction as any other tune I'd written."

IKE'S THUNDER HAD swelled to near-corporate dimensions, his road staff growing to around thirty people which included the band, now officially the Isaac Hayes Movement, the full Bar-Kay lineup dressed in their blindingly colorful body suits with some modeling

Revolutionary War uniforms etched with American flags or draped by capes looking like the flag—Ike's manner of claiming the flag from the racists, a trenchant statement soon copied by James Brown. The retinue included the backup singers, hangers-on from his past or a new circle of ass-kissers and handout-seekers, women he sometimes added on the spot, and a masseuse/barber/manicurist named Delores Jones to keep him looking def and his head smooth as a summer squash. Security was a top concern, as well.

As with most music pilgrims on the road, Ike packed heat inside his waistband just in case, but Bell also sent Johnny Baylor and Dino Woodard out with him, not just for protection but to collect the proceeds, every dollar of it, not trusting promoters to live up to the contracts. Ike was no easy mark, yet he wasn't expected to confront promoters who screwed him. Baylor and Woodard were. And this simple fact led Ike to accept them as had Bell, even as nearly everyone else at Stax could barely breathe knowing they were lurking around. Ike took a particular liking to Johnny as a sort of buffer, countering his own affability with fans, many of whom would approach him. One young man who did at the airport in Chicago recalled decades later that "We had a fairly lengthy conversation about music and some people we mutually knew, even to the point of his asking me if he could continue walking and talking with me down the corridor to my plane, even though his gate was in a different direction. [He was] just an outstanding down-to-earth human being."

Baylor, not so much, which is why those conversations with fans happened less after Ike began to think more like Johnny, growing suspicious of people for little or no reason. When he or Baylor believed someone crossed him, even if it was in his imagination, it prompted Johnny to nonchalantly stick his gun in that someone's face. Around Stax, almost no one felt safe from being cornered by Baylor; not even Dave Porter was insulated. During the summer of '69 when, Woodard recalled in an interview with author Rob Bowman, "They were supposed to have been writing partners and all of a sudden man—boom—Isaac wasn't even respected as his partner.... Something was going on between [them about] money and finances. Isaac was always on the bottom end. [Johnny] felt that Isaac was the man and so like—boom—he had to be protected. So Johnny spoke [to Porter] on some issues.... I don't know if [Johnny] put a gun to his head but I know that he did go in and speak with him."

As Wayne Jackson heard the story, "One day they put a gun up to David Porter's head and threatened to kill him if he messed with Isaac anymore."

On the surface, this was eminently bizarre. Indeed, by then the bonded rise of Ike and Dave was inviolate, with each being handsomely rewarded. In fact, their mutual enrichment had led to the end of the idealistic "Big Six" profit-sharing arrangement late in 1969—inasmuch as Hayes and Porter had so far transcended everyone else that there was little sharing going on, only continual windfalls to them. Al Bell had massaged Ike even more by refusing to allow the four others in the combine to collect a penny in profits from any of Ike's staggering solo sales, and even more unilaterally, Ike was all but awarded Enterprise for making it profitable—doing what Otis Redding did for Volt with few of the same perks—and given creative control of who would record on it. Porter was also cut in on the label's royalties.

Thus, few around Stax would have believed there was any financial grudge by Ike for his longtime partner—the kind of grudges being held against *them* and Ike in particular now. Booker T. Jones recalled that "because [*Hot Buttered Soul* was] on the Enterprise label, we don't get nothing. He had them by the ass.... Good for Isaac. And I guarantee that if it has been up to Isaac, as fair as Isaac was, I don't even think Isaac knew anything about it. But when we went in and said, 'Where's our percentage?', all of a sudden it's a whole different game. Fuck it. Boy, we all hit the ceiling over that."

Porter, for his part, strongly denies that there was any bad blood between he and Ike, or that Johnny Baylor ever stuck a gun in his face for some reason. Rather, he said of the latter, "I told him if he ever fucked with me, it would be a major problem," which, if so, would have made him brave indeed. "There's twelve boys in the Porter family, one of them would get [his] ass. He wouldn't make it out of Memphis."

Still, there were small matters of pride that Ike had not settled in his mind. He had wanted to go on his own as a singer for years and might have believed Dave had crimped him by perhaps privately turning Jim Stewart and Al Bell off to the idea. If so, Ike may have believed—or was prodded to by Johnny Baylor—that Dave was resentful of Ike's subsequent solo success and needed a good talking to. Also pertinent is that, as Ike's solo stardom riveted upward, he seemed to sidestep songs the two of them had written but not recorded.

"A lot of people have asked why I didn't sing some of the things I wrote with David Porter," Ike once said, "but that was not my personal preference. As a singer my idols were Nat King Cole and Brook Benton, people like that. I'd listen to Tony Bennett, Frank Sinatra, Billy Eckstine, Sarah Vaughn, and Arthur Prysock. So [when I sang], that's how it came out."

But Porter, who released several nifty funk albums on Enterprise collaborating with a new co-writer, Ronnie Williams, worked with Ike on Dave's 1971 LP *Into a Real Thing*, and Ike arranged Porter's version of Chuck Jackson's "I Don't Wanna Cry" as well as co-producing and singing duets with him on Porter's singles "Ain't That Loving You" and its B-side, a cover of Bread's "Baby I'm-a Want You," on both of which Ike had the Movement singers perform background vocals. Though it would take until 1995 for them to write together again, Ike would not utter a negative word about Porter, with whom he would be inducted into the Songwriters Hall of Fame in 2005 (as was Steve Cropper). He said that, contrary to resenting his solo flight, Porter told him—ironically, in the same somewhat biting language Ike had about Dave getting to Stax first— "One of us was going to become a star, and you did it first."

119

When they were named, underratedly so, the seventy-fifth best songwriting team in rock history by *Rolling Stone*, Porter remarked, "I'm no musician but I was able to relate to Isaac, we could communicate together." And that was a bond that not even Johnny Baylor could have destroyed. Still, Baylor so impressed Ike that it certainly paid off for Johnny, big time. Not by coincidence, Baylor "persuaded" Ike to tour with Baylor's meal ticket at KoKo, Luther Ingram, as the opening act, raising Ingram's public profile and sales and ingraining him at Stax where he had also written the Staple Singers' first million-selling record, the 1971 Black-empowerment anthem "Respect Yourself." At Stax, common law was that whatever Ike wanted, Ike got. Because he had Johnny Baylor to get it.

INURED AS IKE was to him, Johnny had begun affectionately calling him "Moses"—which *Jet* magazine editor Chester Higgins had expanded into "Black Moses" in articles about the man he also called a "strutting, virile peacock"—and Baylor's glaring eyes were aimed even at those on tour with Ike. This included Marvell Thomas. During a rehearsal before a show in Cleveland, Thomas took offense at Baylor pinching one of the three backup singers on the ass. Ike said nothing, but Thomas, from behind his keyboard, told Johnny, "Get your silly ass off the stage." Not used to sass, Baylor whipped out his gun and held it to Thomas's head. Petrified but not shrinking, Thomas said later that he challenged him to pull the trigger or get off the stage, whereupon Baylor backed off. But not long after, Thomas was fired by Ike, which left a bad taste in his mouth; after having helped steer Ike's solo career, Thomas quit Stax and became musical director for his sister Carla, who also fled the label, and later Etta James and Peabo Bryson.

Baylor went even further with another in Ike's circle, Johnny Keyes, who had written Clarence Carter's soul hit "Too Weak to Fight" and had recently bought Estelle Axton's Satellite record store from her son Packy, the original Mar-Keys sax man. After becoming friendly with Ike, Keyes began going on the road as his stage manager, but his spending became a problem. Ike and his retinue flew to New York in January 1970 for a benefit show that Ike and other acts played for free at New York's Hunter College for the Soledad Brothers, three Black inmates charged with killing a white guard at Soledad Prison. Ike called the brothers "political prisoners" and told the press, "This is where I'm at. I'm not the turn-the-other-cheek kind of person, no. But I believe in using tact and intelligence."

However, he exercised neither when Keyes asked him for some kind of payment, saying later that while Ike could "donate" his money, Keyes, who had no similar financial comforts, had no reason to donate *his*. Rebuffed, Keyes then went on a spending spree at the hotel, charging room service and other benefits to Ike's account. When Ike learned of this, he told Baylor, "Man, handle it any way you want to handle it." Baylor and Woodard then barged through Keyes's door as he was partying with the Movement girls. As the women scrambled in terror out of the room, the two thugs pounded Keyes with nine-millimeter pistols, leaving him bleeding profusely and hiding under the bed. Barely able to move, he pulled the phone down and called friends who took him to safety, not to return to Memphis for weeks, after which he quickly sold the record shop and moved to Chicago, free of Baylor and the madness around Isaac Hayes.

Ike, who took these "interventions" with barely a shrug, would euphemistically refer to Baylor and Woodard as no more than necessary evils, saying that his mooks merely "corrected" promoters' rip-offs with "gangster stuff" that "protected me. A lot of people didn't like it but I think they were necessary."

Suffice to say, Ike never was stiffed by a promoter. And as far as Baylor's role went, not only did he protect Ike, he was credited by Stax officials for "persuading" radio stations to play the company's records—Ike's as a priority—and record stores to slap huge posters of the company's records in their windows. He also was instrumental in having Stax host industry conventions, one of which, in Atlanta around Christmas time, featured H. Rap Brown as the invited guest speaker, growling about reparations. Naturally, there were more rumors that Bell was being threatened by Baylor to do things his way, possibly not all legal. But Bell hardly minded, not with Stax's reputation in the industry having been transformed from a Southern rube to a major industry player.

As far as Baylor's role as Ike's enforcer, it included making sure the star attraction was never alone in his hotel rooms, that he'd have endless rounds of booze and willing women at his disposal. And there would be a *lot* of time in hotel rooms. The gigs multiplied in 1970, keeping the records so flush at Stax that the sound Al Bell wanted to hear most—*ca-ching*—was really the new sound of soul, and just as importantly, the best way to keep the company's credit line high enough to borrow even more.

WITH THE PROFITS from *Hot Buttered Soul* and *The Isaac Hayes Movement*—which, as the name of the band, led Ike to now dub the backup chorale of Rose Williams and sisters Pat and Diane Lewis Hot, Butter, and Soul—Bell turned Stax even more into Isaac Hayes's personal kingdom. Yet Ike, with all his wealth and perquisites, still wasn't completely contented. He had been waiting for Bell to give him stock shares in Stax, which he had sent sky high. Bell still didn't do it. Nonetheless, Ike was committed to the company, unlike Booker T. Jones and Steve Cropper, who were at long last unable to stomach the vibes that had turned so poisonous. Booker T. went first. He bid adieu and moved to LA, where he received an offer from A&M Records to lure away the M.G.'s. Cropper and Dunn begged off, and early in 1971, Booker T. agreed to join his old bandmates for one last successful album, *Melting Pot*, which took much from Ike's free-range funk. However, Booker T. was adamant about not going back to Memphis, and the work was recorded in New York.

But by then Cropper also had enough of the freak show on East McLemore. Still irate about the beating of Marvell Thomas, Cropper bridled more when Bell nixed him from agreeing to Paul Simon's wish to have the M.G.'s play on Simon & Garfunkel's 1970 recording of "Bridge over Troubled Water." So Cropper, who was so eager to split now that he forfeited the two remaining years on his contract and what he made out to be $100,000 in royalties, finally took off and opened his own Memphis studio, renewing his old connections with Packy Axton, who would die untimely early in '74 from cirrhosis at thirty-two. That left only Dunn and Jackson from the house band, with Jackson writing and producing for Albert King and moonlighting on a side deal with producer Willie Mitchell to back up the soulful gospel singer Al Green, who recorded for Memphis's Hi Records. Soon, Jackson walked as well, signing with Mitchell to be the regular drummer in Green's backup crew just as he burst out as the newest avatar of yearning, burning soul. And William Bell also had enough, moving to Atlanta and starting his own label, Peachtree Records, saying later that Stax had sadly gone from "a little family company to a multi-million-dollar corporation where everybody was a number. I would come in, and somebody would say, 'Have you met William Bell?' 'Oh, yes, [he's] Stax number ST124.'"

Duck Dunn would have gone, too, had not for the plans for him to join Creedence Clearwater Revival (for whom the M.G.'s had opened on a 1970 tour) fallen through. Duck stayed put, lost in a thicket of unfamiliar "numbers" shuffling in and out. The Bar-Kays stuck around only because of their association with Ike that led to them recording new Bar-Kays albums when disco began to bubble up. Ike, meanwhile, was broadening his stage dimension, hiring new musicians in an expanded Isaac Hayes Movement lineup, one of whom—repaying a favor he had not forgotten—was his old mentor on the club scene, Sid Kirk, along with another keyboardist Lester Snell, guitarist Charles "Skip" Pitts, and trumpeter Mickey Gregory. Each of the crew was paid seventy dollars per gig, which mounted up quickly. Snell remembered that when he first stepped onto a stage to play behind Ike, he looked out into a sea of 70,000 Black and white faces. He had gotten no setlist in advance nor any rehearsal time, and the first song of the set was one he had never heard.

"It was fast," he said. "Chords coming, and here comes the breaks, and it's got all kinds of stops. And then right in the middle of that, the tune breaks down into 'Oh mama let me light your fire....' I'm like, what? Then it comes back to going fast again, then into triplets, now totally ripping. That's the first tune." Of the recording process, Hall said of Ike, "He was a night owl. He'd say, 'Hey, man—session tomorrow night at 7.' But then he may not show up until 11, depending on which chick had just flown into town."

To keep the session cats from boredom, Ike would send one of his retinue out to pick up a few of Ike's steady women friends and bring them to the studio. "At that point, all the crooked backs straightened up, everybody's got their hips shaking, and grinning, and boy, now you got something going on." Sometimes, Ike would provide other types of performance enhancers, which Hall boils down to a simple act, which he said was to "just drop a tab of acid, and go crazy." Whatever the stimuli, "We were the tightest band you'd ever find. It could be straight-out jazz or Jimi Hendrix, but no matter what was going on, you never lost the groove."

That of course could have been Isaac Hayes's epitaph. Yet, as oversized as he had gotten, he couldn't help feeling more and more like a stranger in the old theater, which even he had less to do with now. He had grown accustomed to the acoustics and production crew at Ardent. Stax was almost a ghost town, with many acts, including Dave Porter, given the leeway to record at Muscle Shoals. But Ike still took seriously his role as vice president, something the other veeps simply wore as a badge rather than a commitment of purpose. Sitting in his large, expensively furnished office, its walls covered with vertical black and white striped wallpaper and a massive horseshoe-shaped, red and white desk and an Eames chair stacked with music sheets and fan letters, several secretaries would dart in and out along with Stax executives and community leaders with whom he would discuss his new nonprofit, Isaac Hayes Foundation, which he told the newspapers would "alleviate suffering wherever and whenever possible."

On the letterhead were names of board of directors like Jesse Jackson, Georgia state representative Julian Bond, and Odell Horton, president of LeMoyne-Owen College. In 1972, he was invited to Washington by the Congressional Black Caucus to testify before a committee hearing, at which he sat in a modest suit, mingling with heavyweights like Barbara Jordan, Walter Fauntroy, and Ralph Metcalfe. He also appeared at the National Black Political Convention in Gary, Indiana, schmoozing with Harry Belafonte, Dick Gregory, Al Freeman, Jr. and Gary Mayor Richard Hatcher and performing at a show emceed by actor Richard Roundtree. With such important links to the government and showbiz, he was able to secure $8 million from HUD for the housing project he sponsored in the Virgin Islands, a twenty-acre community of apartment complexes, and he had learned some vital lessons.

"White people play it smart," he once said. "They have the right counsel at their fingertips and when they retire, everything is cool. That same kind of financial guidance is available to me and I'm taking advantage of it.... You see, I *could* be shooting my money into my arms or I *could* be chasing whores. What I *am* doing is making a sound investment. The only thing this country respects is money, because it's power. If you get it, you can break down a lot of doors."

AND HE DID. When not recording or out on the road, he would be an administrator doling out money to local Black causes and performing at fundraising concerts; one of which was billed as the "Give a Damn Extravaganza," for which he brought with him The Bar-Kays, Soul Children, Emotions, and Short-Cuts. Alarmed at the fading aura of the town's historical music scene, he entertained and handed out awards to native talent each year at a show held by the preservationist Memphis Music Inc., on whose board of directors he served—the only Black member of the twenty-one directors. A ubiquitous presence on the political scene, he campaigned for Black candidates such as Harold Ford, who was elected to the state legislature in 1970 and became Tennessee's first Black US Congressman. Aware of his leverage, he pulled no punches about Stax's mostly white upper crust. "I forced issue after issue," he said. "I approached Jim Stewart saying: here's a white-owned company selling Black product to a predominantly Black audience. You gotta have some Black employees around here other than musicians and custodians."

The problem was that as much as he wanted Stax to be Blacker; his lifestyle was so excessive that it began to mock, not magnify, Black pride. Outside his garish office were only dilapidated streets and a progression of empty storefronts of downtown Memphis, streets which not only saw Ike's wheels but those on the Cadillacs owned by, among others, Porter, Bell, Johnny Baylor, Eddie Floyd, and Johnnie Taylor. This stamped an era that Stanley Booth referenced in a *Saturday Evening Post* commentary, writing with distaste of the "matched sets of Cadillacs" on otherwise poverty-covered streets. Indeed, while Ike would feel like he had to explain that the Caddy made a trenchant point in that it blunted the notion that such rolling tanks were only seen as "pimp-mobiles," it seemed to some that a "soulmobile" wasn't much more tasteful.

For Ike, wealth and materialism gave him a winning hand in the game of life still beclouded by vest-pocket racism. As *Ebony* writer B.J. Mason waxed in a long fluff piece of him in 1973,

> There are a number of things the sultan of sound doesn't like about show business and bigotry is first on his list. It appears that even an Isaac Hayes can be caught in a racial trap—usually triggered by phonies who treat him cold until they discover who he is, by slickers who foolishly regard him as just a dumb

country nigger, by hotel managers who withhold their best suites, by promoters who attempt to lock out black entertainers, and by the subtle discrimination that black stars have to deal with in general. "It's a hassle, sometimes," Hayes concedes, "but I don't let it get to me."

Not that Ike was unaware of the thorny edges of this bramble bush, for which he had a ready comeback: "Success has placed me on a high level in society, but I can still relate to the dudes on the block. The money, the cars, all of it is just fringe, but Isaac Hayes is roots."

Indeed, he would often alight from the Ed Dorado to rap out with the dudes, sit in the barber shop, mess around with old buddies, and shoot some crap on the corner. He gave handouts worth thousands to people he might barely know. The story was told that when a local shopkeeper was being closed down by the IRS after not paying taxes, the man pulled out a gun and held the FBI agents at bay and wanted to speak to Ike; as cops surrounded the store, Ike ran over and talked the keeper into putting down the gun and the crisis ended peacefully. That was how he rolled. He wanted to be populist, not pompous, a people's Moses. Yet those gold wheels were quite a useful metaphor for him, more so for the backlash it seemed to stir. As it was, the '50s Broadway play and movie *The Solid Gold Cadillac* used such wheels as a metaphor of no less than a too-capitalistic America, which as one critic mused "will give you an interesting ride, but don't expect it to take you or your intelligence very far."

And this cynicism, hinted at by Booth, was inculcated by the soul community itself in 1974 with Philadelphia soul singer William DeVaughn's "Be Thankful for What You Got," reminding all that even if you didn't have a diamond in the back, a sunroof top—or a car at all—you could dig the scene with a gangsta lean (the original title for the song being the ironic "A Cadillac Don't Come Easy"), The record assuredly sold two million copies; its follow-up,

"Blood Is Thicker Than Water," may as well have been titled "Black Blood Is Thicker than Hi-Test Gasoline." And so while Ike certainly had all that he had fantasized as a kid with ripped shoes and lint in his pockets, lurking ahead was a pothole in the fast lane: the reality that neither he nor Al Bell believed was remotely possible for men like them, Black men who had indeed proven that money was power: the reality that neither of them would ever be rich enough to conquer their own mortal faults.

10

A Bad Mutha

Ike never said much about his songs being in Norman Mailer's chaotic 1970 indie flick *Maidstone*, the last of three avant-garde movies written, produced, directed, and acted by the rambunctious author himself. But the Mailer gig represented an upward move for Isaac Hayes into the anteroom of the white glitterati, which had been a key crossover path for Otis Redding. At the time, Hayes had only performed for a mass audience on a TV variety show called *Music Scene*, singing "Walk on By." Mailer deserved props for knowing how riveting Ike's gritty, soulful voice could be, which it surely was in the three songs he sang for the soundtrack: "Precious, Precious," "I Just Want to Make Love to You," and "Rock Me Baby." And Al Bell this entree used as a prop for more movie outreach as the cinema became manna for pop music.

Bell had foreseen these possibilities when he had Booker T. & the M.G.'s record the soundtrack for *Uptight* three years before. He was aware that an oddball but potentially revenue-rich "black" movie was being produced, directed, written, scored, and acted in by the Black gadfly Melvin Van Peebles, who had directed the racial comedy *Watermelon Man*. It was called *Sweet Sweetback's Baadasssss Song* and Van Peebles had to put up $100,000 of his own money and borrow $50,000 more from Bill Cosby to make what he heralded as "the first black power film" and give the finger to "The Man"—every reason why no studio would touch it, another being that Van Peebles would play a man framed for murder who escapes, has indiscriminate sex, teams with Black Panthers, burns down buildings, kills a bunch of cops, and gets away with all of it.

Van Peebles could get away with this due to his ironic, wry humor, and his resume. He had recorded a stirring jazz-soul album and for *Sweetback* hired the then-nascent Earth, Wind & Fire to record a jazzy score that included one of the first instances of rapping. It was released in April 1971 and became a public fascination that would earn over $15 million, with real Black Panther Huey Newton calling it "revolutionary." Jumping in on all this, Bell had paid Van Peebles to have Stax release the soundtrack album, which would be sold in the lobbies of the few theaters showing the film at the start, soon to be followed by hundreds of theaters. The album sold over 100,000 copies and reached number thirteen on the soul album chart. It also had begat the portmanteau "blaxploitation," not from a cynical white critic but a highly admirable Black man, Junius Griffin, who had written the Pulitzer Prize-nominated *New York Times* series on the racial scene called "The Deepening Crisis," worked as Martin Luther King, Jr.'s speechwriter, then as Motown's public relations director, as well as being president of the Beverly Hills NAACP. If Griffin meant the new word as a slight, he would be stunned when the Black literati picked up on it with a sense of pride.

Bell was all in on Van Peebles. He would also profit from his work by releasing the cast album of his hit 1972 Broadway musical *Don't Play Us Cheap*, which claimed two Tony nominations. But Bell was after an even more handsome return on investment. Weeks before *Sweetback* came out, he held a meeting with Mike Curb, the youngish president of MGM Records, the music arm of MGM Studios. Curb, who had written and produced a load of songs and movie scores, seemed the last executive suited to soul. A Republican, he had campaigned for Richard Nixon and Ronald

Reagan, and later was elected Lieutenant Governor of California, yet he steered Bell to an MGM Studios project—the studio having optioned former *New York Times* reporter Ernest Tidyman's 1970 pulp novel about a Black New York detective. MGM had hired Gordon Parks to direct it, as he had with the 1969 "black" movie *The Learning Tree*. Tidyman, who was co-writing the screenplay, created the detective—John Shaft—as a sophisticated man of the street who "used black rage as one of his resources, along with intelligence and courage." Yet, just before shooting began, MGM wanted to alter the story and make Shaft white. Livid, Parks threatened to quit, and the studio backed down. And that was when Bell drove a bargain with MGM to record and release the score via Stax.

Bell broached Ike about writing the score and set a meeting for him with the studio heads, although Ike wanted more to play Shaft in the film, despite having never acted. They told him he could audition for the role, provided he agreed to do the score as well. Once he agreed, the audition never occurred, and Parks moved in on him with assurances that the movie would light a fuse; even if MGM's budget was a mere million dollars and could afford no major actors, the lead going to the relatively obscure Richard Roundtree. Not that Ike was ready to throw himself into it. "I wasn't too confident about it at first," he said. "I was a little nervous. I had never recorded a soundtrack before and I was scared that I would mess up. But I talked things over with Quincy Jones, who is just about the number one in film music composers, and he encouraged me to take [it] on."

He approached it as, he said, "a concept to sell to Black consumers. It was as if they just discovered there was a Black market out there. Now they wanted a Black composer and they picked me." Parks kept reminding him that Shaft was a hero—a Black hero. "Zero in on the character!" Parks kept telling him, "A relentless guy, always in pursuit, always on the move." Much like Muhammad Ali, whose "trainer" and second banana, Drew "Bundini" Brown, had a small role in the movie. Not incidentally, the role of Blacks in sports also grew dominant in the early '70s. Another "superman," Hank Aaron, broke the home run record of the most fabled of white supermen, Babe Ruth, in '71.

And so, in the very pit of Black exceptionalism, Ike came to New York with The Bar-Kays during the shooting of the movie to watch daily rushes of the film. He sat at a piano, sucking on a toothpick as Parks kept peppering him with suggestions. Because Ike hadn't learned how to chart music, he would turn to his Stax cohort Johnny Allen to do the charts when he returned to Memphis. Then Ike and the band took off for LA to cut the album in MGM's studio. Parks was eager for the riff of the opening scene, when Shaft emerges from hell out of a Times Square subway station clad in an expensive brown leather trench coat and hip yellow turtleneck sweater and before threading his way through the dregs below porn theater marquees. Ike found a rhythm for it, as he usually found them, on the fly. He had no chords, no set melody. As Skip Pitts remembered, Ike and the musicians were looking for a beat; Ike at the piano, Willie Hall on the drum kit, and Pitts on guitar. Ike's first idea was to have Hall create, as Ike would say, "a relentless, dramatic effect," by swishing busy sixteenth notes on the hi-hat cymbal, a *chug-a-chug-a-chug-a* sound rarely heard in rock or soul, as producers disfavored cluttering the sound with cymbal effects. But Ike had helped chart Otis Redding's "Try A Little Tenderness" with sixteenths, and it felt right here too.

Ike went with it on the keyboard, the bass settled in, and now it was Skip's turn to riff, though really all he was doing was tuning up by joining in on the sixteenths on an F chord.

"And Ike looked at me and said, 'Keep playing that, keep playin' that riff.' When he changed his key to G, I changed, too, but then went back to the F. But he said, 'No, no, no! Keep playing on your G.' And all through the whole damn structure, I kept on my G. He'd say, 'Bang it twice' to the guys, to double up on the beat, but I'd still be on my G—all except for the end, when I hit an F for that last note that kinda went *woiiiinng*. That was the only time I didn't play that damn G!"

As Ike explained it, "Before I even presented [the guitar line] to Skip, I had that wah-wah in mind. When Skip played, I got on my knees and worked the wah-wah pedal [the floor-standing, vocal-sounding guitar tone modifier invented in 1965 by Vox and popularized by Jimi Hendrix] with my hands, then he got the feel and took over." He smiled. "It all worked, man."

To Pitt's amazement: "I mean, I didn't think what I did was the way to go. Man, when I hit that last note I was so damn glad. Because to me the song sounded repetitious, redundant, and ridiculous. And when it came out and I was in the car and heard it, I still didn't like it. Like, *Why'd he have me do that same thing all through that song?* Shows you what you know, alright? Only later on, it started hitting on me, why it worked. And it changed my life, too, because people believed I made the song what it was. No, Ike did, we all did. People even started saying [the pedal] I played on, on an old Baby Box kick block, what they called a stomp pedal, was a new thing. Well, it wasn't, but what I did with it made history."

"THEME FROM SHAFT" was one of those accidental but perfectly tuned Isaac Hayes masterpieces; the smooth, snappy intro bulked up by funky, almost sarcastic sounding horns. It worked really well for Parks, and when someone in the MGM office told Ike that a song would be more worthy of Oscar consideration if it had lyrics, he scribbled fanciful lines on an envelope that he thought would mesh best as a climactic vapor, a minute-long deviation near the end. "Shaft was a form of rap, really, before that term was used," he noted. "It was a back-and-forth thing, a conversation, done in rhythm. The lyrics came easy. I did censor myself, though—'This cat Shaft is a bad mother...shut your mouth.' I did it that way, otherwise somebody would have told me to shut my damn mouth."

In fact, even tempered "blue" lyrics were daring, for example, the word "damn," possibly marking the first time even that mild vulgarity was used in a song. Ike had watched Roundtree utter the endless curses in the script and sensed a rhythm to it, similar to Ali's boxing poetry. That carved out the rhythm of the lyrics. In a simple call and response, he semi-rapped and semi-sung about the "black private dick" and "sex machine to all the chicks." He had the background singers, Telma Hopkins and Joyce Wilson, shout "Shaft!" Then his retort: "Damn right!" followed by similar call and response repartee with the singers, also throwing in "Can you dig it?"—the question asked three years before by the Friends of Distinction on the poppy "Grazing in the Grass." He lauded Shaft as "a bad mutha," the updated "soul man." The final shtick was that Shaft was a complicated man, understood only by his woman, so with the last words from Hopkins and Wilson deferentially crooning came the full identity of our hero:

"John Shaft!"

This pastiche, so quaint and well-known now, was back then a long jump into the deep end of white culture. And the most amazing thing about it was how easy it was for Ike to make it sound so authentic. Because Shaft was something Hayes wasn't—the latter being a complicated man who was never completely understood by *any* woman except one, his grandmother Rushia Wade. But the score gave Parks nearly seventy minutes of funky, jazzy wonder, enough for a double album—another rarity for movie soundtracks and the first double album of original material by any soul artist.

The fifteen tracks on *Shaft* were an endless stream—and sometimes a raging river—of soul crosscurrents and undercurrents. It segued from coolly blithe to still-cool discordance; to the point that the groove and intensity were so instinctive that, in "Soulsville," Pitts began playing a riff that sounded like the ding-dong-ding NBC network jingle, just before Ike terminated the song by saying, with streetwise perfection, "Fuck it, we're out of time." This was another Isaac Hayes on-the-spot riff, and would be the score's final words. Such anything-goes instincts can be best heard in the 2009 remastered soundtrack *Shaft* album on CD, with full studio versions of the tracks. Indeed, much had to be trimmed before the original album went out. And Ike, unhappy that the acoustics in the MGM studios weren't optimum, insisted that he re-record the soundtrack back in Memphis, embellished with conga and bongo runs by Gary Jones, a lead trumpet added by Richard Davis, and philharmonic, quarter tone notes by flutist John Fonville.

MGM knew they had a winner. The theme was used as a conscious publicity tool for the campaign of TV commercials and posters that hung all over big cities of Roundtree firing a smoking gun and the words "THE MOB WANTED HARLEM. INSTEAD, THEY GOT SHAFT. UP TO HERE." By the time the movie debuted on June 25, the theme was being played via selective leaking of the record to key radio stations prior to its official release on Enterprise Records in the last week of September, with "Cafe Regio's" (Shaft's Greenwich Village hangout) on the B-side. Within a week, the movie was the top box-office hit, en route to taking in over $10 million, surely an undercount, since a new method of theft, pirated copies of movies, had hit Stax hard, with an estimated 800,000 such copies being hawked.

This all happened despite reviews for *Shaft* as a work of film that were fairly blah—two and a half stars from Roger Ebert being one indicator. A review by N. Owano in the *Village Voice* chafed Roundtree for looking like "the men in billboards plastered all over the Bronx, Brooklyn, and Harlem—of SUPERCOOL, smoking Salems, or spritzing Afro-Sheen, or flexing his dimples in a pair of Alexander's knit bellbottoms." Shaft, in this take, was James Bond "put into blackface...a Madison Avenue dummy, and not a real brother at all." Yet Owano could admit, "*Shaft* is not the film you walk out on."

This was freely attested in the music press—though Robert Christgau still seemed not to make up his mind about Hayes, judging that the album was "Pretty rhythmic for a soundtrack—if a backup band played this stuff before the star-of-our-show came on, you wouldn't get bored until midway into the second number. Proving that not only do black people make better pop-schlock movies than white people, they also make better pop-schlock music. As if we didn't know." The grade was an almost insulting C+. Not that it mattered a whit that a good number of white critics, and a few Black ones, took easily to these kinds of halfway slurs. The theme song would lurch to number one on the pop single chart on November 20, and the week after, above a passel of white megastar commodities—Cher's "Gypsies, Tramps & Thieves," John Lennon's "Imagine," and Bread's "Baby I'm-A Want You."

"When it hit so big," Ike would say, "I was in severe disbelief. I walked around thinking, *Did I really do that?*"

It had cruised to number two on the soul chart by Halloween and would stay there for three weeks, kept out of the top only by Marvin Gaye's equally stately and provocative "Inner City Blues (Make Me Wanna Holler)" and the Chi-Lites' soothing "Have You Seen Her." And yet, leaving aside the pirate factor, a marker of remarkable consistency was that the album would sell more soul records than any other that year, beating The Temptations' sedating "Just My Imagination (Running Away with Me)." The album, which also went Gold within weeks, ate up the soul chart, going number one for fourteen weeks and finishing '71 as the tenth-ranked soul album, one slot behind Gil Scott-Heron's *Pieces of a Man*. And as if by rote, Ike again topped the jazz album chart and also hit number four in England.

All of which, despite the reviews, actualized Parks' goal of making *Shaft* a crossover tool like none before with the single also earning a gold record, Ike's only one as a performer. The album did not leave the pop chart for *sixty* weeks. Hayes won Oscar and Grammy nominations, and decades and cultural eras later, it is really his work that has kept the movie bronzed; retro-reviews by people not born until years after the movie cover it in laurels of coolness, far more so than the spate of much-later sequels for which Ike spent his final years scoring the same sort of scenes by memory. Indeed, the original soundtrack has never lost its hold on hip Black cultural tropes. One retro-review on *Pitchfork* by Nate Patrin, upon the release of that "deluxe" edition of the soundtrack in 2009, pegged not only the ageless theme song but "Soulsville" as "a guided tour of the ghetto, as if from above on a cloud, charting welfare lines, tricks on the corner, ditching reality to get high only to find you can't touch the sky...clearly written as an entreaty for otherwise-oblivious whites to sympathize with Black America's troubles."

That is a pretty effective back view of the *Shaft* thing, as was Jacob Heilbrunn opining in *The Spectator* in 2020 that, in the song "Soulsville," "Hayes echoes Rousseau's observation that man is born free and everywhere in chains [but] might be more powerful," that black men were born free but, as the song went, 'The chains that bind him are hard to see/ Unless you take this walk with me.'"

IN THE WAKE of Shaftmania, other movies studios could see a golden rainbow in even the lowest rungs of Blaxploitation. One after another they came; some surprisingly cogent, some gag-inducing bad. Many pimped the progenitor of the idiom; when MGM hurried another, called *Cool Breeze*, the company's ads began "FROM MGM, THE COMPANY THAT GAVE YOU SHAFT..." summarizing in faux Black-speak that the main character "hit the Man for $3 million. Right where it hurts. In the diamonds." On the other hand, the best of the rest was Warner Brothers' 1972 *Super Fly*, also directed by Gordon Parks and blessed with a score by another soul master, Curtis Mayfield, who refused to let the typically violent and vulgar amorality dictate his music. Unlike Ike, he didn't lionize any ghetto supermen; rather, he torched the whole damn ghetto with the funkiest scolding ever. For the pimp in the title song, he reproofed, "The only game you know is do or die," a message repeated in other outstanding tracks like "Freddie's Dead"

and "Pusherman." Mayfield's score made the movie bigger than *Shaft*, netting $30 million on a half-million budget—though paradoxically, the movement found less to praise without a Shaft-like superhero. A most curious turn in the progression of Black power, in no small way owing to Isaac Hayes.

Indeed, *Shaft* pricked '70s culture in large and small ways. Telma Hopkins would also ride her "Shut your mouth" refrain into a ready one-liner in TV sitcoms. Ernest Tidyman became the first white writer to win an NAACP Image Award. Gordon Parks was handed the director's job by MGM for an inevitable *Shaft* sequel with Roundtree and much of the cast back and Tidyman the screenwriter. Naturally, Ike had been expected to join as well, but he was not keen to compose more of the same thing with a lesser movie. The monetary factor was irrelevant, being so enmeshed in touring (during this period he went off on mega tours in America, Europe, and Canada) that he could pull off a squeeze play with MGM, asking for such poison-pill compensation in the sequel so that he could back off by blaming the studio.

As a result, MGM took back the soundtrack for its own record label and opted not to use Ike's "Theme from Shaft" or any of his original soundtrack—a self-destructive decision that, as if in spite, had them prohibiting any other movie borrowing the songs from it until 1978. Parks wrote the score to the sequel himself, trying somehow to replicate Ike's priceless riffs, and did well enough with it that the sequel, *Shaft's Big Score*, with twice the original's budget, was glossier and more conventional. It made $10 million despite some critical stoning that often blamed the loss of Hayes's touch. "You miss that sound," wrote one, "which gave 'Shaft' a persistent, rhythmic drive and undercurrent." As Nate Patrin noted decades later, "There was nothing quite like the convergence of popular and cinematic music in *Shaft*, at least not since Duke Ellington was tapped to soundtrack *Anatomy of a Murder* 12 years previous."

Any iteration of Shaft, then, renewed Ike's aura, just out of familiarity, even in other Blaxploitation potboilers like *Black*

Caesar, which was also released in '72 and was a mess, but a profitable mess—*its* score composed by James Brown, whose usual funk jams sounded a lot like the man's world of Isaac Hayes, whose name and presence seemed as integral on any piece of music within this format. Indeed, when "Son of Shaft," a follow-up to his *Shaft* theme about a crime fighter chipped off the old block—quite a ludicrous notion since Shaft was a still young man—did come out, it was recorded by The Bar-Kays as a near note-for-note copy (though it was written not by Ike but Allen Jones, Homer Banks, and William C. Brown and produced by Jones), but it was dead on arrival as a single. Actually, the closest anyone came to channeling Ike's layered, barbed grooves was Willie Hutch, a Motown writer for The Jackson 5 and Marvin Gaye, who wrote soundtracks for notable later Blaxploitation flicks like *The Mack* and *Foxy Brown*. (Hutch's single release of "Slick" from Motown's *The Mack* soundtrack was essentially "Shaft" with the word "Slick" substituted, and went to number eighteen in soul and number sixty-five in pop.)

The much alive spoils for Ike carried into 1973, first at the Grammy Awards on March 14 at Madison Square Garden's Felt Forum. The *Shaft* theme song, nominated for Best Instrumental Composition for a Motion Picture or Television, was up against Elton John and Bernie Taupin's "Friends," Barry De Vorzon/Perry Botkin, Jr.'s "Bless the Beasts and Children," Francis Lai's "Love Story," and Maurice Jarre's "Ryan's Daughter." The presenter of the award, the British actor/singer Richard Harris, tipped off the result: "I was promised I could kiss the winner, but Isaac you can relax." So announced, Ike strode to the stage in a foamy, two-tone, full-body brown leather caftan, silver chains dipping from neck to navel, and a raised a fist amid a loud ovation. He thanked Stax Records and "the record buyers and many fans" without whom "this wouldn't have happened." In all, he was up for eight Grammys; one was for Best Rhythm and Blues Performance for "Never Can Say Goodbye," but lost to Lou Rawls's "Natural Man." Ike and Johnny Allen shared Best Instrumental Arrangement, and he and

Allen shared with Henry Bush, Ron Capone, and Dave Purple for Best Engineered Recording.

These conquests were among a record seventeen Grammys won by Black artists, others being Aretha Franklin, Quincy Jones, Bill Withers, and Ike and Tina Turner (plus special lifetime awards for Louis Armstrong and Mahalia Jackson who both died in 1972). Yet there was a sour footnote to the event. When no Motown nominee won—Marvin Gaye lost twice—company executives stormed out of the hall, with Marvin bitching afterward that James Brown wasn't nominated at all. An irate Miles Davis split when Herbie Hancock lost Best Jazz Performer to white pianist Bill Evans. Given this flak, the Grammy people could be grateful that Ike dominated the headlines.

A month later, the Academy Awards were in LA's Dorothy Chandler Pavilion. "Theme from Shaft," nominated for Best Original Song, had brought about another kerfuffle among some Academy parliamentarians. Ike recalled, "The Academy tried to disqualify it, saying because I can't write music it wasn't my composition. Quincy Jones got in there and argued my case, saying that even if I didn't physically write it down [in notes on a music chart] they were my ideas." Ike would perform the song before a nearly all-white audience, head to toe in formal attire. The performance could have been called "Shaft in Hollywood," a lip-synced ballyhoo that started with a female dancer's bump and grind as Willie Hall pretended to play the hi-hat opening. Scantily clad dancers jiggled and chicken-walked as Ike, in his chain-mesh vest that dangled down his bare chest, sat at a rainbow piano all ultra-cool. At song's end, a smoke cloud rose over everybody, leaving host Sammy Davis, Jr. to display his characteristic exuberance, wildly applauding and exclaiming, "Wow! Was that something? Whooo! Talk about heavy!"

Inane as it was, it was another in-your-face stride within the culture evolution. (Forty-four years later, a *Rolling Stone* ranking of the twenty best Oscar performances ranked it seventh, writing, "Daaaamn right. The Oscars have never shied away from serious spectacle du Velveeta...but this blend of time-capsule showbiz goofiness and hot buttered soul is the perfect combination of sweet and salty.") His fellow nominees for the top honor were music royalty: Henry Mancini, Marvin Hamlisch, Perry Botkin, Jr., and Robert and Richard Sherman. But history had made the musical ligature between Black and white force fields complete. A year before, Phil Spector had made some history for rock by winning for his score of The Beatles' *Let It Be*. Now, making history for Black music men, when Ike's win was announced by the actor Joel Gray, he became the first African American to win an Oscar for a movie score and just the third to win one of any kind behind Hattie McDaniel and Sidney Poitier. Black Moses came jogging down the aisle in a white striped exercise tuxedo trimmed at the neck and wrists with white ermine, including a big bow tie. He remembered later that he was "trembling" that night and "felt an enormous weight on my shoulders. There was a lot riding on that Oscar—not so much for me as the brothers across the country. I didn't want to let them down." Taking the statuette, there he stood, Black, bald, and beautiful, thanking Stax for "encouraging me to score a motion picture." Then, looking into the audience for Rushia Wade, he went on, "Most of all, I would like to thank a lady who's here with me tonight, because years ago her prayers kept my feet on a path of righteousness, and that's my grandmother. This is a thrill for me and in a few days it's her eightieth birthday and this is her present."

Looking back years later, he would explain, "Guys would say, hey, you gonna take a fine babe to that show? I said, hell no, I'm gonna take my grandmother. I prayed every day for her to keep on living so I could tell her how much I thanked her. And when I won, I gave it to her. That was a big thing for me. It brought it all back home."

Shaft lost that night for Original Dramatic Score to Michel Legrand's *Summer of '42*. (As a related sidebar, Ernest Tidyman took home the Best Writing Adaptation Screenplay award for *The French Connection*.) The National Association of Television

ﾟﾟﾟ

and Radio Announcers would name *Shaft* Album of the Year. The galactic impact was that by then the template was already set in the stone of street crime dramas in the new genre of Blaxploitation—which branched into sub-genres including western, (*Buck and the Preacher*), horror (*Blacula*), and comedic put-ons. While many decried the trend of underlining stereotypical Black behavior without redemption, the counterpoint was that Black actors suddenly had an inside track for jobs. Though a few, like ex-football-players-turned-actors Jim Brown and Fred Williamson and the delectable badass Pam Grier, had the lion's share.

As could be predicted, claims would surface that Ike had not written the lyrics to the *Shaft* theme and had prevailed on songwriter Clarence "Blowfly" Reid for help. But Reid, who co-wrote and co-produced Betty Wright's 1971 "Clean Up Woman," revered Ike (years later inviting him to appear in a video of Reid's disco put-on "Fonky Party"), and Blowfly never backed up the claim made about him. To be certain, whatever else Ike would record, John Shaft would be lurking somewhere in the grooves. The first new work to follow the movie would rub off its glitter, allowing him to take himself up another notch, into another racial identity for himself drawn from no less than the Bible.

11

"I Apologize"

Ike began to record the *Black Moses* album in March 1971, even as the *Shaft* album was still in development. He laid down preliminary tracks in his usual opalescent soul, and put them on hold for *Shaft* then, reversing that style of ghetto-wise similitude, returning to covering pop hits in free-form funk blues, including two more Bacharach/David standards in the genre, the Dionne Warwick "I'll Never Fall in Love Again," the Carpenters' soothing "(They Long to Be) Close to You," and The Jackson 5's "Never Can Say Goodbye." With an almighty respect for the soul men he admired, he covered Curtis Mayfield's "Man's Temptation" and "Need to Belong to Someone"; the Gamble/Huff/Jerry Butler "Never Gonna Give You Up"; The Friends of Distinction's "Going in Circles"; Clay Hammond's "Part-Time Love" (a hit for Little Johnny Taylor in 1963); and Toussaint McCall's "Nothing Takes the Place of You." The real curve was Kris Kristofferson's country blues "For the Good Times."

Ike co-wrote four songs for what would be a double album: the cheeky "Good Love 6-9969" with Mickey Gregory and three intros that maintained the self-identifying, self-enriching rap fold he'd started with "Ike's Rap I" on *To Be Continued...*—"Ike's Rap II/"Help Me Love" (co-written by Luther Ingram and Johnny Baylor), "Ike's Rap III/Your Love Is So Doggone Good" (a cover of

Ray Charles), and "Ike's Rap IV/A Brand New Me" (a Jerry Butler number co-written with Gamble and Huff). "Rap II" stood out as an emotionally overpowering rap with Ike starkly and convincingly unburdening himself with simple self-bludgeoning lines about taking advantage of and using a woman, for which "I apologize now."

As the titles suggested, most tunes carried a distinct ruefulness in a languid and almost lachrymose pall swirled by the aural images of storms, sunsets, and uncertain next mornings. Not by accident, at the time of the sessions, his marriage to Emily was in tatters, the fault being all his own and something he could not duck. He spoke of the album as a kind of self-therapy, connecting scattered thoughts that could have come from an hour on a shrink's couch. It was his way of purifying his soul that had prospered but gone off track—not that owning up to this would stem his addictions to adultery, booze, and conspicuous consumption. He made his confessionals with fewer syllables and notes than on his previous works; none reaching ten minutes and most lasting around five. He and the Isaac Hayes Movement provided the material for no less than five sound engineers—Capone, Bush, William Brown, Eddie Marion, and Dave Purple—to massage and hammer a throbbing, smoothly rhythmic work.

Titling the album *Black Moses* was not as easy a call as it might seem. Ike had originally believed using the term for an album was sacrilegious, but was convinced to go with it and take the dare of courting obvious mockery. He would explain that it only meant he was purging himself of ill thoughts in order to "reform as a black man delivered to the epitome of black masculinity," and that "Chains that once represented bondage and slavery now can be a sign of power and strength and sexuality and virility." Gilding that lily, the liner notes by Chester Higgins justified this concept of Black Moses as a history lesson dating back to the Egyptian kings.

Stax creative director Larry Shaw framed the cropped cover image of him as a gate fold, photographed by Joe Brodsky, with Ike seen from the neck up, robe top on his head, rectangular shades over his eyes, peering beyond the camera against a pale blue sky. When the image was fully unfolded, he stood head to sandal-covered toes in that pastoral attire with his arms stretched wide, forming the effect of a cross. On the back cover he was stripped nearly nude, again his arms thrust out and upward, chains dangling down to black and white striped Egyptian *piloi* anklets. The song list was styled as if they were the Commandments, which of course for Ike, they were.

If all this indeed was a tad hard to take, Ike succeeded again on a hunch, now making pretension part of the soul litany, if done right. After the album was released in November 1971, it took only five weeks to rise on a Biblical path to number one on the soul chart the week of January 15, 1972—a year after *To Be Continued...* sat in the same spot. It was just ahead of *Shaft*, which had moved up from number three which was now occupied by Sly and the Family Stone's *There's a Riot Goin' On* after its own run at the top. This clearly was when all the stars and moons parted for Isaac Hayes, and *Black Moses* would remain in place for seven weeks to be displaced by The Temptations' *Solid Rock* and Al Green's *Let's Stay Together* thereafter.

While *Shaft* would park at the top of the pop album chart in November, *Black Moses* peaked at number ten on that compilation.

The single "Never Can Say Goodbye," which lifted off from a slow, percussive heartbeat into to a convincingly sexy pant with his breathy vocals one of his most melodic, eased its way to number five in R&B and number twenty-two in pop, not quite cracking the formula for soul singles in a year when half of the top dozen singles on the Top 100 chart were by soft-soul singers including Al Green's "Let's Stay Together," Michael Jackson's "Got to Be There," Betty Wright's "Clean Up Woman," and The Stylistics' "You Are Everything."

Two other forthcoming Ike singles in '71 and '72 came from the *Shaft* soundtrack:

"Do Your Thing" and "Soulsville." The former reaching number three in soul and thirty in pop, and the latter failing to chart; though the record was saved when the B-side, an instrumental cover of "Let's Stay Together," became a mild hit on both charts. Nothing else came from *Black Moses*.

And the album, as well as it sold, would foment a backlash, based on the conundrum that the *Shaft* composer had worn out his welcome with uptown funk and his co-option of white pop. *Rolling Stone*'s Russell Gersten's review of the LP had predictable snark about the kitschy cover images and liner notes with "appropriately pompous history of the 'soulful prophet,' printed in Germanic script, written by the editor of *Jet*." The work, he wrote, had "taken the poetry and life out of every single song," all of which were "dissipated and self-pitying." Ike was "a mediocre vocalist [who] even when he hits on a good idea, like the vocal backups on 'Close to You,' kills it by lethargy, schlocky strings, and drawing the song out beyond the lengths of human endurance....Even by Andy Williams' easy listening standards, Black Moses is dull and enervated, and, need I say, pretentious. Sly's recent music has mainly been about feeling down, zonked-out, being in pain; Isaac Hayes' music just wallows in those states of mind."

Rolling Stone's Tim Crouse contributed his ounce of salt in the February 17, 1972 issue, sticking Ike as a "Sunset Strip African." Surveying the bombast of Ike's shows, Crouse chaffed that "the Number One Black Entertainer in the World" was no more than one of those Black actors in the 1940s who played African savages: "Tall and broad-shouldered, he appears to be cleverly disguised as a grass hut. He moves rigidly, as if on stilts...wearing a sort of British magistrate's wig fashioned out of straw, a long mantle of African cloth and a grass skirt....He and [his dancer] go through a routine of choreographed lasciviousness that climaxes as she tears off his mantle. He raises his bare arms as if to say, 'I am king at this festival,' and the crowd goes crazy."

Other deprecation awaited: "Ike fried his mind on acid and his music's never been the same;" another said that he was "the black [Rod] McKuen," which *really* had to hurt. Then there was the Shakespeare who thought it cool to use a little old-time stereotyping: "Ol' Ike aims at honkies who want some soul music." This was the price for keeping *Shaft* distant from his usual self-mirroring fodder, propelling a white British reviewer, of all things, to write that Hayes was "amazingly turgid," his audience a "cult," and, worst of all, not "aggressively black." This while Ike was being kept off TV for being too "militant" as John Shaft's virtual body double. Talk about a complicated man!

Hayes of course lived to see himself vindicated; the very same *Rolling Stone*, for instance, would retro-review *Black Moses* decades later as a work that "flexes masculine strength through vulnerability," and samples from its grooves found their way onto such motley diversions as Tricky's "Hell Is Around the Corner," Portishead's "Glory Box," and the Brazilian rap unit Racionais MC's "Jorge da Capadócia" and "Salve." "Ike's Rap II" was sampled in Alessia Cara's "Here." Those grooves lived on, never needing to be apologized for.

AS *SHAFT* AND IKE's other work raged on, Al Bell figured the time was right to celebrate the new order of Black music, which had become the lever of political/social/artistic change, something Al figured was his doing in many ways. Hollywood was again his focus. He had created the job of West Coast Director for Stax as a way to attract more movie projects, and his hire, Forrest Hamilton, suggested a "Black Woodstock" event as part of the seventh edition of the week-long Watts Summer Festival in mid-August. The festival was established to pull together and put some money into the scarified East LA community after the 1965 Watts riots. A music festival could centralize that effort and not incidentally further engorge Stax's profits. With Bell calling in chits and enlisting a who's who of Black performers and public figures, Stax would take the lead role in the festival, arrange the concert, and release a subsequent movie documentary, for which he aligned with the respected documentarian David Wolper. Bell also secured a distribution agreement with Columbia Pictures.

Wolper came at a high price. He would receive the first $400,000 of the box-office proceeds and a cut from the rest. Hamilton would cash in one-half of the profits from the film, but Bell retained the exclusive rights to produce and release a double album, on which Hamilton would be given a ceremonial sop as executive producer. Still, there was no guarantee of success. At the time, Black mass outdoor concerts were rare, and even a mega event like the 1969 Harlem Cultural Festival concert was overlooked by the general public, film footage of it left unseen until the 2021 documentary *Summer of Soul* emerged. The biggest concerts were those by Ike, who would be the closing act for this one. Bell could sell the concert around him and line up a host of other Stax acts who would follow the leader. The concept, Bell told the press, was that soul would "demonstrate the positive attributes of Black pride and the unique substance found in the lives, living and lifestyle of the African-American working class and middle class."

Bell, Hamilton, and Tommy Jacquette, the prominent civil rights activist who had founded the festival, knew the event needed to be held outside of Watts if it hoped to draw enough people to be a success. They lobbied the directors of the cavernous Los Angeles Coliseum, who worried that "a little record company" couldn't manage such an endeavor and would kick in only limited capital. Bell would have to finance the rest, at sky-high overcharges. With that done, Bell set the concert—originally named "Woodstax" but then changed, mercifully, to Wattstax, a better acronym for principle and profit—for Sunday afternoon, August 20, which happened to be Hayes's thirtieth birthday, one of the subtexts of the day in pre-event advertising.

Besides Ike, Bell received commitments from The Bar-Kays, Dave Porter, The Staple Singers, William Bell, Eddie Floyd, Carla and Rufus Thomas, Albert King, The Soul Children, Luther Ingram, and lesser-known soul acts like Eric Mercury, Little Sonny, The Temprees, The Newcomers, Ernie Hines, and The Rance Allen Group—clearly, the most stupendous matrix of soul stars ever assembled on a stage. All would perform for a basic minimum, even Ike, who of course had performed for free at similar Black awareness concerts. All tickets would be sold for exactly one dollar to allow attendance by the community at large and for the promoters to hire local Black workers to build the stage and be in the film crew. Bell would produce the songs with Dave Purple and Tom Nixon, and the stage and security manager would be none other than Melvin Van Peebles, who would also deliver an oration.

The garrulous, publicity-conscious Jesse Jackson would reap large donations from Bell and Hamilton for Operation PUSH as well as being the emcee and opening the show by reciting his poem "I Am Somebody." When the movie was put in motion, however, the host would be a still-formative Richard Pryor, who would do a comedy set at Wattstax though his hosting scenes would be filmed separately at a local bar. During the seven hours of entertainment, the crowd of over 112,000—the largest of any music event and any public event save for Martin Luther King, Jr.'s March on Washington—fed on vibes that ran Black, strong, and cool as hell despite ninety-degree temperatures. The performances were on a ramshackle stage built only the day before after a Rams-Raiders football game was played in the stadium. The house band, conducted by Dale Warren, who had arranged the last three of Ike's albums, stayed on the stage all day and most of the night.

Ike's role reached beyond just the concert. That morning, he was grand marshal of the Watts Festival and conducted several interviews. He was nowhere near the Coliseum most of the day until around 8:30 p.m., with the crowd itching to get a look at him, most of whom could not have afforded the price to see him on his concert tours, when he got into a gold—of course—station wagon and was driven into the building and to the stage. As the crowd surged toward the stage, Jackson announced, "If you wanna see Isaac Hayes, you must keep your seats!" Then, his voice screeched, "Do you wanna see Isaac Hayes? Now, here's the brother we all been waitin' for! The bad...bad brother...Isaac Hayes!"

Ike climbed from the car, hooded, and in a floor-length cloak, an entrance Bell had planned as fit for a king. Bell, in fact, had shot down The Bar-Kays' plan to come to the stage for their set riding in horse-drawn chariots, so as to save the histrionics for Ike. As a scoreboard lit up "BLACK MOSES," the latest edition of the Movement broke into "Theme from Shaft," a song that Ike usually saved for his encore. He stood staring into the crowd through his shades, then began slowly taking bows. When he doffed the cloak and was down to orange tunnel pants and his gold-chain vest against his bare barrel chest, he banged on a tambourine. When the vocal part came, he drew out each familiar syllable—the longest "Dammmmmn riiiiggght!"—and held the microphone toward the crowd for them to mass-chant the "Shaft!" chorale thrusts.

Skip Pitts, recalling that version of a tune he played hundreds of times, summed it up in one word: "fire." The rest of the set was equally funky and feverish as Ike seamlessly stitched "Soulsville," buffed by his own searing sax solo, "Never Can Say Goodbye," "Part Time Love," "Your Love Is So Doggone Good," "I Stand Accused," and an extended "Ain't No Sunshine," which he stretched to twenty minutes and drilled into with more blistering sax solos. When he left the stage, the crowd had indeed left their seats, nearly swallowing him as he squeezed back into the wagon. For sure, the concert, for all its variety and seven hours of soul, was another Isaac Hayes ten-strike.

However, there was a snag. When MGM discovered that two *Shaft* tunes were in the upcoming movie, *Wattstax: The Living Word*, due out in February 1973, with the album preceding it by a month, it informed Columbia that the movie would be breaching

MGM's exclusive rights on all *Shaft* songs. Bell, who apparently hoped to bypass that roadblock on grounds that the songs were part of a documentary, could only sit by helplessly as Columbia had the movie's director and co-producer, Mel Stuart, remove them. Bell would need to scramble to fill the void. The album (which also added a few studio recordings to cover for the bad sound equipment at the site) needed no great revision. Just one long Ike song from the show, "Ain't No Sunshine," would suffice. However, for the movie, Bell wanted Ike to sing original hit material.

He had recently recorded one in Memphis, "Rolling Down a Mountainside," an obscure tune written by soul singer and former Motown writer Leon Ware with Jacqueline Hilliard, cut in breezy, up-tempo Curtis Mayfield style, its pithy coda being that "We've got strength and we got pride / 'Cause God is on our side." Al wanted to go with it, but to do that, he would need to fly Ike and the musicians back to LA, wear the same garb, and in an empty Coliseum at night, perform the song as it had been done at Wattstax, whereupon the director and film editors would splice it into the original cut, with the end of the picture being him intoning to the nonexistent crowd, "We're the cause. Right on!" The process was a nightmare, and by then, Ike was touring in the Netherlands. But, the good company soldier that he was, he complied, flying all the way back and recreating the vibes with amazing elan and accuracy, perhaps his best acting job.

IKE PRAISED THE Wattstax sojourn as "a wonderful experience" and that was the collective judgment. It seemed a minor miracle. While there had been a few casualties at the admittedly larger and longer Woodstock, its Black counterpart was free of issues beyond people dancing in the aisles. The organizers had bet their reputations on this by not allowing security guards to be armed. And as commanding as Ike had been, the ubiquitous presence of Bell did not go unnoticed—not if Al could help it. Despite almost no one in the sea of the crowd knowing who he was, he lurked about the VIP section in designer glasses and a perfectly tailored white suit. On stage, he stuck a clenched fist into the air with the dashiki-clad Jackson, wrapped an arm around Melvin Van Peebles, and exchanged high-fives with performers as they clamored onto the stage.

Bell had to battle what he said was Hamilton's rip-off charges and would donate $100,000 of Stax money to the sickle-cell anemia charity, the Martin Luther King, Jr. hospital in Watts, and Jackson's Operation PUSH. But in the end, he profited a good deal from the "nonprofit" event that more than realized the Black empowerment goals he had set out to achieve. Black power groups showered Wattstax with unqualified acclaim, and even the racially insensitive—to put it mildly—Mayor of LA, Sam Yorty, christened August 20 as "Wattstax Day."

The back end for Bell was the success of the event's ancillary spin-offs, something he had specifically kept to himself when ceding so much of the festival's live gate to Hamilton. The two-hour album, which few on the outside knew was embellished with other songs recorded after the fact, greased the way. Within two months it hit number one on the R&B album chart the weeks of March 31 and April 7 and number twenty-eight on the pop chart, selling around 225,000 units. A second, much lower quality volume would come out later in the year with an ink-rendering of Ike in song on the cover but would sell far fewer copies. And in the end, Bell, who believed he had a sure thing with the rights to record the next five Wattstax festivals, had gone through all that work for a live "Mountainside" only to release it as the B-side of a cover of "If Loving You is Wrong," without charting (it would have a second life when covered in again by the Harlem soul band The Main Ingredient in '74, hitting number seven in soul). Not that any isolated blip really mattered. With Ike the drawing card for all these properties, the movie was a breadwinner. At the premiere, a red-carpet event in Los Angeles, it still included "Theme from Shaft" and "Soulsville." When MGM again laid down the law, it went out for national release with only "Never Can Say Goodbye" as Ike's contribution, as the last song of the film.

For reasons unexplained, Stax's latter-day corporate proprietors would not re-release the album until the latter-day owners of the the Stax post-Atlantic catalog, Fantasy Records, in 2004 issued a three-CD package and a thirty-five-year anniversary set in 2007, nor would there be a re-release of the film with Ike's full set until a 2000 limited-run restoration and again in 2003 as a DVD set by Warner Brothers. (A twelve-minute DVD issue, *Isaac Hayes at Wattstax*, also surfaced, minus the *Shaft* numbers.) But in its time, the documentary made Columbia several million dollars—$1.5 million in rentals on the new VCR cassette format alone. Nominated for the Best Documentary Golden Globe, with its slam-bang soundtrack and cut-in shots of ghetto life and determination, it is one of history's best aural and visual portrayal of extant Black culture of the '70s, with Hayes the sine qua non. As for Bell, it was such a personal triumph that even his own stable would wonder what had been in it for the performers or the region. Years later, Duck Dunn mused to author Peter Guralnick, "Whose cause was it—Wattstax or Al Bell's? Were they doing it for the people of LA, or were they doing it to promote Al Bell in LA? And what did they ever do for Memphis? Not a goddamn thing."

Among its other beneficiaries was Pryor, who soon after recorded his third comedy album for Stax's Partee label, *That Nigger's Crazy*, a punchline he'd used during the concert; released in May 1974, it would hit number one on the R&B album chart and win the Grammy for Best Comedy Album. Also scoring sales was Jesse Jackson's Stax album *I Am Somebody*, produced by Tom Nixon, the title being the emotive poem he had recited at Wattstax and took up the whole first side. In fact, the overall theme of that soul train in LA, and the glittery performers that carried it out, kept delivering as Wattstax albums were released in sundry editions for years, all over the world, sundry singles from the show's amazing array of talent also springing onto the soul chart. This was all part of Bell's long-range strategy, which included his plans for other film projects. As long as he had Ike, it all seemed not just possible, but as good as done.

BELL HAD A real empire now, and he was feeling good about it. He was the man who made Stax go, and was in the same position as Jim Stewart when The Beatles entertained doing some recording in the studio, despite Stewart banning outside acts. Bell did the same for Elvis Presley, who had watched from his Graceland palace as Stax grew to dizzying heights. As The King's relevance fell, he wisely wanted to help himself to that magical studio, and did sessions periodically from 1973 to 1975. Despite the static of Elvis's retinue of musicians and his own "Memphis Mafia" virtually taking over the building at those times, Stax reaped heavy session fees from RCA, and everyone profited when his *Good Times* and *Promised Land* albums, and the six singles from them including the cover of Chuck Berry as the former's title song, became pop and country "comeback" hits. (In 2011, an album was released of all forty-eight songs from the sessions.)

From his own stock, Bell fattened his profits. Ike was at the center of many projects, another being a deal Bell made with TV host/producer Merv Griffin, for a series of Stax-hosted concerts taped at Caesars Palace in Las Vegas to be shown as TV specials. The first had been done in December 1972, billed long-handed as "Isaac Hayes and the Stax Organization Presenting the Memphis Sound," with performances by Hayes, The Emotions, Johnnie Taylor, Luther Ingram, Albert King, and The Staple Singers. The unknown Jean Knight had broken out when "Mr. Big Stuff" went to number one soul and number two pop, winning a Grammy nomination. The Stax version of The Temptations, the Don Davis-produced Dramatics (a Detroit unit who had been held hostage and their valet killed during the riots that inspired Ike to write "Soul Man"), took the funky stomp "Whatcha See Is Whatcha Get" to number three in soul and top ten in pop. The Staple Singers hit the big top with the wistful pop funk promise to find a place with no crying, worrying, or lying to the races. "I'll Take You There," written and produced by Bell when his younger brother Louis was murdered in their home town of Little Rock, Arkansas went to number one in pop and R&B. Johnnie Taylor would have another Gold record with the Don Davis co-written and produced "I Believe in You (You Believe in Me)," and Luther Ingram took "(If Loving You is Wrong) I Don't Want to Be Right," produced by Johnny Baylor and co-written by Homer Banks, to number one in R&B and pop.

The last was a real coup for Baylor, who apparently believed he could now muscle even further into the Ike's circle and vat of wealth. He did this stealthily, by helping himself to more of Ike's concert receipts than even he had a right to. When the Stax accounting department discovered a gap between Ike's fees and what he took home, Ike was furious. His toleration for the shady Baylor suddenly evaporated. As it was, he had become uncomfortable with the bad blood Baylor left, if only because, as Ike said, "People started being afraid to come around me." And so he left word for Baylor—at a safe distance—that his services were no longer needed. This was good timing for another reason, as word had filtered down that Baylor was, inevitably, under investigation by the IRS. With Ike's finances having fattened more after *Shaft*, the last thing he needed was to be drawn into a widespread tax probe of his earnings.

But if Ike thought he could cut that cord and simply walk away from Baylor, he learned how naive that was when Baylor and Dino dropped in on him in his office one day, their guns again drawn, and asking for an explanation. Ike, thrown off balance, tried to defuse the situation by telling Baylor he hadn't fired him, Stax had. But the three of them then got into a loud shouting match and security guards outside the office decided it would be wise to clear the building and call the cops. When they arrived, they banged on Ike's door with shotguns in their hands. The two wiseguys stuffed their weapons in a garbage can, and Ike played it cool, telling the cops that he was simply "having a family discussion."

The cops bought it and left, and Baylor thanked Ike for not ratting him out. The two of them man-hugged, and Baylor and Dino left. But never again did Baylor go on the road with Ike. Instead, he spent most of his time working with Ingram, whose success more than made up for the income hit Baylor took being pried away from Ike's pockets. Demanding and getting from Bell a new agreement for KoKo Records, Baylor was given a higher level of publishing royalties from Stax for KoKo products.

That was yet another Bell outlay that erased Stax's bottom line, from which Baylor was all but living now. Among Bell's other alms for Baylor were a yearly salary of $1.89 million, a chic pad on New York's Upper East Side, an expensive suite for Baylor and Dino to live in at Memphis's Holiday Inn Central, and a home for the latter in Memphis. While Baylor's looming tax problems posed a serious quake, Bell ignored what might happen for what was happening in the here and now. Stax was being stoked by million-selling records, movie deals, and highly successful acts. Bell had signed new talent that in '71 and opened the new specialty labels Hip, Partee, Respect, and Gospel Truth, the latter explicitly for the release of Jesse Jackson's album. Bell also formed a partnership with Don Davis's own vanity label Groovesville, for which The Dramatics recorded their Stax records. Bell, who had believed when he got to Stax that Ike was too impatient for the spoils of success, spared no expense funneling money into all manner of Black causes such as business and prison reform agencies, the Miss Essence of Tennessee beauty pageant, and a Jim Brown celebrity golf tournament. He even thought there was room for a *Stax country* sub-label. He was rarely wrong, but that one, ominously, tanked.

THESE WERE SURELY some wild and crazy—and never cheap— ideas. But Bell, who could point to Stax's dramatic revival under his watch, by '73 raking in around $185 million, was so confident of his authority and magic wand that not only did he—like Ike, his protégé—ignore the dangerous curves of overspending, but by 1972, Bell was ready to buy Jim Stewart out. This was something long in the wind, and something Jim was all for, no longer much involved in his own company. For this to happen, though, Bell had to once again bring Stax into the arc of another giant corporation. Waving the baton of *Shaft*, he talked RCA Records into making an offer of $16 million, but it was rejected by Stewart because the payoff would be only in stock, which both men had learned from the Gulf and Western deal was a trap. Bell next turned to Columbia Records President Clive Davis, a surprising turn as the label, which had released jazz albums in the '50s as part of its catalog, had avoided soul music for rock giants like Bob Dylan and Simon & Garfunkel. Bell too was wary, but Davis, who had shown his appreciation for soul by not only approving Columbia's financial participation in the Wattstax venture but bankrolling a distribution deal for Gamble and Huff's Philadelphia International in 1971, was hot for the Stax deal. Davis had begun a soul music division at Columbia, and he wanted to buy half of Stax's stock but because of antitrust laws, the deal could only be for distribution. The price tag was $6 million, as a loan, all in cash.

The deal, consummated in late October 1972, was for ten years and applied only to the company's three main labels: Stax, Volt, and Enterprise, and with the cash, Bell could buy out Stewart for $4 million, $2.5 million up front—though the buyout, to Bell's chagrin, was to be kept publicly mum in order to disabuse the industry from knowing Stax was now officially ruled by a Black man. Stewart would thus remain titular president until 1975, saying later, "I was president in name only" and Bell "the chairman and only director." Incredibly, Johnny Baylor also profited from the deal, with Bell kicking back at least $1 million to him, leading some to gossip that Bell was either in Dutch with him—or so intimidated—that Baylor wound up with *all* of it. Whatever the case, Bell had moved so precipitously on the deal that he all but ignored a New York power broker and the owner of Sussex Records named Clarence Avant, known in the industry as "The Black Godfather," who he had enlisted to scout possible deals. Avant, who had helped secure the Gulf and Western agreement, was stunned. Having cooked up another pact with RCA for $16 million, he watched Bell precipitously take less than half that, upon which Avant said Bell's deal was "the biggest fuckup he ever made."

People like Avant would see gaping holes in CBS's lawyers demanding, and getting, what they wanted. In addition to a two-cent override per each record sold, Stax would be paid higher amounts not for *sales* but for insane levels of records being merely *released*, turning Stax into a sweat shop assembly line. Those people tried to warn Bell that Davis had more in mind than a simple distribution arrangement—that his goal was to strip Stax to the bone as Atlantic had done and eventually force Bell and Stewart out altogether. While Bell did achieve neutering Stewart and reaping the publicity value of the deal, CBS would do little for Stax's looming financial problems. Bell was in fact in the same place he always was: needing to keep taking out numbing loans from Union Planters Bank, which had actually eased off on Stax's already hefty payments in order to help the CBS deal happen so Bell wouldn't have to default. Worse, it became clear why Bell was greasing Baylor. Bell had become disgruntled when CBS refused to distribute Stax records still on store shelves when the deal was made, only new ones. It wasn't long before guess-who showed up at the doors of CBS executives, suggesting they change their minds—and that if they didn't, they would need "a helicopter ride" to be able to get away from Baylor.

All of which seemed blithely normal in these circles. No one at CBS held it against Bell, and Bell could con himself into thinking he was big enough now to make literally anything happen. Why not? By 1972, Isaac Hayes had soul in his grip, peeling away more and more of its former hurdles. He wasn't alone. At Motown, The Temptations had outgrown the soul middle ground with powerful songs like "Ball of Confusion" and "Papa Was a Rolling Stone." As Otis Williams points out, "We sang of ripoff landlords, abortion, poverty, of a no-good black man cheating on his wife, leaving his kids. We sang, 'Rap on, brother, rap on.' We sang (on the original version of the song later covered so massively by Edwin Starr), 'War, what is it good for?' That war meant 'destruction of innocent lives' and 'tears to thousands of mother's eyes.' We didn't avoid reality, but we didn't pander to it. We kept it upbeat." He didn't state the obvious: that while Ike's scope excluded those too-strident and too-political themes, going street a la *Shaft* would have killed The Temptations' affable image and their regular Las Vegas hotel and casino gigs. "But I'll tell you something, Isaac, he could play anywhere. He was a great performer and put all he had into taking his music in different directions. We envied that. And, man, was he cool. That man didn't even have to try to be cool. He just was."

But even as white acceptance of Black cool now outdistanced the tentative inroads of the "Soul Man" era, Stanley Booth presciently wondered if this was a mixed blessing for Black art. Writing in the *Saturday Evening Post*, he averred, "Across the country...soul is not the exclusive property of any one race. Nor, in spite of soul music's origins in rural poverty, does it belong to any one economic class. It might have at one time, but it has become too prosperous for that." The other shoe in that equation of profitable Black redirection of white culture was that playing to all classes and races might have been as much a pitfall as a blessing, losing its elemental oneness. If so, neither Ike nor Al Bell gave it a second thought.

12

The Feeling That Keeps on Coming

Exhibit A in Booth's premise was of course Isaac Hayes, who was playing for packed audiences at the biggest venues in America and across Europe, including several rousing concerts at Frankfurt's Jahrhunderthalle. He was now so separated from any sense of a home and family life that Emily was no longer even trying to get him to change his ways and sued for divorce. Reluctant to admit his failures, he contested it in court, yet the wreckage of his promises of reconciliation were so real that it had sparked the tortured confessions of *Black Moses*, which made him even wealthier, a lucrative repercussion of personal pain. His lawyers pushed back the final court ruling by asking for continuations but the judge had no tolerance for his smug alibis and granted the divorce on Emily's terms, awarding her sole parental rights and $6,000-a-month in alimony and child support. He filed an objection but was denied. He then relented and bought Emily and the kids a smaller but opulent home in the same neighborhood, the latest in what was becoming a side-business-footing-expense for children he had fathered.

By then, he had his next wife chosen: the bank teller Mignon Hartley. Eager to find the salve of redemption, in November, Ike took her along with his toadies and road crew on a private Learjet during the Thanksgiving holiday and flew to Lake Tahoe. He was about to record his first live album at the Sahara Hotel and Casino, a handsomely packaged gate-fold, double-LP that would showcase fifteen songs amid a din of screams, clapping, whistling, and obligatory cries of "right on!" that tied together Ike's usual eclectic grab-bag of rap and funk-drenched pop and soul—kicked off by "Theme from Shaft" then summoning his hit covers and others like The Doors' "Light My Fire," Bill Withers's "Use Me" and "Ain't No Sunshine," Carole King's "It's Too Late," Roberta Flack's "The First Time Ever I Saw Your Face," and Dave Mason's "Feelin' Alright."

He threw in two more from *Shaft*—a twenty-minute rendering of the psychedelic funk "Do Your Thing" and "Ellie's Love Theme"—two "Ike raps," and four new songs: his "Type Thang" and "The Come On," T-Bone Walker's "Stormy Monday," and B.B. King's "Rock Me Baby," and he filled his Bacharach/David hunger with "Windows of the World." The tracks, spliced from tapes of two shows, were meant as feel-good funk, or "funky lounge lizard charm," as one retro-review put it, and not the exhausting psychological meat rack of *Black Moses*. Most tunes were under six minutes. He handled it deftly, his rap on one tune or between songs sometimes carrying over to the next track, and he spent most of his stage time in mock sexual interplay with the now four-strong backup singers; joined by Barbara McCoy, the group was now trademarked by Ike as Hot Buttered Soul Ltd.

But his big move came after the gig was over. He had for months teased Mignon, seeming on the edge of proposing, once even giving her fourteen diamond rings, apparently one for each finger and four toes, but then backed off. Now, she could sense he would go through with it, and, she said, "I got scared. Then I got sick. I always get sick when he surprises me like that." She said yes and they were married in Las Vegas, where the troupe partied like it was 1973. Then when the musicians headed back to Memphis, the newlyweds stayed for two weeks on the West Coast in LA at the hilltop mansion Ike had recently purchased on a whim—and for which Stax reimbursed him $25,000 each year—in the city's chic Wilshire district as a getaway from the rigors of Memphis (he also bought a town home in Washington, DC for when he went there on his activist chores).

He seemed almost like a new man now, and even a monogamous one on the surface However, he was soon back on the prowl again with rumors in the air about him and a long-legged dancer he had hired for the stage show, Helen Washington, who was David Porter's niece. Ike met her when she was a guest of the state at the Tennessee State women's prison, serving five years for credit card theft. He'd done a show for the inmates there and afterward she told him how much *Black Moses* had changed her life and made her, she said, "realize that I was somebody and I owed it to myself to be that somebody." After he pushed for her early release, she was released, and he had her hired by Stax as a songwriter, something she had never been. Ike then put her into the act as a dancer, immediately noticeable because of her own shaven head, usually drawing gasps when she would introduce him at the start of shows.

They made quite a pair. *Ebony* put them on the cover of their May 1972 issue and decorated a story about her reclamation with pictures of them acting more than chummy. Both denied anything beyond showmanship. Perhaps trying to make that case, Ike, who'd had almost no photos taken with either of his first two wives or children, invited the Black papers to regularly take shots of him and his new happy family, which soon included a daughter named Heather and a year later, their son Isaac Lee Hayes III. Mignon was clearly an accommodating wife.

"Some women," she told *Ebony* in October 1973, "expect their husbands to stay home all the time. That's impossible. Our marriage wouldn't work if I decided to be suspicious and neurotic. I have complete faith in Isaac and I understand the demands of his business."

No doubt contented by her words, he said, "I tell Mignon that I don't belong 100 percent to her. She has to be—and is—a very generous person. We both have to make sacrifices."

What his sacrifices were, he didn't say. But he was relieved of any Helen Washington complications by, of all people, Johnny Baylor, who became romantically involved with her and signed her to a recording contract at KoKo Records. She lived in high style at Stax even though she would never record a single song.

RELEASED IN APRIL 1973, *Live at the Sahara Tahoe* zoomed to the head of the soul album pack the weeks of June 23 and 30, moving out Al Green's *Call Me*, and reaching number fourteen on the pop list. With it, Robert Christgau finally found an Isaac Hayes he could sort-of understand, grading it a B-minus and writing, "I like Ike live because he makes fun of himself, but though I hear the patrons laughing I miss his turquoise tights. Can't even say I wish I'd been there—not in Tahoe, thanks. But the band is crisp and funky, and he does talk more on stage than on record if you can believe that, and I even find 'Rock Me Baby' sexy myself. Not 'First Time Ever I Saw Your Face,' though." And *so Sahara* became one more Gold record. Still, no singles from it were released, and in the Stax boardroom, one could assume that while the heady days of *Shaft*-like "right on" magic still resounded, it could not be repeated.

While Ike had always said that hit singles didn't "mean shit to me" and that he was a "concept" man best appreciated on his long-form albums, the "Theme from Shaft" was both a bauble and a curse. He could have sharpened his songs to fit the three-minute turf but resisted—a rare dissent from what was "happening" in '70s culture when all the best of intentions seemed to still be crimped by conditioned racial tropes. Consider that on the most influential medium of TV, the new wave of realism was undercut all the time. Archie Bunker sputtering about "jigaboos" and "spades" was intended as a satire of racism, yet a good many racists took it as bias confirmation. Black-cast sitcoms were belied by clownish roles like Jimmie Walker's monumentally moronic "J.J." and the stupendously clownish Black businessman George Jefferson, and a high school dimwit named "Rerun" for all the times he'd been left back. The only truly Black character was Redd Foxx's screamingly funny reverse-racist Fred Sanford, but the most familiar Black image of the next decade would be a vacuous variation of the "tough" Isaac Hayes: Mr. T, scowling, "I pity the fool!"

Yet if TV fairly avoided him, Ike for now was the epitome of cultural Blackness. As of 1973, for example, George Clinton had climbed on Hayes's grooves for P-Funk albums like *Funkentelechy* and *Aqua Boogie (A Psychoalphadiscobetabioaquadoloop)*, not to mention the chorus "We gonna turn this mutha out" in their 1975 (as Parliament) amulet "Give Up the Funk." The alarmingly large and lovelorn Barry White came along the year before, writing, arranging, and producing a girl group he had discovered on a very Hayes-like album, *Love Unlimited*, the lush, string-laden single "Walking in the Rain with the One I Love" going Gold and introducing his indelibly deep, grunting basso as the lover boy on a simulated phone call and conducting the funk anthem "Love's Theme," which went number one on the pop and soul charts, and his 20th Century Fox album *I've Got So Much to Give* reached number one in soul—by displacing *Live at the Sahara Tahoe*.

White would clearly bloom directly in Ike's shadow and then beyond it, his métier also imploring soul and dramatic rapping. But even a sometimes Hayes-denier like Robert Christgau noted that "White's hustle is to combine Isaac Hayes's power with Al Green's niceness, and he succeeds, in his way, but the synthesis has its drawbacks—[it] tends to compound his humorlessness and mendacity as well." That v ̣ ̣ ı grudging way of saying that Hayes brought more plausible human feeling to the table, as could be judged by the success of other soul performers spinning off him. The relentless Gamble and Huff unleashed The O'Jays' declarations of both brotherhood ("Love Train"), betrayal ("Back Stabbers"), and avarice ("For the Love of Money"). They also profited from the empty soul of unrequited love with Harold Melvin & the Blue Notes' "If You Don't Know Me by Now," the opening being a pleading rap by Teddy Pendergrass. Motown had gone cynical with The Undisputed Truth's "Smiling Faces Sometimes," in which smiling faces pretend to be your friend but mask the "evil within."

These three-minute doubloons proved that the new parameters of soul weren't, in life, tales told as a twenty-minute soliloquy but simple, slick messages—the undying common law of rock 'n' roll. Another Gamble and Huff tune, instructively titled "Love Is the Message" on an instrumental album of the same name that went to number one on the soul chart for six weeks in '74, was performed by their Barry White-like house band MFSB—ostensibly for Mother, Father, Sister, Brother but to the musicians, Motherfuckin' Soul Band—a priceless rhythm machine led by guitarist Norman Harris and drummer Earl Young. Two years earlier, they had caught the wind when their high-stepping "The Sound of Philadelphia" was chosen as the theme of TV's syndicated "Black American Bandstand," *Soul Train*, which seemed more interested in newer flavors of soul than that of Isaac Hayes. Indeed, it seemed that Philly had overtaken Memphis as the soul Mecca, taking these catchy up-tempo tunes and Utopian love vanities that Thom Bell rolled out steadily with the Stylistics in tunes like "You Are Everything" to maximum profitability. Gamble and Huff's paean to grown men with lifetime gratitude to their maternal bonds, The Intruders' "I'll Always Love My Mama," was something right up Ike's alley when it came to grandmama Rushia Wade—if only he could have torn himself from the never-ending battleground of love and the spigot of money that was still running on full blast.

As far as the imitations went, Ike didn't take these reductive copies personally, not with his bank account and fixed godly status. It was flattery, sure, but on a deeper level, he saw them as a cheapening of Black art, leaning in on his genius and attachment with Black and white audiences, and the results made the first half of the decade perhaps the most pervasive ever for Black cultural inroads; being beaten by other soul acts to the simple message did begin to make him idly ponder his place in the galactic order. Smart as he was, he knew how vulnerable the business, and he himself, would be to interlopers. As it was, his work was less sure; his first of just two singles in 1973 a cover of Luther Ingram's "(If Loving You is Wrong) I Don't Want to Be Right / Rolling Down a Mountainside," failed to chart. The other would be the title track from his next studio album, *Joy*, which, when it was recorded in April, went back to the well, with Ike writing all but one track, which was kept in-house, co-penned and co-produced by Willie Hall and Stax writer Randall Stewart. Even so, it was a rather streamlined work, the double-LP format peeled back to two sides and five songs, two of which extended length, the opening title cut at nearly sixteen minutes and the closing "I'm Gonna Make It (Without You)" at over eleven.

Arranged by Johnny Allen, it was big and ballsy, pumped and primed by the requisite strings and chorale coatings, the near-single message being his continued self-resurrection; at thirty-three, after putting himself through the meat grinder of infidelity, he was a virtual sandwich board for monogamy, at least for those who would buy it. The first track, "Joy," expressed just that within frontal strings and deep soul vocals. The repetitive beat was mesmerizing, almost hypnotic, all too ironically similar to a Barry White tune. In effect, he was mimicking someone who had mimicked *him*. The theme was replayed, and hopefully his moral debt repaid, on all the songs. The understated funk of "A Man Will Be a Man" especially wore a wreath of redemption with Ike conceding that after a failed love, "I lost you, and I feel so bad."

The last two cuts, "The Feeling Keeps on Coming" and the easy-jazz "I'm Gonna Make It (Without You)," were part-rap, part-croon *billets-doux* to the unnamed Mignon, whom he assayed as "the perfect example of sexuality" and himself as "like a dog in heat." The laid-back funk of "Make It" was when he could say, "I'm a changed man now," but not without a cheap shot at a jilted lover— no doubt meaning Emily—for "teasing me" and insisting he felt no pain for the breakup.

In a sense, these separate yet interrelated, to-the-bone feelings were not unlike The Delfonics' "La-La (Means I Love You)" and "Didn't I (Blow Your Mind This Time)." And perhaps this is why they weren't quite as compelling, or marketable, as already-trod-den ground. Not that some of the usual suspects in the white rock press needed additional grievance or white entitlement to review it harshly; Mark Vining wrote in *Rolling Stone*, "It isn't the bogus orgasms or the blustery soul-baring that are embarrassing. It's the fact that Hayes has systematically substituted these gimmicks for the native sensuality of black music." Of course, the truth was that "native sensuality" only provoked fear for many whites stuck in throwback racist conditioning. Yet, as with all his works, *Joy* had a built-in appeal to soul seekers.

While its only single was the title cut, divided into parts one and two on the 45 release, it only rose to number seven in R&B and number thirty in pop late in '73; the LP, released in October, barged up the charts to become another Gold record, kept from the top of the soul chart by Gladys Knight & The Pips' *Imagination* and then Barry White's *Stone Gon'*. As a historical marker, however, even this slight dip in fortune suggests that the album was something like the last shot of the wad, which was reflected by Ike's public state-ments at the time. Late in '73, while on another tour of England, he told Roger St. Pierre of the British music rag *New Musical Express* that he actually *was* a changed man, and acting was where his head was at. When the calendar turned to 1974, the year that would send Richard Nixon into highly deserved infamy six years after playing the race card, Ike and Al Bell moved to movie diversions. He had now been seen performing in three documentaries, *Wattstax* being preceded by a September 1973 movie adaptation of the '72 "Save the Children" concert in Chicago that also headlined The Jackson 5, Marvin Gaye, and Roberta Flack, and a low-budget video of one of his gigs that popped up in November, *Isaac Hayes—The Black Moses of Soul*, both filmed on cheap stock that made them seem like pirated movies. He had also hosted the 1972 Stax tribute TV show produced by Merv Griffin, and while "Theme from Shaft" was under the MGM ban, it somehow slipped through and was heard in *very* low-budget porno flicks with titles like *The Lumberjack, Sons and Mothers*, and, yes, *Black Heat.*

His first acting role, however, would be within the idiom he had helped seed. Also in late '73, he was signed to co-star with Fred Williamson in an Italian-made spaghetti Blaxploitation film. Shot on location in Chicago, *Three Tough Guys* was produced by the eminent Dino De Laurentiis, who cast him in an amoral buddy piece as a splendidly dressed ex-cop private dick who teams with a corrupt priest and a money-fixated hood named Brother Snake to avenge the death of the priest's associate by an on-the-loose bank robber, a plot not far from *Shaft.* The trailer had the usual over-baked "hood" speak, "They plowed down the meanest streets into every ghetto hellhole!" His part was intentionally based on Dirty Harry, his lines soft-spoken through ever-present cigars, but he was pitched in the ads as the central focus: "Isaac Hayes as Soul Brother Number One gets hard in his first movie!" In an era when tough, cool Black men were allowed, even expected, to slap down women who challenged them, he did so, and also outwitted the priest's goal to eliminate the two comrades and keep the loot. With Ike kneeling over him, he asks, "Who are you?" says Soul Brother Number One, with metaphorical perfection, "I'm the guy who arrived at the right moment."

As with *Shaft,* the deal for Ike was contingent on his compos-ing the score, a real get for the producers, given that he had turned down doing the score for both of the *Shaft* sequels, though the *Tough Guys* score began not surprisingly with *Shaft*-style chords. Hitting hard and brassy, it was enough to fill a double album to be distributed on Enterprise and recorded at a studio Ike was permitted by Stax to operate, Hot Buttered Soul Recording, at 247 Chelsea Avenue. Not scrimping, he employed The Bar-Kays and the same bulging flotilla of musicians and Movement singers who had filled the studio for *Black Moses*.

Soon after, he also acted in and composed the score for *Truck Turner*, which was produced by the B-movie studio American International as a tag-along for the studio's *Foxy Brown*, the first Blaxploitation entry starring a woman, who else but a barely dressed Pam Grier. The *Truck Turner* character was an ex-football player turned LA skip tracer whose violent nature, smooth vulgarity, and air of cool Black superiority was made palatable by an easygoing, almost familial wit, à la *Shaft*. Jonathan Kaplan, who had directed only movies such as *Night Call Nurses*, made this one a classic OG as seen from today—the opening scene an animation of the *Hot Buttered Soul* cover, Ike's shiny pate jutting from the covers. The posters had him nude from the waist up, covered only by a shoulder holster, with a menacing gun across his bare chest, and the recommendation, "Hide yo mamas, big brother is coming." Clips had him fighting or shooting his Magnum, telling one subdued victim, "Tell 'em you've been hit by a truck—Mack Truck Turner."

Actually, as the reluctant super-dick, he was less showy than his latest bounty meed, the scintillating Nichelle Nichols—a briny pimp-ette of "junkie whores" like Turnpike ("You gotta pay to get on and pay to get off") and Colonel Sanders ("She's finger-lickin' good"), whose pimp had been busted by Truck. Snarling as she never did on *Star Trek*, she informs would-be hit men, "I want that black bastard Truck Turner and I want him dead! The man who kills him gets my broads. And I'll run the stable," to which one mob guy played by Yaphet Kotto warns, "You'll need the United States Army to get Truck Turner off your ass."

These so-bad-they're-good movies, with their obligatory car chase crashes, off-the-cuff sex, and over-the-top dialogue, were of a period that practically screamed Isaac Hayes's name, who, as the trailers reminded audiences, was "the magic man of music makin' a new kind of music—and it's mean jive!" Not just grist for the mill, his scores of mainly instrumental booty-call-ready numbers were cleverly interspersed with occasional cool, guttural vocals such as an against-the-grit romantic song like "You're in My Arms Again." However, for Ike there was a glitch to all his mainlining of the Black underground. Since both films would not be seen or the albums heard until the late spring of 1974, circumstances would be working against what so effortlessly seemed to be an unstoppable fortune.

ON THE SURFACE, '73 had been a hell of a year for Ike and Stax. The label had cleared over $14 million and moved to fifth place, just behind Motown, among Black businesses, most of which were owned by the Johnson family that owned *Ebony* and *Jet*. So flush was Stax that it could pay their overlords at Union Planters Bank all that had been loaned, plus interest, and another $800,000 loan that had been made to Stax through an investment firm, Lynn & Associates, which had been brought into Stax to make tax-sheltered investments. Having loans technically made to Lynn (some could, and did, call that money laundering) allowed Stax, already $6 million in the hole to CBS, to take out more loans, and Union Planters was all too eager to extend another $3 million to a human sponge with enormous income. Even more loans went to East/Memphis Music, including a half-million to build new office space for Stax, almost cloyingly in an abandoned church on Avalon Avenue, as well as refurbishing the associated Ardent studio.

But it seemed every dime of that came into Stax almost immediately went out, an avalanche of it to Ike. Bell would go on spending, always sure he would be able to repay loans the size of a small country's national product, because he had. Stax was a worldwide money-making machine, and Bell was anticipating a flow of new funding, including a $20 million contract from Polydor

Inc. to distribute Stax's products globally, which he would need badly given that by the end of the year he had fallen behind on the loan payments to Union Planters. The bank's president, William Matthews, was so enmeshed in getting those loans paid back that he sometimes traveled to New York with Bell and Stax lawyers for business meetings at CBS, just to ascertain the exact figures of the deal; some of which were not on paper at all but rather handshake agreements with Bell or Stewart.

By then, these numbers had become more of a thorn, since Clive Davis was fired in May 1973 for bilking his expense account for $94,000, which was discovered three days before he was indicted by a grand jury for not paying taxes on that money. Davis would have an amazingly lenient aftermath, during which he was sued by CBS yet hired as a consultant to the company. Within a year, still in the clear, he founded Arista Records, which became a kingly rock 'n' roll label. Finally, in 1976, he paid a skimpy $10,000 fine and settled up with CBS, the firing all but forgotten. Bell was not as lucky, nor was Stax, whose existence was tied to him and for which Bell would fight to the death when the two companies began a cold war. Suspicions ran high, CBS assuming Bell was inflating Stax's value on paper to acquire loans and, at the same time, hiding income on the books in order to undercut CBS. Bell denied any such thing and ventured that CBS had no interest in soul music, only in stealing his company, his money, and, in his imagination, his blood.

Bell had come to believe Davis had backtracked on his original vision for the deal. Davis said Bell thought Clive was "sabotaging" Stax. When Bell stopped returning his calls and didn't invite him to Wattstax movie premieres, they never again spoke, and Davis turned away from Stax. That led to open warfare post-Davis between Bell and CBS, who enraged Bell by cutting its inventory of Stax records as well as the per-record guarantee on sales by 40 percent. Bell, in turn, went behind CBS's back, selling records secretly through his network of community-based sellers who

CBS had ignored. Bell complained, with cause, that CBS only cared about their rock artists and that it had conspired with Union Planters to bankrupt Stax.

The war got uglier through the end of 1973 and into 1974, which would only damage Stax, not CBS. Stax's sales and profits came crashing down, putting the company on death watch. Yet it wasn't corporate jealousy and back-alley jabbing that put Stax in disarray; it was Bell's sanguine attitude about debt, and the dire in-house consequences of slavishly greasing Johnny Baylor. As with his carefree overspending, Bell refused to recognize the clear and present danger of turning the minatory Baylor loose, his fingerprints all over the company business. Even when he stepped over the line, Bell shrugged. But Baylor could not sidestep trouble for long and when an innocent event blew up into big trouble, Bell couldn't duck or dodge any longer.

As it was, Isaac Hayes for the first time was feeling the pressure. "Once you make it," he told *Ebony*, "it's not over with because the *real* test is being able to sustain. And even when you stick, you don't belong to yourself anymore. You have an image to uphold, like me. Every *day* I have to *know*, Jack. I have to know that I can stay on this perch until *I* decide to step down."

But as it happened, the choice wasn't his to make.

13

And the Walls Came Tumbling Down

In November 1972, Johnny Baylor had gotten off a flight at the Memphis airport and was going through a routine search when airport officers asked to see what was in his carry-on bag. In it was $130,000 in cash and a check to him from Stax for $500,000. Baylor's explanations for the stash meandered; some of it he said was a loan, some were record earnings due Luther Ingram, some were for promotion, and some were winnings from horse races. The money was confiscated, and an investigation began. But the Stax brass didn't flinch. Jim Stewart, even years later, shrugged it off, saying "it was Johnny's money." Nothing nefarious about it. Baylor was even able to get most of it back, though the investigation went on to become the light the fuse of a bomb.

In July 1973, the first fuse was lit when the IRS found that Stax, as it was reported in a *New York Times* story, had "uncovered" a $406,737 kickback scheme in a payola scandal run by two employees, Herb Kolesky and Ewell Roussell, in '71, but Stax had not reported it to the feds. Instead, Bell and Stewart had filed an insurance claim with Aetna Casualty, and the employees settled with the company and were fired. A US Attorney told the *Times* that

Stax had tried to "thwart" a grand jury hearing the case by hiding information and had lied to their own attorneys. A grand jury subsequently stuck a $1.8 million lien on Baylor. Bell and Stewart were also summoned to testify about the payola scandal in New York, and while no charges would be filed against the label on the payola matters, that was scant relief as the IRS was looking into every nook and cranny of Stax's account books, including Ike's finances.

As things stood, Ike's yearly salary was only $50,000, implicitly for tax protection. But Bell was so nervous that Ike would walk away and sign with or start his own label, he tore up the contract Ike had signed only a year before and early in 1974 slid him a new one, rife with insanely generous terms. He was guaranteed $1.9 million a year, to be paid out in two installments a year with an initial payment of $270,000. Bell would also pay over a hundred grand a year for Ike's private security, a credit card with a $6,000 credit line, and two more cars, neither of which he ever drove or even got in. His royalty rates were mind-blowing, nearly 25 percent, making him one of the few performers in the world to clear more from the sale of each record than his record company. He was also given the freedom to open his own recording company and self-incorporate into an entity he named Hot Buttered Soul, Inc.

Bell made it part of the pact that Ike would be expected to record forty-eight masters a year, but also gave him the leeway to produce records for others, even non-Stax acts, at any studio. The only cut Stax would levy was a half-million dollars from royalties in 1975; all else he could keep. Hungrily grabbing at the green, Ike threw loads of it into tax shelter deals for properties he didn't even care to know about but Lynn and Associates swore were winners. Even with all that, much like Bell, Ike could not resist wanting more, more, more, as a famous disco hit of the era went. And the golden fleece, or fleecers, was Union Planters. The loan officers there only encouraged this cash runaround, given that Ike was the lowest risk they could imagine. Indeed, even with all the talent at Stax, the joint was in actuality Isaac Hayes, Inc., even if Bell stubbornly clung to his one exception: not cutting Ike in on Stax stock, which was still a burr under Ike's saddle.

Even so, only a piker could have complained. Ike was on the highest rung. And then, when he deposited his first $270,000 check into his account at Union Planters, it bounced. Almost kicking down Bell's office door, he confronted Bell, who had not signed the check, and left it to the loan officer at the bank, Joe Harwell, to send it out—ordered to do so by Bell despite warnings that things at the bank were getting more than a tad squirrely. As it was, Ike recently had a run-in with Bell over rebuffing more of the Hayes corporation's civic plans for Memphis. In a brusque missive, Ike demanded Bell not "subjugate" him, nor give him a "run-around." Bell pledged to make it right but Ike was now seriously close to doing what no Stax employee had ever done: sue Al Bell.

He had done no recording since the two movie soundtracks, nor had he gone on the road since a show in Baltimore on July 29, 1973. Most seriously for Bell, Ike had begun feeling out other record companies for potential deals, the breach of payment sufficient cause to consider breaching his contract. It did seem providential for both Ike and Bell that *Three Tough Guys* and *Truck Turner* would be hitting theaters in May and June respectively and Stax hoping the soundtrack albums would inject some desperately needed cash flow. But the lack of promotional aid being lost in the glut of inter-corporate warfare with CBS did not bode well.

Still, Bell conned himself into believing he could work out the wrinkles with CBS. However, in November 1975, Union Planters took a giant step of its own, suing basically everyone—CBS, Bell, Stewart—alleging that they had been running a con game all along, that CBS had rigged it to control the soul market, and that Stax had conned the bank out of so many illegal loans that it now owed over $10 million. It said nothing about Joe Harwell and the bank's own malfeasance in these matters. As if by rote, Stax stuck its nose into the legal cesspool, seeking to annul the original $6 million deal by suing CBS on anti-trust grounds for $67 million.

CBS then countersued Stax and Union Planters. The sky was lit up with so many legal fireworks that few could figure out who was right or wrong, or if everybody was wrong, which seemed a more distinct possibility.

Bell and the bank were right in one respect: the old warhorse conglomerate CBS was clearly uninterested in promoting Stax records, and when Stax fell behind in its payments, CBS deducted what it owed Stax on royalties. It was another corporate Catch-22: while keeping the legendary soul label like a chained-up dog in the backyard and cutting inventory and royalty rates, CBS feared setting it loose under the banner of another big label that might prosper from it. Bell had his own Catch-22. He wanted to avoid bankruptcy and losing Stax to Union Planters, but could only do so by falling further behind economically by taking on more loans. As strained as things were between Stax and Union Planters, he swung another $3 million loan, but only by agreeing to put up a hundred shares of Stax stock as collateral, giving them even more sway. This was in every sense the definition of insanity. Or, in the record industry, just another day.

ALL THE WHILE, the Johnny Baylor lesion kept metastasizing. All the alms and kickbacks Bell had slipped to Baylor came to light, with the New York apartment particularly concerning the investigators. The investigation of Stax became a flurry of rumors that Bell's loans may have been fraudulently obtained and Bell's dealings with Baylor money-laundering gimmicks. Caught in all these traps, with Stax revenues being held hostage by CBS and Union Planters, by early 1974, the company existed mainly as a meeting place for furrowed-brow executives, lawyers, and accountants to fret and fantasize about how to pay all the debts. It was so bad that Jim Stewart, whose "retirement" was nothing but nonstop meetings with money lenders at the bank where he once worked, concluded that Bell was letting Stax slip through his fingers. Trying to reclaim some sense of stability for his drowning duchy, he mortgaged his opulent Memphis mansion to provide the label with over $4 million in capital.

However, this money went down the same sinkhole, with Bell frittering it away on his quiver of projects and both CBS and Union Planters still owed, by some estimates, over $10 million. Stewart was left with no return on that investment, the bitter end being when Joe Harwell was indicted and convicted for his embezzlement and sent to prison. In the fallout, the bank seemed to know the roof was going to fall in, and until it did, it needed to pull up stakes with Stax. For Bell, this was fatal. Those pending deals with Polydor and Merv Griffin fell away due to the bad publicity. And music now seemed to be an afterthought. The last chart hit for the label was "Woman to Woman" in November 1974 from Shirley Brown, co-produced by Al Jackson, Jr., though Brown's long "phone-call" monologue to the other woman in the song (arguably the first female rap) was clearly inspired by Ike and Barry White. The record came out on the Truth sub-label and was handled by independent distributors, not CBS. To Bell's delight, it was a million-selling, number one soul hit and Grammy nominee, helping to delay the end times for at least several months and stoke Bell's pipe dream to thrive without CBS.

Ike himself clearly had other things on his mind than recording, mainly his cinematic explorations that were released in late spring. But there were complications. *Three Tough Guys* was released mainly in Italy and France, where ads for the flick were unwittingly funny European attempts at the American soul idiom, such as "THE BLACK MOSES, THE HAMMER, AND THE PREACHER MAN. THEY'VE GOT THEIR OWN KIND OF MEAN GAME." Thus, it didn't do much business in the States but did prove that there was more to Isaac Hayes's movie presence than *Shaft*. In fact, the *Tough Guys* soundtrack did much to kick off the '70s paradigm of "urban" funk/pop that soon would be all over the movies and even as jingles for white TV fare like cop shows and the pro football broadcasts, not to mention filling the song catalogs of Billy Preston and The Isley Brothers. Indeed, most shows seemed to feature at least one Black character—though save for the few all-Black series generally not in the lead role—as if, at least, in the cosmetic sense, Black was part of a new white. Fittingly enough, Ike had also composed the theme song for an ABC crime/drama series *The Men*. It lasted only one season, but the theme again received as much buzz as the show, an elongated version released as a single became a top-twenty soul hit and later covered in disco and jazz styles, a form of collective soul that future generations would poke fun at for how *mainstream* it was. Ike's acting was a perfect complement: ballsy and given to reverse racial stereotyping but also mellow and prone to bouts of moral guilt. *Truck Turner* would overachieve its pedestrian standing, pulling in $2.2 million and again scoring big as a rental. But Stax was in no position to do anything with the albums; both dropped only on vinyl with Stax not able to foot the cost of separate editions on cassette. Few albums made it to the stores, and its fetching selections were barely heard until a 1993 CD re-release of both movies' soundtracks and in 2003 when a standalone *Turner* album was released.

Still, the films kept him in a spotlight, one that he had no doubt would keep shining. The release of the movies came just when he had sunk millions more into a long-held dream to own a pro basketball team in Memphis. And, with his new deal at Stax the talk of the industry, he was at the center of an effort to buy one that already existed, sort of. He, soul singer Al Wilson ("Show and Tell"), and a well-heeled heavyweight, Holiday Inn hotel founder, Kemmons Wilson (who owned the rockabilly label Holiday Inn Records), were recruited to buy the American Basketball Association Memphis Tams by Mike Storen, who had quit as league commissioner to head a new team renamed the Sounds. Ike was highly visible, as usual, in a courtside seat each game and had a hand in personnel decisions, such as signing ABA free agents Rick Mount and Mel Daniels. When the season began in October, crowds would suddenly discover there was a team in town, and though they lost money, there was an undeniable buzz around town about the games.

Even so, the instability at Stax ensured that by the time the season ended in May 1975, Ike would no longer be employed there. In September, Ike and his lawyer, the wonderfully named McDonald Yawn, shocked Al Bell by filing a $5.3 million lawsuit against Stax for lost earnings and damages, claiming that Bell had illegally purloined over $1 million alone in Ike's royalties and prevented him from promised equity in the company. The suit was quickly settled, with Union Planters stepping in and brazenly siding with Ike, its best loan candidate, and demanding that Bell capitulate or else lose Ike to another label. Capitulate he did, with the $270,000 in arrears footed by the bank. But that was only the first step of a more shocking move. While Bell made the accommodation to keep Ike from jumping ship, soon after his legal team demanded his outright release, followed by a blatant threat by the bank not to loan Stax anything more unless they gave Ike the release, which would be the only way to get him back in the studio and making money again. In fact, clued in that Ike was prepared to sign with ABC Records for a $7.5 million advance, the bank was already salivating about reeling in several million for outstanding Ike loans.

The sad but necessary release happened after an emergency meeting (as they all were now) on September 14, 1975, with all of Stax's high council in attendance. Unable to resist the bank's threats and Union Planters being the only institution that they could turn to for sustenance, Bell signed an agreement that ceded to Ike the master recordings for the two movie soundtracks and the only recording he'd made at Stax in recent months, the wistfully titled "Wonderful." Decades later, Bell would grimace at the deed, insisting that the bank was more avid about "crippling" the Black company and driving it out of the city's white business cradle than helping Ike's career; this may be correct, given that Ike's debt, like that of Stax, was all but written off.

Whatever the motives, which were typically confusing, after over a decade reaching the summit and beyond, Isaac Lee Hayes would need to find a new way forward within a soul music infrastructure that by the day was moving further ahead of him, and no longer related to the kinship of Stax. This was no small undertaking, but Ike believed he could simply transfer his Stax-bred soul to less soul-flavored labels. As rock journalist Pete Wingfield noted, "Whatever bizarre circumstances caused the [fall of Stax and Hayes's defection], they had little to do with the music." So, while he could have demanded the rights to his songs upon leaving the company, he let them go to just make the same sort of chart hits. Another mistake turned out to be his basketball reverie. The Sounds somehow made the playoffs with a 27-57 record and drew acceptable crowds, leading the owners to think they could qualify for inclusion in the impending ABA merger with the NBA, but when the season ended, the red ink was too much to continue, and after just one season, they sold the team. This was perhaps one more hint that, for Ike, who'd had everything go his way, there was perhaps more to winning than it seemed.

HIS EXODUS WAS followed by The Staple Singers, Eddie Floyd, The Dramatics, and Richard Pryor's hit comedy album needing to be transferred mid-stream to a different label. Another would-be Stax soundtrack, produced by Dale Warren for the Richard Burton-Lee Marvin movie *The Klansman,* was canceled and given to another studio, and a group under Warren's wing, 24-Carat Black, was now financed by Warren out of his own pocket. Johnnie Taylor split for none other than Columbia Records (which had merged with the Japanese global giant Sony, Inc.), recording in '76 the biggest soul hit ever up to that point, "Disco Lady," produced by Don Davis, its vibraphone-coated, leering sexual lyrics taking it to number one on the pop and R&B charts as the first Platinum single, selling two million copies. Taylor slyly paid homage to Ike by titling the album that spawned the record *Eargasm* (though unlike Ike, the advances he received from Columbia/Sony kept him from earning his full due until his estate sued the company decades later).

Moreover, it seemed like a final tragic metaphor when the great Stax drum maven Al Jackson, Jr. didn't live out the year. On September 30, 1975, just about when Ike was set free, Jackson, who had already survived being shot in the chest by his estranged wife, was shot five times in the back by an intruder in his home. He died in the street as his wife screamed for help. (The murderer would be killed by police a few months later.) Inside the crumbling Stax walls, the talk was not of music but shady characters and lots of dirty deals.

In January 1975, the beleaguered Al Bell had peremptorily fired over two hundred Stax employees, carrying on with a skeletal staff. Union Planters was in effect the owner of Stax, having gained control by dint of its majority stock shares, and was reluctant to extend any further loans to a moribund Stax. In fact, the bank was itself enjoined from doing such by the bankruptcy court. Bell still spent all his time still trying to pull off a Lazarus-like deal. But that same September, a Memphis grand jury issued a shocking fourteen-count bank fraud indictment for he and Joe Harwell, the charges stemming from Harwell singing while in custody. Bell was in his office, unaware of the indictment, when armed guards came in and, much in the way Johnny Baylor and Dino Woodard had with their prey, had a few simple words for him, which according to Bell went like this:

"Nigger, you got fifteen minutes to get out of the building."

Still shaken, Bell recalls, "They came to physically kill me. One was ex-CIA, another ex-FBI. Both were Black. They were from a private security firm and CBS got a judge to federalize them so that white men wouldn't be killing a Black man in Memphis. I am alive today only because a Black federal marshal happened to be there when they came in. That marshal saved my life."

These claims were never confirmed but when he was released on bail and went back to the office, he was for many a victim and hero. Some Black leaders and opinion writers in the Memphis papers began alleging the charges were bogus, that for all of Bell's missteps the fact was that his signature had been forged by Harwell. The phrase "legal lynching" was commonly used in the Black media. Bell himself cast the entire episode as blatant racism, a context he still echoes when he says things like, "In its own way, Stax Records was fighting the same fight as Dr. King, and Stax Records was assassinated too."

Bell found himself with a stockpile of sympathy, his reputation intact as a respected music maven who had been screwed over by The Man. Doggedly, he burned up the phone line trying to make deals that would liberate Stax from the dead. He even took $50,000 from his father for the cause, and there was chatter that Stax might relocate to Gary, Indiana, the idea floated by the city's Black mayor, Richard Hatcher. Looking to play the best legal angle, the company's lawyers first settled up with CBS, who proposed that Stax could pay only half of its debt to the giant label if CBS kept the inventory it had on hand. Bell signed the settlement, albeit "under duress," he said—then tried to backtrack, sending scathing memos to CBS vowing: "We shall win—only strong survives." The deal would crumble when Stax ultimately filed Chapter 11 bankruptcy, turning its fate over to the bankruptcy court to figure out how to dispense with a *$30 million* mountain of combined debt to CBS and Union Planters.

In the end, no one would really "win" this demented, mortifying power game among grown men acting more like spoiled brat children, which would still not reach a final dispensation for another year. But Union Planters did own exclusive rights to post-1968 Stax masters and catalog—an all too familiar, nauseating replay of the sacking by Atlantic, which kicked Jim Stewart in the gut once again. Having sunk every cent he had into the abyss, he later rued the doomed mission that "destroyed me personally. I had plenty of money, I was wealthy, but I just lost everything," including his twelve-acre estate, which was sold at auction. Al Bell was looted as well when Union Planters foreclosed on his personal income and belongings, leaving him with little but the shirt on his back; his wife needed to sell her diamond jewelry to feed and house them and their children, though they lost their stylish home and had to live on the poor side of town.

Isaac Hayes, who had not been indicted, was nonetheless shucked, his royalties and other compensation all thrown into cold storage by Union Planters, to whom he had an enormous debt. He had done well to escape the house of cards before they all fell, using his leverage to sign a recording and producing deal with ABC Records. But Hayes was hardly untouched by the wreckage of the defining context of his life, its zephyr of perpetually comforting annuities all sold off to a white bank. At thirty-five, his fortune to be wiped out, he would always be the quintessential hybrid: the Soul Man, the bad mutha Shaft, and Black Moses. But now he faced his own crossroads, as if he was being punished for all that. His marketability was undeniable, but his work force was now subject to shapeshifting not of his making and his life in arrears to something he had thought he'd never have to revisit: poverty.

14

Black Moses Is Dead

Ike's record deal with ABC put him in good company. The label had been Ray Charles's home base until 1973 and since then had drawn The Four Tops away from Motown reaping the crossover hit "Ain't No Woman (Like the One I've Got)" and B.B. King. It was a comfy place to roost; his royalty rate higher than anyone, his independent label Hot Buttered Soul partnered with ABC, and his records were to be released on a joint label. Even so, in the transition he lost the unheard-of financial leverage he had at Stax. In fact, the losses were deep and ongoing. Already burdened by paying two ex-wives and child support, Stax's takeover by Union Planters and his tanked investments were bringing him ever closer to personal bankruptcy.

Naturally, he had to continually respond to questions about the traumatic dim-out of Stax. But while he privately blamed Al Bell for having gotten him and the company into a financial hole, he could not dismiss the reality that Bell had gotten him way up the ladder and almost alone fomented the Isaac Hayes delirium. Bell says there were no hard feelings between them and that they would frequently speak through the coming years on professional matters. And Ike kept him out of his recriminations. When interviewed by

Jet's Mark Stansbury for the June 26, 1975 issue, he spoke of misguided reliance, but didn't name names:

> *"The Stax situation cost me tremendously.... I trusted the wrong people. But I didn't lose my spirit. Because I realized that I came from nothing, so I can start all over again. I wasn't going to jump off a roof. 'Cause it's all just material things anyway. I could do it again. I'd made contacts. I had to use 'em. I was relaxed, because I'd been there, done that."*

His split from Stax, he said, was irreconcilable. "If we had been able to work something out, I would have stayed. But there was a situation where their backs were against the walls. You can't get blood from a turnip." He added that he had lost "a handsome amount" and that, "Yes, you can say that the break was a distasteful one" but fudged over the fact that Al Bell had severely overspent on perks for him, nor did he mention that his own loan debts were abominable. Moreover, if he thought about publicly laying on hands about Bell's "persecution" by the white establishment, he abstained on that too.

Clearly, he wanted to put Stax behind him, as if that could ever happen, needing to deliver his first non-Stax work to ABC. The sessions for an album were over two weeks in June 1975 at the Hot Buttered Soul studio, for which he now had to pay operating costs though the sessions were covered by ABC—mercifully, since the room was packed with fourteen musicians, including himself, and the sound board run by old friend Henry Bush, with engineer Roosevelt "Head" Green doing the final mixing at ABC's studios in LA. It was a big production, to be sure, and ABC signed on to the work as a reflection of the older, no-longer Black Moses-in-chains, an angle *Jet* reported along with the news that Ike had yanked the BLACK MOSES plates from the El Dorado for the calmer ISAAC. To Stansbury, this was a major turn of events, writing, "Black Moses, Hayes has decided, is dead." As Ike saw it, "I would like to be looked upon simply as an entertainer...and Black Moses restricts me, because people look upon me as some type of saviour [*sic*]. They don't look at me as being human."

Toward that end, the album, called *Chocolate Chip*, would have him on the cover in a three-quarter pose, black clothing merging into a plain black background, his hand holding a half-eaten cookie. This was the meme of a "new" Isaac Hayes, grabbing deep inside himself for what was in the simple base of his soul, which here came out as a mainly slow jam entry, joining the romanticized minarets of the Gamble and Huff brand, getting in and out with dispatch. Of the seven tracks on the LP, the longest were three that ran six and a half minutes; the opening cut, "That Loving Feeling," and the final two, "Come Live with Me" and "I Can't Turn Around." The briefest, self-explanatory "I Want to Make Love to You So Bad," was a relative shortcut. "That Loving Feeling," co-written with Tony Joe White, wound around a heartbeat-like bass taken from "Ike's Mood 1," with a mandolin picking around Ike's Barry White-ish moans of "Come, come closer, baby...I feel my heart pounding inside me."

The title cut and its separate instrumental track were his concessions to the reality of disco, a horny, *wocka-wocka* stream and backing *whoo-whoos*, the first with barely coherent James Brown-style lyrics about being "a walking sex machine," and the funky, churning stomp "I Can't Turn Around" hitting the disco cylinder, rotating over and over into a long fade-out. "Come Live with Me" and "Body Language" were pop-romantic lulls, slow-dance funk that wrapped around the soul. And so it was rewarding that after his absence from the scene, the LP went Gold, number one on the R&B album chart and number eighteen on the pop chart. Not terrible, by any means. But after his interregnum, it was a tad disappointing, as was the return on the singles ABC hoped would detonate the fire, the title song that reached number thirteen in soul and number eighty-two in pop, and "Come Live with Me" / "Body Language" that hit number twenty on the R&B list but failed to dent the pop chart.

Chocolate Chip was another winner, but even as a new thing for Ike there was the same old curiously mixed racial messages: Black listeners needed to have it in their Isaac Hayes collections but were not overly into paying big bucks to see him live, while white listeners were just the opposite. It was confusing to try and figure out, and Ike had no idea that the Gold-Record comfort zone, a given since 1969, was something he needed now to enjoy while he could, and that *Chocolate Chip* would be his last taste of it.

BACK OUT ON the hustings after a year, he began wearing finely tailored white suits and shoes, looking through conventional non-tinted eyeglasses. The bald dancer was gone from the act, as were the grass skirts and full-length tunics. The backup band was prim and proper, and while that could not be said of his performances, he mainly sat on his piano stool, weaving and bobbing, or standing to lead the orchestra with a frenetic baton much like Barry White, a reverse take on the copycatting he despised. Worse was that when he complied with ABC's two-albums-per-year requirement, he went back into the studio in the fall for the next chain link, he could no longer avoid the disco pocket. The album was indeed called *Disco Connection*, which on the Isaac Hayes omnibus of heartfelt commitment sits last, on the back seat of his soul.

Although dance vibes had been in the bloodstream of his work from the start, he had shied from going full disco. But Baby Boomer-populated dance clubs running wild with coke, 'ludes, and mushrooms had become a subculture, undercutting the "serious" soul that had vaulted Ike, Barry White, and Stevie Wonder's searing albums to Grammy awards, Stevie seemingly every year. But with some desperation he was impelled to join the new party, even if he deemed it conditional, and with the understanding that, technically, disco had fused the same ingredients he had mastered: high strings, electric keyboards/synthesizers, swarming horns, double and triple bass lines, raw sexuality, rap. One could even say disco was another step in the inclusion process of all races wanting to seem sufficiently Black or, in 1977, imitating Travolta dancing like he was Black. At least he tried to explain it that way, though it was surely no small wonder to him that a whole scene had cemented within the obnoxious décor of white guys with fluffy perm-waved Afros, polyester shirts open to the navel, and women's spandex catsuits. Disco meant money, easy money given the ardor of shamelessly repetitive syncopation. So here we were.

Again, he was there already, since Willie Hall's hi-hat, four-by-four patterns had firmly sunk into dance-beat songs, and Ike's song texture of heartfelt growls and raps backed by lushly orchestrated arrangements needed no tutelage. Neither did he scrimp, putting over twenty musicians into it, including his old honchos Sid Kirk and Floyd Newman, all of The Bar-Kays and *fourteen* horn players alone, one on bass trombone, two on French horn. He then polished it all with The Memphis Strings. Searching for a groove, he injected the usual suspects of disco-ism in percussive and stringed notches but never really took off for disco-land, the connection still being to melodic R&B, deciding at the start to bag vocals and go with the instrumental flow of his important movie soundtracks—the "disco" here being the soft, mystic interior of the genre, in tune with the romanticism of Barry White, Gamble/Huff, Norman Whitfield's production of Rose Royce's "Car Wash," and the biggest hit of the summer of '75, the DC-based Van McCoy's Soul City Symphony's "The Hustle."

This made Ike a disco miner, borrowing from here and there and hearing his own inner commands for songs with nomadic titles like the title tune, "The First Day of Forever," "St. Thomas Square," "Vykkii," "Disco Shuffle," "Choppers," "After Five," and "Aruba." The album was lovely and lifting, and the most he would bend for disco, which is a pity since he may have beaten Giorgio Moroder's seventeen-minute album version of Donna Summer's ersatz orgasms in '75, "Love to Love You Baby" or the gasping female spasms on ex-Delfonics singer Major Harris's "Love Won't Let Me

Wait," had he chosen to weaponize his own moaning "eargasms."
As it was, the album's title track was a funky jag with rolling synth
and stabbing drum effects that would be appropriated by *Soul
Train* for its line-dance spot, another marker for the generation.
However, *Disco Connection*, released under the name of *The Isaac
Hayes Movement*, its cover not of him but a generic Black dancing
couple lost in reverie, barely got into the soul top twenty and lagged
at number eighty-five on the pop chart, the "Disco Connection"
track making it onto the soul chart at number sixty, and curiously,
number ten in England.

By the end of 1975, then, his fan base was deep but thinning.
Even t]The Bee Gees scored higher on the disco and soul charts.
Partly in frustration, his two albums of '76, *Groove-a-Thon* and
Juicy Fruit (Disco Freak) were almost mockery. On the title cut of
Groove, on which he let the songs run longer, up to ten minutes, he
reached back for the horn flourishes of *Shaft* as if to remind everyone who he was. *Fruit* (the semi-comical cover of which might
have been from a highlight reel of his carousing—a butt-naked Ike
in a pool surrounded by six ladies laying hands on him wearing
only Carmen Miranda-type fruit headgear) had him rapping that
disco "will never go away" was a facetious riff on rock 'n' roll's
enduring epitaph, uttered during what was a group-speak intro
similar to Marvin Gaye's immortal "What's Going On," as a peek
into an imbibed night at a disco. Yet he was too confident that
such wryness would be appreciated. Few did; even decades later,
a retro-review of *Fruit* on the AllMusic site blisters him for "lazy
singing" and "irritatingly banal lyrics." To be sure, his overdubbed
vocals on the *Groove* slow jams "Rock Me Easy Baby" and "Make a
Little Love to Me" were facile hat-tips to Barry White, but they also
took the sheen off more daring original numbers like *Fruit*'s "Lady
of the Night," a tale of woe about falling in love with a hooker, wondering about "How many Johns have come and gone" before him.
Again, these works were perfectly intriguing, if not earth-shatter-
ing. *Groove* peaked at number eleven in soul and number forty-five

in pop, *Fruit* number eighteen in soul and a gut-punching number 124 on the pop. Accordingly, ABC was now starting to rethink his long-term presence on the label, and Ike felt as if he was in a tightening vise. As his royalty train continued to slow, he fell into a panic. The Gold records stopped coming in to hang on the wall, and with the final dispensation of Stax, his homes, his lifestyle, and his future were all up in the air.

As IKE TRIED to hang tough, Stax officially died. Bankruptcy judge William B. Leffler, who himself labeled Stax a "financial holocaust," closed the old theater on January 12, 1976. Boards were nailed onto its windows and doors, with no one able to collect any items from offices or the studio pending what would be a public sale of those items. While all this kicked around the court, Union Planters would be savaged within the Black community of Memphis, with Operation PUSH distributing fliers on lamp posts urging a boycott of the bank, warning that while Stax "is struggling for life, UP Bank is in the process of liquidating the STAX property...and using every method that can destroy the company, and the people behind it!" For a time, the bank itself seemed on the brink when its vice president and several other officers were convicted of fraud, joining Joe Harwell behind bars.

Al Bell then had to fight for his freedom. At his trial in the summer of 1976, he was portrayed by the defense as the victim of a corporate version of racist profiling. Jesse Jackson and Ralph Abernathy sat in the front row behind him, and they helped raise $7,500 to help defray Bell's legal expenses. And the jurors were more taken by Bell's insouciance and the angle that he was being prosecuted for being successful and Black than the numbing financial statistics reiterated by the prosecution. It ended with an acquittal and Bell angrily pointing out that he had gone from "a man that owned a company whose masters were valued by Price Waterhouse at sixty-seven million dollars to a man that could scrape together fifteen cents." When he was acquitted, all he could do was wait for the bankruptcy court to hand down the final exaction of Stax Records.

Ike, meanwhile, who bore the glory of what Stax had been, pushed his former sanctuary further behind him as he and his troupe, hangers-on, and security force went where the demand was. His first gig after two years in dry dock was at Philadelphia's Spectrum in September 1975, then at Detroit's Olympia Stadium, the Frankfort Arena, Toronto's Maple Leaf Gardens, and in September he hosted a seven-hour "cause concert" at the cavernous, half-filled Houston Astrodome to foot legal bills for Rubin "Hurricane" Carter, the boxer who had been framed for murder; the show also featuring Bob Dylan and his Rolling Thunder Revue, Stevie Wonder, Carlos Santana, Stephen Stills, and Ringo Starr. And though apathetic performances by some limited the impact, Ike, wearing a "Hurricane" t-shirt, sang with gusto, backed by Stevie's Wonderland band, leading chants of "Free the Hurricane!" He also crossed the pond for dates in England, to take the usual flak from Brit critics, one of whom, Simon Frith, regurgitated criticisms of Ike's "self-indulgent black muzak" and "supper lounge soul" while admitting he had an "alarming genius [for] the contemporary soul formula...The album is not very original. But Hayes' genius has always been for arrangement and production and they're impeccable. You can dance to this and make out."

This skill kept him in star-land, but only bordering on the stratospheric level. But his earnings were of pressing interest to the IRS. In the fall of 1976 they entered again, filing a lien for $464,000 in unpaid federal taxes from 1974. And when that became public knowledge, creditors who he had been dodging filed their own claims, including the Memphis clothier Woolf Brothers for $11,000, Saks Fifth Avenue in Beverly Hills for $10,500, and the Saks in Washington, DC for $10,000. With no way to satisfy these debts with his biannual royalties, Ike, pulling Mignon into it as though a ploy for sympathy, declared dual bankruptcy on December 31, 1976, claiming an astonishing debt of $6.5 million and declaring that he and Mignon were in a state of "survival in destitute circumstances" without "having enough money to pay for a place to live, utilities, food and transportation," although he did note that they had "a chauffeured limousine to take my children to school."

The bankruptcy did not prevent the IRS from taking the mansion, the ten acres of land it sat on, and all of the possessions inside it. A few weeks later a foreclosure sale was held on the steps of the Shelby County courthouse, the winning bid a relatively cheap $375,000, a hundred thousand less than Ike had paid, and the buyer was none other than Union Planters Bank, which was logical as they already owned practically everything else of his, and still owed millions. This meant he would need to find a new home, and when he would go, it would be without most of the possessions he could boast of, as the bank mercilessly held a public auction, with basically everything in the house up for sale. On the day of the auction, items from paper clips to his grand piano went out the door, including all of his cars, the famous gold-encrusted El Dorado fetching $13,750 and the Cadillac limo that ferried the children to school $6,100. An unlikely-named buyer named Jim Velvet spent $15,000 for a lot consisting of Ike's grand piano (for $7,200), organ, and three xylophones. (His Oscar statue would be gone, too; having allowed Al Bell to show it off in his office, it was legally out of Rushia's hands when the IRS ordered everything to remain where it was.)

The total of all the sales came to $54,000, leading an auctioneer to say, "We were pleased with the auction. Everything was sold," with none of the money going to the Soul Man.

This actually amounted to little, a drop in the bucket of his mélange of debts, but it represented the ultimate object lesson of a high life gone haywire. No matter that he could sell out large arenas and sell thousands of records, he was damaged property. Indeed, from now on, any mention of him in the press not only carried an epitaph of Stax but some religiously retold the ugly business of his home and belongings being sold out from under him. This was, in effect, a main spoke of his legacy, one that for a spectacularly successful Black artist bore unspoken tribute to such men being disciplined and ripped off enough to keep their fortune from being sullied or stolen. Another kick in the gut was the failure of a highly promoted live double album he recorded while on tour with Dionne Warwick at Atlanta's Fox Theater. It happened after Warwick had been so impressed with his cover of "Walk on By" that she asked him to tour, and when ABC Records proposed an album, she obtained permission from her label, Warner Brothers.

On tour, each had their own backup bands, arrangers, and conductors (Ike's arranger was Lester Snell) and backing singers—and a series of love-song medleys. They both were listed as executive producers. It was surely an odd-couple pairing, but Warwick's tightly mannered soprano melded with Ike's balls-to-the-wall soul. "Walk on By" was the second track, paired with "I Just Don't Know What to Do with Myself," and there were peaceful, easy renditions of her "I Say a Little Prayer" and his juiced up "Come Live with Me" and for the finale, "Chocolate Chip." Others were takes on hit-makers such as Gamble and Huff on the opening track, "Unity," Paul McCartney's "My Love," Olivia Newton John's "Have You Never Been Mellow," and KC and The Sunshine Band's "That's the Way I Like It" and "Get Down Tonight." It was enough for a double album of Vegas-style glitz, the nadir a lachrymose cover of Morris Albert's much-mocked tearjerker "Feelings." The album, *A Man and a Woman*, had them on the cover in high-tone, Ike in a dark suit, and a reflection that the work lacked the hardscrabble flash of the Lake Tahoe album.

It was a rather sloppy project, with several misspellings on the album's inner jacket compilation of lyrics, and it missed all the charts. Robert Christgau roasted it as "an embarrassing blot on both artists' careers. Almost everything is slowed-down and schmaltzed up, including past Warwick hits...and several of the worst pop tunes of all time: 'Feelings,' 'Love Will Keep Us Together,' 'My Eyes Adored You.'" Yet the pairing had a silver (actually gold) lining. During their tour, Ike wrote a song called "Deja Vu" after they'd had dinner, then cut a track of it when he was recording his next album, sans lyrics. The melody he wrote was similar to "Walk on By," slow and sexy with perky chords. He sent her a demo tape, but as she recalled, "He kept promising me a lyric for it and the weeks went by and finally I had to threaten his life. It seemed like the only way I'd get the song." While she waited, she had a song-writing partner of her friend Barry Manilow, Adrienne Anderson, write the words about finding a love that "awaited all my life."

Dionne sent Ike a rough copy of her recording for his approval. "The next thing you know," she said, "my phone's ringing at 5 AM—it's Ike telling me it's the best lyric anyone's ever written for one of his songs!"

Anticipating a hit, Ike set up IkeCo. Music Ltd. to control the publishing rights with Anderson's publishing company. But while the song waited for Warwick to sign with her next label, Clive Davis's Arista Records, Ike too landed with a new label, Polydor—the very one Al Bell had hoped to heaven would save *him*. Such were the crazy paradoxes of the record game, in which winners and losers can change places as suddenly as a game of checkers.

ALMOST IN DIRECT parallel to Ike's ongoing financial woes, the toll at Stax was complete. In July 1977, Al Bell had filed a last-ditch $20 million suit against Union Planters, which got nowhere, and in November, bankruptcy trustee A.J. Calhoun announced the disbursement of the Stax debts. Both CBS and Union Planters, having figured they would be left with enormous debts, were right. CBS was given $750,000, UP around $500,000, the IRS collecting another $100,000. CBS got to keep the Stax inventory it had, Union Planters got the licensing rights on post-'68 royalties. The old theater had been unassigned and left for dead, suffering its own added indignity when its offices and studio were opened to a public auction, Calhoun running an ad in *Billboard* simply reading "Sale,

Stax Records." As with the sweep of Ike's home, memorabilia could be had for a song, and out the door went 1,500 master recordings that had eluded the grip of Atlantic, CBS, and Union Planters, and 200,000 tapes, recording equipment, furniture, typewriters, and stereos—and the Oscar. A Memphis newspaper's headline read: STAX RECORDS: THE DREAM THAT DIED.

This was surely true in the abstract, but whatever lingering rights Union Planters had on Stax history were enough to prompt Fantasy Records, the Berkeley, California-based jazz label of the '50s that had broken the rock 'n' roll bank with Creedence Clearwater Revival, to buy the Stax imprimatur from the bank in '77. Fantasy hired Dave Porter to run its affairs from his office on Union Avenue, but after some talk about rebooting the label, Fantasy chose to make Stax a memory lane, only re-releasing oldies. The first one was an album called *Hotbed*, a pasticcio of Ike's Lake Tahoe recordings as well as his unreleased songs like "The Ten Commandments of Love" and a re-release of "By the Time I Get to Phoenix" / "Walk on By" that made it to number sixty-five on the R&B chart. This opened a small door of auxiliary royalties for Ike and Dave. However, when Union Planters pawned the Stax publishing companies East/Memphis and Birdees to West Coast record executive Al Bennett for $1.8 million, they would get nothing from the Birdees stockpile. Worse, Ike feared that if he started a new publishing company, it too would be waylaid by the IRS, thus his publishing rights for his first post-Stax songs were shared with ABC.

On other fronts, bag man Johnny Baylor was charged with $2.5 million in fraudulent loans and would serve time in prison, and then return to KoKo Records without Luther Ingram, who signed with Profile Records, an early hip hop label. Baylor died in obscurity in 1984. Al Bell meanwhile fled Memphis to pick up the pieces of his shattered life in DC, finding backers for a new soul label but ran dry of money and went back to his home town, Little Rock, Arkansas, to try to keep the label going.

For Ike, climbing back up was also the context of *his* life, and for that, he too moved to new ground. Because Mignon's family owned a home in Atlanta, he took his leave from the city that spawned him and soul and moved the family to the lesser music outpost. His studio would be Atlanta's Mastersound, run by local producer Bob Richardson. For Richardson, who had produced the frat-rock classic "Double Shot of My Baby's Love," Ike's symphonic windstorms were a far cry. But Ike was taken by how other hits made there such as "Dueling Banjos" and "You and Me and a Dog Named Boo," meshed so transparently with the studio's acoustics. His first piece of business was the mixing of the Warwick album. He then turned to bringing a new coterie of musicians and technical experts into Mastersound for his first Polydor album, which would be released solely by the company, having folded the Hot Buttered Soul label and studio when he fled Memphis (the only other act to record there having been the disco band The Masqueraders, their 1975 *Everybody Wanna Live On* album produced by Ike for ABC).

The album, *New Horizon,* was arranged by old confrere Johnny Allen and engineered and mixed by Joe Neil. The only returning musician was Willie Hall; the new crew included guitarist Kim Palumu, bassist Derek Galbrieth, keyboardists Jessie Butler and Travis Biggs, percussionist Daniel Zebulon, and The Atlanta Horns and Strings. With Ike also on keys, the first two tracks were a trembling cover of the torch song from *Kismet*: "Stranger in Paradise," with five minutes of wind chimes, xylophone, and a gong banging before the vocals kicked in and Hayes's "Moonlight Lovin' (Mènage Á Trois)," each running over ten minutes.

The latter cadged Barry White but went where Barry never would have: to the previously taboo topic of threesome love, the pelvic-thrusting beat ringing as he rapped on about "a rendezvous of me and you and you;" the hook sung with the backing choir going *"Mènage á Trois, Mènage á Trois."* It was a song one had to wipe his or her brow to. Yet of the other three cuts, "Don't Take Your Love Away," "Out of the Ghetto," and "It's Heaven to Me," only "Ghetto" was a disco rag—the flammable word "ghetto" losing its fire when the sophomoric lyrics centered on wanting to take a "foxy lady" out of the ghetto but you "could not get that ghetto out of you." The other cuts were reliable slow jams with the needless reminder from him on "It's Heaven" that he was singing "a melody that mesmerizes me."

On the LP's cover was a tight shot of him, shoulders covered in a sporty pink T-shirt, a weirdly non-committal pose, not endemic of any theme. And maybe this was the problem. No one really knew Isaac Hayes now as a specific *thing*. He was still a noble Soul Man with Shaft-like prickliness but part-crooning lover boy and part disco rambler put him in too much company. Additionally, Polydor issued hundreds of records a year during this era, including albums by The Bee Gees, Andy Gibb, The Who, Eric Clapton, Golden Earring, and The Jam, and in the soul/disco category: Gloria Gaynor, the Silver Convention, and James Brown. In this glut, Ike's albums were not among the most heavily promoted. *New Horizon* was neither dissed nor ignored. It peaked fitfully at number twenty-six on the soul chart; the singles "Out of the Ghetto" and "Moonlight Lovin' (Mènage Á Trois)," both with "It's Heaven to Me" as the B-side, tracked at numbers forty-three and ninety-six, respectively, on the soul chart.

As gorgeous as the material was (later releases would add a sixteen-minute version of "Moonlight" and "single" versions of "Ghetto" and "Moonlight"), fans clearly were more drawn to the Barry White model of high-tone soul that was, of course, based on the earlier work of Isaac Hayes, even if, as one critic rightly noted, White "had the voice but none of the physical beauty or political impact of Isaac's iconic *Black Moses*." Actually, both Ike and Barry strongly denied there was any intrinsic similarity between them, each believing in their own singularity. White smugly told music writer Joe Nick Patoski in 1975, "Isaac Hayes? I defend him now. People started to say Isaac is copping Barry White and I defend him now, have for the past nine months. But he really doesn't sound like me, he still doesn't. He's into his own thing and I'm in mine. I just feel I'm better in mine than he is in his."

More to the point was that Ike's "thing" should have been spunkier in the new soul mold of Ray Parker, Jr., Brothers Johnson, and Earth, Wind & Fire, not fixed in quickly-aging rhythmic mold—in fact, White and Philadelphia International were starting to lose their hold, too, especially on younger ears. Staying on top in soul was far easier imagined than done. And apparently this stoked a need for Ike to sell himself to the highest bidders. In 1977, two aides of Tennessee Governor Ray Blanton, one nicknamed "Speedy," had tried to line him up to entertain for what the newspapers called "a Saudi Arabian sheik." The pair flew to LA to meet with Ike but, not only did they not report their travel costs, a larger stink broke out about the aides selling paroles to convicted felons for which they were sent to jail and Blanton removed from office. Sadly, the Soul Man never did pocket any Saudi bread. Considering the possibilities, that must have hurt like hell.

His FOLLOW-UP WAS his lone album release in 1978, *For the Sake of Love*, which faced the same uneasy parameters, leading Ike to reach back into the past for reassurance, creating a sequel to "Theme from Shaft," something he had refrained from for either of the two *Shaft* sequels—a favorite gripe of critics and fans of the franchise. "Shaft II," essentially a "Shaft" EP, was a disco-fied, ten-minute Xerox of the original that softened horns and strings amid a chugging beat, adding a bongo-tambourine bridge and skipping into the famous *wah-wah* closing, but without his raunchy, heavy-breathing vocal. It was really "Shaft Light," though as a disco piece it was, as one retro-reviewer would call it, "ear-buzzing." The problem it would encounter, though, was that the primordial song was just as easily danceable and is one that cannot be improved upon.

Additionally, his back-to-the-future covers of Billy Joel's "Just the Way You Are" and James Taylor's "Don't Let Me Be Lonely

Tonight" were better revivals of his artful, semi-rapped pop, the
three-minute rap intro of the former another self-dissection of his
caddish impulses, purring the alibi that checking other women out
only meant that he had an "eye for beauty" that justified "my adoration for you." The slowed, toned-down cover of the song itself was,
if anything, an anti-disco statement, his torchy, emotional vocal
reaching maximum credibility. "Lonely" and his original "Believe
in Me" and "If We Ever Needed Peace" fell into the same fold, his
vocal delayed on the Taylor cover by three minutes of aural sex, on
"Believe" attesting to "being right here to kiss away every tear," and
on "Peace" preaching a trite sermon that "the sunlight of peace" was
the way to brotherhood." Yet, Polydor had slotted him into the disco
market, and the album's core was "Zeke the Freak," a bass-charged,
horn/synth instrumental hacked off of the electro-pop dance idiom
of Billy Preston and the Silver Convention's "Fly, Robin, Fly." The
cover this time had him silhouetted side-face against a vivid red
sunset, a darker image in keeping with his post-Stax underside, but
it was fighting trends. Given Ike's personal travails, there were those
who rooted for its success. One Brit critic, Pete Wingfield, wrote,
"An odd album—but I wish the man luck with it. After all the shit
that's been hitting the fan, I imagine he could do with the breaks."
However, a two-sided single of "Just the Way You Are" (the single
version of which, with an expanded "Shaft II," would be added to
later releases of the album), missed the charts. But when "Zeke the
Freak" would go out on the singles market next, it caught a break
that rose like a stiff wind from the past.

In late November, John Belushi and Dan Aykroyd's novelty
soul act, The Blues Brothers, which included Steve Cropper and
Duck Dunn (and in the 1980 *Blues Brothers* movie, Willie Hall),
debuted on *Saturday Night Live* with their version of "Soul Man,"
complete with Belushi's black-suited, sunglassed "Jake Blues"
bellowing "Play it, Steve!" This ignited a fad that sent their album
of otherwise arcane blues riffs by the likes of Big Joe Turner and
King Floyd (and an intro using Otis Redding's "I Can't Turn You

Loose") to top-ranked, double-Platinum status after the new year. The "Soul Man" cover hit number fourteen on the pop chart but far outselling the Sam & Dave classic, its appeal almost solely among the thirtyish white Baby-Boomer audience.

The raw power of "Soul Man" is that its subtle mysteries are always being discovered. Steve Jordan, who was the drummer on The Blues Brothers' cover and recorded live at the Universal Amphitheatre, says now that he missed the groove. "You can't imitate something that was already perfect and timeless. I was so proud of what we did. But knowing what I do now about the blues, I can't listen to it. I listen to the original and I almost have a nervous breakdown. 'Cause mine ain't workin'. My tempos were way too fast. I played too much. Al Jackson never did that. He got inside the song but it was laid back. He could cut a note down, to a half-note, a quarter-note, which regular people don't even hear but it's workin', man, it's workin' on your senses, no matter how many times you hear it."

Duck Dunn said virtually the same thing about Ike. The producer of the record, and all four Blues Brothers albums, was Bob Tischler, a *National Lampoon* writer who had done some music engineering and got the gig mainly because he was tight with Belushi. Because "Soul Man," which was also on the fourth best-of album, was recorded live, Tischler "had little to do. We just let it fly, on memory, with almost no rehearsal." Dunn laughed. "With Ike and Dave, *nothin'* went down without hours of rehearsal and last-second changes. Our Blues Brothers thing was good for what it was, we went for a feel not a piece of art—Belushi's 'Play it Steve' gave me chills down my back. But if it came out as a new record, it would have died on the spot."

Benefiting from the groove that never will die, the renewal of "Soul Man"—though, again, it came with zero financial gain for Ike—ticked up the sales of *For the Sake of Love*, which early in '79 reached number fifteen in soul and seventy-five in pop, with the "Zeke" single rolling to number fifteen in soul. That was a rewarding turn. Yet if '78 was a revival, '79 was a relapse. On July 21, 1979, the top six records on the US music charts were disco songs. By September 22—post-Disco Demolition Night, when thousands of people set disco records, and almost Chicago's Comiskey Park, afire on the field between games of an aborted doubleheader— there were no disco songs on the US Top 10 chart.

Ike had been circumspect about disco, not selling his soul to it but trying to fit it into his general soul grooves. This guided his next album, *Don't Let Go*, as a five-song, good-time jangle. The title tune, a semi-disco cover of the late Roy Hamilton's chirpy 1957 blues pop hit written by Jesse Stone and produced by the great Otis Black-well, set the mood; its "ooh-wee" and "aw shucks" diversions met by horn and string movements Ike had worked out with arranger Bill Purse. He also paid another homage to a pop classic, "Fever," basting it in the disco beat, his squealing vocal sounding alarm-ingly like Barry White. But the album boasted his new reliance on slower-than-slow moodiness. "What Does It Take" (not the 1969 Junior Walker Motown hit), featured a sharp funk guitar and crept into the Earth, Wind & Fire bag, his vocal begging, "Please don't go away." The dreamy "A Few More Kisses to Go," was his obliga-tory foreplay song attesting, "Girl's gonna be a full-grown woman before this night is through." The final cut was his self-pitying "Someone Who Will Take the Place of You," the phrase repeated by the backing singers as he rode on pity and revenge, warning a jilting lover, "Someone's gonna take the place of you" This was clearly his most carefree and least stressful work, and it broke into the top ten soul albums and top forty pop albums. The "Don't Let Go" single also crossed over, to number eleven in soul and number eighteen in pop; a later release of "A Few More Kisses" went to number eighty-nine in soul. His viability may have wavered a tad, but he still was a standard who never seemed to fall. Even a moon-lighting gig singing with Millie Jackson on her *Royal Rappin's* album, recorded at Muscle Shoals, energized a fairly listless effort, its arguable high point their soul cover of Foreigner's "Feels Like the First Time," appropriating the growling bass line of Peaches & Herb's disco "Shake Your Groove Thing."

That year, as well, the song that had arisen during the Dionne Warwick tour two years before, "Deja Vu," rose again when, produced by Barry Manilow, it went to number fifteen on the pop chart, twenty-five on the soul, and number one on the Adult Contemporary chart, which was mocked by some as the Narcolepsy Chart, its province being acts like the Carpenters and John Denver, though it also was conquered by Stevie Wonder's "You Are the Sunshine of My Life." The song helped Warwick to a Platinum Album and a Grammy. It also made for some welcome writer's royalties for Ike, who with it seemed to have survived the Stax meltdown quite well, thank you. But with the restless and amazingly convertible decade he had formatted almost to the last G-clef nearing its end, the times in which he would distinctly matter would become ever more scarce.

15

Transition

For Isaac Hayes, 1980 was a comforting sinecure, notwithstanding the sad fact that Isaac Hayes Sr. died at sixty-seven in March in Jackson. Ike Sr. had remarried and had another daughter and was a regular at the Mount Moriah Baptist Church. He had almost no contact with his famous son. When Ike Sr.'s funeral was held at the church, he was laid to rest at Highland Memorial Gardens cemetery, but Ike Jr. found no reason to attend. At the time, Ike Jr. was busy preparing his next album, which for him was a far more pressing priority.

The album, *And Once Again*, stayed true to the formula of *Don't Let Go*, melding disco fluff and lovelorn longing. Again arranged by Bill Purse, cut one of the LP's five tracks was another withdrawal from the sacred soul bin, "It's All in the Game," Tommy Edwards's mammoth 1958 big-band ballad that went to the top of both the pop and soul charts. Ike slow-rolled it, with an intro rap about love and then massaged the song with understated pop orchestration and a languid lounge-style vocal. The LP's long track, thirteen minutes, merged "Ike's Rap VII" with "This Time I'll Be Sweeter," a mid-tempo dance tune co-written by Gwen Guthrie and recorded often by female disco singers during the decade.

Ike took it down to a crawl, his rap almost identical to the don't-let-me-be-lonely lover on *Don't Let Go,* vowing, "I won't let you down. Have faith in me"—the urge to unburden these thoughts deriving from the growing cracks in his marriage to Mignon. What he wanted, he and the chorale sang over and over, for his woman's forgiveness. The same thoughts filled out "I Ain't Never,", "Love Has Been Good to Us," and one more self-imprecation, "Wherever You Are" ("Stop this pain in my heart").

That he still had it was confirmed when the LP was released, presenting him on the cover not as "mature" Ike but a revived Black Moses—an almost anatomically correct illustration by Mike McCarty had him in a loin cloth, wings sprouting behind him, brawny arms reaching for the sky, hands shooting fire against a raging hellscape. Despite his showy renunciation of the image, Ike may have wanted this to be the lingering impression of himself, after all, and its reclamation spirited its path to number twenty-six in soul and number fifty-nine in pop, despite a single of "A Few More Kisses"/"What Does It Take" stalling out at number eighty-nine in soul, though eventually it went Gold. This was a familiar retrenching for him, a dip in sales that had always been reflexively followed by another break back to the top echelon. But it was different this time. Because *And Once Again* was followed by never again.

REVIVED BLACK MOSES or not, he was getting tired. Tired of the grind. Tired of the money he considered stolen from him. Tired of pretending that writing a song rehabilitated him from the adultery and drinking that had by now taken a toll on yet another marriage. Tired of having to be original for his own satisfaction while copying better-selling soul men who had copied *him.* Tired of his frequent depression and self-doubt. And so he resolved to drop out with the arrival of the new decade and the passing of his third decade in the business. He made Atlanta his new playpen of time-wasting, drinking, drugging, and screwing around, surfacing in the studio or on the concert stage with lessening commitment to prime his ego and restock his bank account.

By '81, he was capable of making only one more album, the terminal-sounding *Lifetime Thing*, his very own "Let It Be" theme, the cover of him anything but the fire-breathing Moses; more like a postcard from the 1920s, it had him leaning against a tree in comfy pants and shirt, wooing a woman in a schoolmarm frock and bonnet, a serene gazebo behind them, and on the back cover, carrying her in his arms to the gazebo, a vanilla, county-fair scenario a soul man might not generally imagine, unless the gazebo was a love shack. And maybe that was the point. Serenity was now his state of mind—or desire. Co-arranged with Lester Snell, the work was again marketed as a disco paean, but that idiom had perished and most of the tracks were slow-jam, under-the-sheets collages.

He ripped through covers of The Temptations' and The Supremes' "I'm Gonna Make You Love Me," "Lionel Richie's "Three Times a Lady," and Curtis Mayfield's "I'm So Proud," and three originals, with the title track, "Summer," and "Fugitive" (co-written with Henry Bush). He put the usual care and detail into each. He and the overworked backing singers and string players moved effortlessly from fast to pitched—during the dirge-like "Three Times a Lady," he seemed to break into sobbing—and his cries on "Lifetime Thing" of "All I wanna do is just get next to you," and the yearning for the girl he knew, and lost, in "Summer," sounded extraordinarily sad.

Much like Hayes himself, the album would be enjoyed by his loyal brigades but largely drop from sight after failing to make the charts (it has been his sole album not to be re-released in digital) as he sunk deeper into personal and professional alienation. The charts instead were filled with similar soul-stirring, slow-jam provender like "Endless Love," "Being with You," and a cover of the late-'60s "Love on a Two Way Street" by fifteen-year-old teeny-bopper Stacy Lattisaw, and post-dated disco successors like Earth,

Wind & Fire's "Let's Groove," Rick James's "Give It to Me Baby," and the Gap Band's "Burn Rubber." Almost depressingly, the top *soul* album that year was Hall & Oates's boppy *Private Eyes*. This was an eclecticism that further disoriented Ike, who, like other soul buffs, saw MTV launch in August 1981 with the new wave song "Video Killed the Radio Star." The cable music channel presented almost no videos by Black artists, who seemed to be shunted into a netherworld and were, for now, the casualties.

Naturally, Ike was born for the video format, having all but invented the modern film soundtrack and been a visual lightning bolt in live performances such as in *Wattstax*. But in a new order of visualizing white album-oriented rock left him and other Black blues men in the cold. Even MTV's own head of talent Carolyn Baker, a Black woman, admitted that the network played Rick James's "Super Freak" video only because "there were half-naked women in it" and that "it was a piece of crap" she would have preferred "not represent my people as the first black video on MTV." Rather than stoop to this new industry racism, Ike hesitated to play an updated, rock 'n' roll Uncle Remus to fit in, and would rarely make a video suited to the video generation even after MTV reluctantly began playing those by Black rockers, albeit ones with huge white audiences like Michael and Janet Jackson.

When Ike came up for air during the decade, it was primarily for another kind of video, actual acting, on the big and small screen. He had already staked that ground years before. In 1976, he had popped up for the first of three appearances on *The Rockford Files* as Gandolph "Gandy" Fitch, an ex-prisoner buddy of James Garner seeking to clear his name, and also wrote and sang a phlegmatic song for the episode, "Gandy's Theme." Of course, his work was always on tap somewhere, "Soul Man" in particular, becoming common backing music on TV shows such as *WKRP in Cincinnati, The Fresh Prince of Bel-Air,* and *The Wonder Years*, and flicks like the Bruce Lee karate mash *Dynamo*, Paul Simon's *One-Trick Pony*, and Spike Lee's *Crooklyn*—even Ken Burns's *Baseball* documentary. Additionally, the highly successful *The Blues Brothers* movie had scenes that played over "Soothe Me" and "Hold On, I'm Comin'."

But as for recording, his only product in 1980 was the release of a single from *And Once Again*, "I Ain't Never" / "Love Has Been Good to Us," which rode to number forty-nine in soul. He then went on to produce the estimable jazz trumpeter Donald Byrd's 1981 Elektra/Asylum album *Love Byrd* at Mastersound, on which he also played keyboards with Byrd's 125th St. NYC Band and wrote two songs, "I Feel Like Loving You Today" and "Falling." Byrd, who had put out dozens of albums, had co-produced The Blackbyrds' "progressive" soft soul hit "Walking in Rhythm," but Ike helped usher him into sharper dance music on this and the '82 follow-up *Words, Sounds, Colors and Shapes*, for which Ike co-wrote six songs with Byrd and one on his own, "Star Trippin'." This was, in effect, Ike's counterpoint to the deafening, regimented core of the new dance sound such as in Janet Jackson's "rhythm nation" mien, and he was comfy under the jazz master's wing. One review of *Love Byrd* contended that his gruff but infectious vocal on the William Barrett-written "Love Has Come Around" sounded "more inspired than at just about any time since a certain film theme 10 years ago" and made the R&B hit "a joyous monster with a really loud, happy voice," the Byrd-Hayes collaboration "mighty and inspired."

He didn't completely shut himself down. Indeed, in '81 he was in the biggest movie he would ever act in, *Escape from New York*, John Carpenter's wildly bloody, off-the-wall sci-fi potboiler set in the terrifying future of 1997. Rather than a good/bad guy, he was all bad, as The Duke, the nattily clad, glaring crime boss of the savage streets of postmodern Manhattan, a maximum-security prison (not a totally outlandish proposition at a time when the city was awash in crime, though it was filmed in St. Louis). Duke's gang takes control of the president for ransom and is set against a motley rescue force led by Kurt Russell's former soldier and current eye-patched convict Snake Plissken. The plot weighs on their personal battle, with The Duke at one point beating the crap out of Snake. While he still stands, The Duke can revel being able to scowl at the president, "What did I teach you?" and hearing, "Y-You...You are the Duke of New York! You're A-Number One!" Which is what the movie was; with a $6 million budget, it made over $25 million and became the precursor for the metropolis-as-battle-zone genre.

Still, Ike sometimes seemed almost under wraps. At a Millie Jackson concert, when she spotted him in the audience and tried to pull him up to the stage for a duet, he refrained, a restraint rarely observed in his salad years. However, moderating his public profile did not include staying at home much, and did nothing to save his third marriage, which had gone off the rails for the usual reasons, his indifference and remarkably public cheating, as if the old law of dating six women at once still applied to him, as a carryover of his still propped-up glory.

HOWEVER, FOR A good five years he dropped out. The *Village Voice*'s Carol Cooper years later would note, "Hayes vanished in the early '80s, amid a swarm of prurient speculation about bankruptcy, drugs, Hollywood vice, and government plots. Aside from intermittent film cameos, we simply saw him no more." The withdrawal was something he never could fully explain. In truth, there were shadows lurking around him. His estranged father's death and the aging of Rushia Wade were discomfiting reminders of mortality as he hit forty, an age bracket in which some prominent soul men—Al Jackson, Jr., Dave Prater, Marvin Gaye, Joe Tex—died before their time. Another, the former Stax writer Raymond Jackson, Homer Banks's collaborator in the '60s and early '70s—whose brother Robert was periodically employed by Ike as his manager—died in a 1972 house fire in Memphis at thirty-one. Losses like these tormented him, sending him jetting off to places he thought could ease his mind, living incognito for a year in London, another back in LA in a Malibu cottage, staring at nothing but blue sea.

It appeared almost a redo of Otis Redding's dock of the bay introspection about loneliness and the angst of not being able to do what people told him to do. There were stories told of him getting into drunken or drugged-out psycho scenes in Hollywood, brawling for little reason, insulting record industry people who refused to sign him, mistreating women, being run in to the station house for a night at a time to dry out. As Duck Dunn recalled, "None of us knew where he was at any given time. Isaac and I had talked about getting the old gang at Stax back together for a reunion. Dave Porter was all in on it, and he and Ike writing again would have been a *major* thing. We could have gone out on tour as the *real* Blues Brothers, which is what we were, and rocked those old songs. But we needed him for that. Because he had all the charisma. But I think he'd gotten out of control."

Given his puzzling drop-out, Ike would be asked about whether drugs had made his life run amok. He denied it, with a resentful parry that being Black and high-living made it altogether easy for these assumptions. "An image is just that—an image," he said. "In the entertainment industry, you can't really tell what someone is like by looking at their image. You'd probably be wrong most of the time. Back in the '60s I learned about drugs. I saw what it did to other entertainers. I've worked with musicians who were addicted. We had them on methadone programs. I never wanted to fall into that trap."

A decade later, when he sat for an interview by hard rock musician Henry Rollins for a book by the latter, he went deeper, into a meandering social treatise about drug abuse as "a condition created by a racist society," which he said "started when our forefathers came off the ships as captives...and not allowed to be a man, whenever he stood up and spoke for his family, the Klan would take him outside, beat him and lynch him.... They couldn't get jobs. So what do you do? You turn to drugs as an escape. Entertainers who do drugs have a problem. They are not living up to their responsibilities [of being] bigger than life in the eyes of your fans."

He went on to complain that "a lot of drug programs were cut out by the government by certain administrations" to keep Blacks in a pit of drug dependency from childhood, and that "these kids had no recreational things in the evening to keep them occupied. And as the saying goes, 'An idle mind is the devil's workshop.'" There was more, lots more, much of it not entirely coherent, and as proof that he wasn't on drugs he needed no requests to display his Superman physique, which had only grown more muscular, his hours of daily workouts a form of feverish self-therapy for years. He would soon record a song with a distinctly anti-drug message. If all this was a case of protesting too much, though, no rumors could disturb the Isaac Hayes cachet, ironic indeed given that finding himself was beyond physical solution.

By NO SURPRISE, his marriage to Mignon Hartley was done in the early '80s. He and Mignon had hung on for several years for the sake of Heather and Isaac III, but in September 1982, too tired to keep hoping he would stop his tally-whacking on the outside, she compelled him to pack his bags and live elsewhere; the separation stretched on for four years, Ike continually prevailing on her, echoing his pleading songs, not to file divorce papers. But file she did, on the grounds that the marriage was "irretrievably broken," and after asking for custody of their two children, a division of their property, and permanent alimony and child support of $2,500-a-month for each child, the court approved these terms. That meant Ike would need to reenter the studio and movie sets to make the payments. In '86, he signed with Columbia Records—the very company that had helped to cut Stax to its knees, and which still owned the inventory of post-'68 Stax records, many by Ike himself, not that he could profit from them.

Columbia, now being run by the imperious Walter Yetnikoff, still had Bob Dylan, Simon & Garfunkel, and the kings of Platinum-

selling albums, Pink Floyd, and in two years would enjoy a monumental payoff when it was bought by Sony Music Entertainment,
the ultimate corporate takeover of rock in its elder years. As with
ABC and Polydor, Ike was not on the highest rung of attention but
routinely given the authority to record as he wished. On time and
under budget, he buckled in and brought in an album of six songs,
four recorded at Mastersound, two in a studio in Encino, California, with the mixing done in Columbia's studios in New York. Titled
U-Turn, as if a hard return to past glory, it surely seemed a top-line
project and Ike did press appearances for it, discussing his years
of withdrawal in generic terms, leading the *Los Angeles Times* to
sum up his return this way, "Coping with business and personal
problems—which he didn't explain in detail—have kept him busy.
'I couldn't really get into anything creative until those things were
cleared up,' he said. 'Last year I was finally at a point where I could
really concentrate on work again.'"

He retained an LA personal management firm called Hush
Productions and as his manager Larkin Arnold, who had handled
the careers of Nancy Wilson and Lou Rawls and was credited as
the album's executive producer. Not loath to benefit from other top
soul men, Ike now corralled bassist Bernard Jackson, who wrote
and sang on Stanley Clarke's albums, to co-write and co-produce
three songs with Jackson's collaborators David Conley and David
Townsend, "If You Want My Lovin', Do Me Right," "Flash Backs,"
and "You Turn Me On" (another allusion to the album's title), with
Jackson on backing vocals. Ike himself wrote the deep soul stirring "Doesn't Rain in London" and "Thing for You," and co-wrote
"Thank God for Love" with Pamela Phillips Oland. The remaining
songs were covers of The Four Seasons' "Can't Take My Eyes Off
You" and Freddie Jackson's "Hey Girl," written by Goffin-King,
which he would precede with his latest riveting rap, "Ike's Rap
VIII," allowing for the usual songwriting cribbing but also providing the opening for the anti-drug statement he believed he needed

211

to make—not as a confession but as another of his self-praising yarns, this one about trying to save another lost ghetto girl.

For this, he went rough, running a scalpel through quietly woven stanzas about a May-to-December romance with a girl that was cleaved by her greed and capitulation to the newest and dumbest addiction punishing society from the ghetto up to the pretty people in Hollywood and New York townhouses: freebasing coke by smoking its cooked crystals in a pipe lit by a rum-dipped torch. Ike was quite familiar with this soul sapping, ruinously expensive ticket to the grave or emergency room, and he sounded totally aware, judging by his use of the new street lingo for it, rapping that the girl had "become a resident of Crack City" and asking her, "Is the pipe all that?"

As it happened, the proto hip hop star Oran "Juice" Jones had preceded Ike's album with his song called "The Rain," a screed about being dumped by a gold-digger that became the first number one R&B hit on the new hip-hop oriented Def Jam label. However, while Jones's reaction was to threaten to blow her away like "Rambo" Ike's was to implore her with hopeless romanticism and yearning for salvation. "Ike's Rap VIII"/"Hey Girl" was released as its only single, and he did light a fire this time, the record hitting number nine on the R&B chart, his best showing there since "Joy."

Touring to support the album on his first road trip since a 1981 concert in Spain, he was profusely grateful for his "third comeback," as *Jet* put it, going well. "I didn't realize I was so respected and loved by people," he said. "There are a couple of generations that have become familiar with Isaac Hayes. Let them know I'm here and let the old fans know I'm back." The album's cover photo by Greg Gorman struck an avuncular tone, with a wryly grinning Ike clad in a Cosby-style knit sweater, more Black Mr. Rogers than Soul Man. The record made it to number thirty-two in soul, but in his elder perspective, it was good enough to hit the stage before fans curious about whether the Soul Man was still that. Wearing conservative suits, he was beseeched by audiences to sometimes strip off his jacket and silk shirt, his body not having aged the slightest—the same that could be said about "Theme from Shaft," which always lit up the still mainly white crowds.

This was a stepping stone back to acting gigs. As it was, interludes of "Soul Man" and "Shaft" had never stopped being played almost in rotation on TV and in movies. In 1986, a modest film called *Soul Man*, not about racial as much as teenage coming of age, included both, though like all the others, he was entitled to no royalties for them. The year before, he had entered the acting maw once again in a November episode of *The A-Team*, the fluorescence of Mr. T. a model of barbed Blackness in the '80s. But for Ike, it was another cultural vine to climb onto, playing a cool (what else?) escaped felon in an episode made for him and the other guest stars, Rick James and Huey Lewis and the News, who also performed songs. Ike's were "What Do You Do When the Wonder is Gone," "Don't Let Go," and a duet of James Taylor's blues parody "Steamroller" with Rick James, whose image as a human wrecking ball surpassed even Ike's, with worse repercussions.

One scene during the show also had an eerily perceptive take on the state of Ike's life, the dialogue between him and Mr. T going like this:

B.A. Baracus (Mr. T): *Rock 'n' roll might be here to stay, but not C.J.*

C.J. Mack (Ike): *I've been, B.A. I've been, and now I'm gone.*

B.A.: *That's crazy, man. You ain't no truck driver, or a surgeon. You don't retire or grow too old to do what you do. You can't. What you do is you. It's something inside you. And nothing can get rid of it. Unless you die."*

CULTURAL OVERTONES WERE all over his new life as an elder icon. When TV's first rock-and-roll-juiced show, *Miami Vice*, became the hottest series maybe ever, giving airtime to Boomer music icons, the Soul Man got his time on an October 1987 episode, going against the grain as a cowardly gun runner who gets his head pushed into a pinball machine by the Don Johnson pretty boy cop—definitely requiring some *real* acting by Ike. Some of his roles clearly had a touch of affectionate mockery, such as in the Blaxploitation tribute/parody *I'm Gonna Git You Sucka*, written, directed and starring Keenan Ivory Wayans. As a hit man in a cast with fellow Black movie elders Jim Brown and Bernie Casey, it earned $13 million on a $3 million budget and led to a failed TV pilot in which Ike and the others, save Wayans, reprised their roles. One other project was very low budget, the Mexican-made action movie *Counterforce*, casting him as a special unit military avenger.

His fame and the ongoing jobs it afforded would have seemed to fatten his pockets but good. Yet, in March 1989 he appeared in a new plot: failure to pay his divorce reparations to Mignon. As had Emily Ruth, Mignon had to go to court to get him to pay up, the tab being $346,300, including $22,000 for Heather's college costs and $5,000 in missed child support for Isaac III. When a hearing was held, Ike hastened to make the payments but the judge, Philip Etheridge, was aghast at Ike's sworn statement that he was so strapped he couldn't even afford the five grand, blistering that claim as "categorically ridiculous and almost beyond belief." He then sent Ike off to the Fulton County jail for two days, with Ike, reminiscent of Al Bell, telling the judge that jailing him was "harassment" and repeating the alibi, saying he didn't like to "struggle and scrape, and I don't like coming down here and pouring out my soul to this court."

If he was indeed only outwardly rich, it meant he had learned little about managing and protecting his big paychecks from movie and TV studios, notwithstanding the mountains of royalties he had lost through no real fault of his own. Doing two days in stir was the easy part. That the public knew he had stiffed his own children hurt him much more. To be sure, even with his latest cultural resurrection, he was still off-track. When the calendar passed into another decade, he was back in semi-limbo, living within a bristled state of mind that no film script could erase or ease.

16

Chocolate Salty Balls

Nearing fifty, Ike had the luxury of never really going out of style. He had hits and universal recognition. He was also at peace enough with himself to finally do what soul fans had been waiting for since the '70s, teaming up with his soulmate, Barry White. Despite each having been privately critical of the other for stealing their thunder, such a union had been pushed in the media for years. But Ike never felt the need to do it until he was shy on the dough.

Agreeing to be a side man for the soul man who had outdone him on the charts from the late '70s on as both declined, he sang on White's "Dark and Lovely (You Over There)" for A&M Records, trading off the verses of a snail-like love ballad about a "tantalizing, mesmerizing" woman, produced by White as a kind of who-can-sing-lower-and-slower competition, bereft of his '70s and '80s orchestral overproduction. Released with him ranked as "with Isaac Hayes" on the label, as a profit venture, the record was a good decade late. Memorable only as a curio, it did limited business, reaching number twenty-nine on the R&B chart as a single from White's middling *Put Me in Your Mix* album.

He then turned to a bucket-list phase—the first order of business to, as he said, learn about his roots, as a man and as an African American. Not by coincidence, there was a connection that he rarely spoke of: an infatuation with Scientology. As had a herd of showbiz types, he had begun to cater to indoctrination based on former hypnotist and swami L. Ron Hubbard's ditsy theories about the immortal spirits of a "Galactic Confederacy." The most impressive thing about the absurdities of these goofball teachings (which had it that evil gods sent billions of people to Earth 75 million years ago and then killing them with hydrogen bombs) and earthly "spiritual rebirth" that rejects psychiatry and family bonding, was that the recruits bought it, at a pretty price that for some included their life savings and families. Despite accusations that the "church" was a dangerous cult and money-making scheme, and the fact that it was later convicted of fraud by a French court, it flourished, not ebbing after Hubbard died in 1986.

For Ike, the transition to Scientology coincided with him being made an honorary king in Ghana. For years, Scientology members had gone on pilgrimages to the west African country as "Volunteer Ministers," spreading carefully crafted economic improvement ideals that were essentially Scientology propaganda. By chance, Ike happened to be in Ghana in 1991 making a video with Barry White for "Dark and Lovely (You Over There)." Filming scenes in a beatific church, he came across a reverend who was a Scientologist; he began selling Ike on the "technology" of its principles, a major doctrinal code word of the propaganda. "Brother," he told Ike, "this is a place full of wonders. Our people use this technology to take control of their lives."

When he got home, he looked further into the program, with a bit of skepticism, telling a church official, "Scientology, that's all that Dianetics, L. Ron Hubbard business. I hear you guys brainwash people, you all take folks' money."

But he took a course called "The Ups and Downs of Life," and as he said, "I was blown away." Another course, "Personal Values and Integrity," followed, and "at that point I knew I was about to become a Scientologist. When I learned how powerful this technology was, I knew I had to be a part of it. These were the tools that I had been looking for, to improve my life and other people's lives." That sent him back to Ghana in 1992 for what he said was a journey to find his roots. Dressed in traditional Ashanti tribal garb, he spoke before large gatherings, learned some of the Ashanti dialect, and met the woman who would become his fourth wife, a beautiful native model twenty years his junior named Adjowa. He helped set up the Scientology's so-called Learning and Technology Center of Excellence and Save a Million Lives HIV/AIDS Project—west Africa being where the disease originated and took a severe human toll—which opened a new line of recruitment for the Scientologists.

That was when he received his honorary crown, under the Ghanese name Nene Katey Ocansey I, and the title of Chief for Development in the Ada region. These honors were reported in America with few mentions of Scientology. However, a video made by the church titled "Isaac Hayes Brings L. Ron Hubbard's Study Technology to Ghana," which would be played around the world at Scientology gatherings, showed him telling a crowd that included twelve regional Ghana kings that in their war-torn country people need to "gain their freedom. No more oppression. I want my area, Ada, to move rightfully into the next millennium, to be equipped to take their rightful place in economic development. [For this] you have to have education. This learning technology was invented by humanitarian L. Ron Hubbard. And I tell you, it is second to none."

Propaganda tool or not, unlike many apparently sheepish Scientologists, he was an open pitchman, telling interviewers the church was "the best thing that's ever happened to this planet. Mankind just hasn't caught up with it yet.... You learn so much about yourself, about your mind, about your spirit and when you're ethical, and you do the right thing, your whole environment changes. Suddenly you're in the right place. I could sit here all day and talk to you about it." In Memphis, Ike led a Literacy Crusade that tried to have the "technology" applied to school studies, but the idea was shot down by the city as a church and state issue. He raged that the resistance was "hogwash" and a "travesty," saying, "I begged them, don't do this, because the kids are the ones that are gonna suffer. Don't listen to some canned, country, whitest network with a bad track record, bad ethics and all the rest."

He took a hit in the papers for that "crusade," but to be sure, being a "royal" gave him ascent and renewed swagger at a time he needed it. Ike, who liked being among the Hollywood crowd of true believers, was perhaps less into the details than he seemed. According to actor and study-mate Jason Beghe, who in 2008 would be the first celebrity Scientologist to denounce it and renounce his membership, "This guy was not a student. Not a reader. This guy was in Scientology a lot longer than I was. But he didn't have the first thing about it. You talk about taking advantage of someone. They had helped him, and all he had to do was promote Scientology."

And that he did, likely expecting that the money being sucked from his pocket by the "church" would buy him exposure, good will, and inner peace, or at least a reason to believe he had inner peace. But Scientology would figure heavily in his final fall from grace.

WITH OR WITHOUT a crown, he was enjoying the status of the elder Soul Man/King, and his legacy heard in the new wave of rap and hip hop, as well as the pop acts incorporating hip hop. Some notable examples were Compton's "Most Wanted," the Notorious B.I.G.'s "Warning," Tupac Shakur's "Me Against the World," MF DOOM's "Dead Bent," Wu-Tang Clan's "I Can't Go to Sleep," Hooverphonic's "2 Wicky," and Beyoncé's "6 Inch." Not that Ike was impressed with any of this. His own stalled recording was partly a protest against rappers and hip hoppers' own con game, almost never cutting the soul men in on royalties by listing them as co-writers. And he railed at the recording industry itself, which he held to blame for a Black creative drain.

Referring to the talent he saw rise one day and fall the next, he said, "The best of them doesn't [sic] come across, unfortunately, and I blame the record companies for that. I'm not knocking hip-hop, but there's not enough depth to it. If you think about it, on the charts now, whoever has a hit record, it lasts for a week. Then next week, it's somebody else there. And people can't remember two months ago. When we had hit records, they'd stay at number one for three or four weeks. It stayed in the minds of people because it had more depth, had more meaning. And like I said, I blame record companies, because they're trying to make quotas, how many did we sell this week? But the art itself is suffering. These kids don't even know who their predecessors were. They don't know whose shoulders they're standing on."

Feeling the industry headlock himself, he took the quickest paydays he could, playing gigs at the hip nightclubs from Hollywood's House of Blues to a high-rated show on Paris' premium TV channel Canal+, Nulle Part Ailleurs. He also performed in 1990 at a concert in Nashville arranged by the pernicious right-wing adviser and amateur guitarist Lee Atwater, featuring Ike, Sam & Dave, Carla Thomas, Billy Preston, B.B. King, Arietta Nightingale, and Chuck Jackson. It was recorded for a live album called *Red, Hot and Blue*, Ike playing and singing "I'm in the Mood" in a classic duet with Preston. He also bounced into his next movie, *It Could Happen to You*, not only as an undercover reporter in Andrew Bergman's romantic comedy about a lottery-winning cop starring Nicholas Cage, but also as the narrator of the film, which racked up $37 million at the box office.

It would take Ike until 1995 to get into the studio on his own again. With his Columbia deal expired, he made his usual quick accommodation with another huge label, Virgin Records, which had recently been purchased by the British tech giant EMI for $1 billion but maintained its imprint. He was put on Virgin's Point Blank sub-label, created in 1988 as a sanctuary for long-in-the-tooth blues men like John Lee Hooker, Albert Collins, Pops Staples, John Hammond, and aging white blues-rockers Van Morrison and Johnny Winter. The Atlanta phase over, he would record back in

Memphis, in a MacArthur-like return to the land he'd fled, at a new studio called Kiva Sound on Rayner Street, with an album pointedly soldering old standard soul with the newer twists and turns.

His crew was stripped down, still featuring Skip Pitts, Mike Toles, and Lester Snell but with new faces like drummer James Burke and bassist Jimmy Kinard, but conceding that the new age of techno-pop was here to stay and with great reluctance dabbled with computerized synthesizers for horn effects. But his message was an old one for fellow soul men, which explained the title of the album, *Branded,* reflecting his objection to the industry too often relegating him into compartments of their choosing, not his, such as the tiresome wail of disco; that is, until now, when he could call the shots. And during its development came a long-overdue historical event: his reunion with Dave Porter.

That was hatched when he dropped into Porter's Memphis office with Andrew Love, who, Ike recalled, "suggested Dave and I do something. The next day we had lunch at B.B. King's club, and I think we were both a bit nervous about the prospect because we didn't really get into it until we were walking to our cars afterwards. But once we started talking it was like the gates had opened, we stood there by our cars trading ideas and we knew we could do it again." The ghost of Johnny Baylor long gone, they meshed easily again and wrote "Thanks to the Fool," the agonist a guy who wins over the girl, Ike purring like Lionel Richie in a slow-grinding intro rap that the "fool" of the song "didn't know I needed all the things that you are," then mounting to a full-orchestral assault and emotional vocal surges backed by a chorale, the title as the repeating hook. The work was mesmerizing and it required a tangle of publishing interests being served domestically, including Ike's newest one for the album, Lili Ann Music, Porter's Robosac Music, LA publishers Red Stripe Music, and Nashville's How Ya Doin Publishers, and worldwide by the Don Williams Music Group.

The axiom about patience certainly applied to the re-pairing of the legendary soul men, but beyond this undeniable lure, Ike also had Marvin Gaye in mind. Two decades before, Marvin had revolutionized soul's subject matter with his songs bewailing the trashing of the ecology. Ike would do the same, by covering Sting's post-Police solo song decrying ecological destruction, "Fragile." Putting a lot of thought into it, Ike opened the album with a near-whispered rap called "Ike's Plea," warning that "we forget how fragile we are." Then, on "Fragile," his liquid vocal was swathed by sweeping strings and a bongo and Bossa-Nova sub-current that lent an almost calypso beat; the last two minutes were a cacophony as Ike and the Watoto Children's Choir repeated the phrase "How fragile we are."

He also covered a mid-'60s hit, John Sebastian's "Summer in the City," where the back of a horny man's neck turned dirty and gritty. Ike made it into dirty soul, roiled with a beat harder and more desperate than the original. But "Fragile" and "Summer in the City" were the only songs not written wholly or in part by Ike, who applied the usual flare of funk and conditional disco. The instrumental "Life's Mood" and "Life's Mood II" were mellow guitar blues in the West Montgomery mode. "Let Me Love You" was another slow-motion mating call, going as low on the scale as he could for a bass vocal with which he could coo, "Let me taste, let me savor what I've been so hungry for." The "Branded" track was a funky dance rime making a word once associated with slavery into the funk hook "I'm branded." More pointed was his redo of "Hyperbolicsyllabicsesquedalymistic" with Public Enemy's Chuck D, a huge admirer of his, who added dense raps between verses and repeated "hyperbolic trip" throughout the song.

It was indeed a trip—into postmodern rap's less mannered and darker nature, something he had avoided even as a "renegade," notwithstanding the Shaft image that had limited his mainstream media face time. After all, the sex-obsessed soul man had never limited his willingness to play "white" events such as a bicentennial concert with Pat Boone, Chet Atkins, Carl Perkins, and John Ritter. Now, he was embracing Chuck D, who had incited rage at "the powers that be" and whose bloodthirsty "By the Time I Get to Arizona," a rage-fest against the state for its resistance to adopt Martin Luther King, Jr. Day (its video was a revenge carnage of Black men assassinating white politicians), was not only was condemned by King's widow but banned by MTV's hip-hop franchise *Yo! MTV Raps* as too violent.

Of course, Ike himself had problems with heavy rap's sexism and violence-baiting—as opposed to dirty-mouth profusions, which flowed at his concerts—and the "Hyper..." cover would be his first and last rendezvous on record with the rap generation. More to form, "I'll Do Anything (To Turn You On)," was a friendly slap-bass boogie with a mid-song rap. And if anything, a redo of the visceral "Soulsville," featuring a new tenor sax earful by Andrew Love, was purposely old-world in the Stax-style, even with the searing lyrics that Chuck D could have eaten up if Ike had put him on that one instead. More than ever before, and by choice on this work, Ike was caught between clashing genres and textures but only visited the camp of hard rap without staying over. As he continued to pull shelved demos from the primordial days—ones that the industry vipers hadn't stolen and which not incidentally could earn him royalties—and redoing more of them than he could get on one album, it opened the way for a second LP of mainly instrumental throwbacks, co-produced by former Stax orchestra conductor Benny Mabone. The "co-album" was called *Raw & Refined*—to be sure the competing yardsticks of his music and his life.

Even more Stax-like, it included an early session for the *Shaft* theme song, which he haughtily titled "Birth of Shaft." Others were "Memphis Trax" (re-titled from "Memphis Sounds"), "Urban Nights" (née "Urban Instrumental"), though the best track of the lot was "The 405," so named for a Texas highway, which in its final form was a cool rush and a great road song. The album was filled out with similarly renamed tunes, "Soul Fiddle," "Funky Junky," and "Southern Breeze," and as a disco-funk homage, the retro, organ-based "Funkalicious." Only one song had a vocal, "You Make Me Live," and his backing singers Brenda Jones Williams and Myra Walker voiced "Making Love at the Ocean." Even with these quick remodels, his taste for experimentation was clear, most especially on "Soul Fiddle," mixing in rockabilly violins as if to prove that in the age of sapless techno-disco, the oldest and simplest music was more resonant to the soul. Those were hunches he always seemed to win.

THE CONJUNCTION OF Ike's newest "comeback" albums was necessary when Virgin released them on the same day, May 30, 1995. This made for some confusion that was not alleviated by *Branded* being released (with an inner sleeve of photos and liner notes in the same cross-cut fold-out as on *Black Moses*) under the name of Isaac Hayes, *Raw & Refined* by the Isaac Hayes Movement. When the first single was released on CD by Point Blank, it was also schizoid, with single and album versions of "Thanks to the Fool" along with "Funky Junky." A promotional EP called *Funky Junky*, which also had nearly identical covers created by Thierry le Goues, was a blend of both albums, the famous bald head and shades seen from the right on *Branded* and the left on *Raw*; each set against a black sky that turned his head into a full moon.

Branded was well reviewed, while *Raw & Refined* was a vanity some would detest. The *Village Voice*'s Carol Cooper proclaimed it "the better of the two albums, largely because on instrumentals Hayes is freed from the natural limitations of gender and personality as the music talks about the things that really matter to him." Cooper posited that "There's always been something a little witchy about Isaac's backing tracks, something about how they grab and manipulate your attention, like a Catholic spiritual exercise. [It's] a synesthesia of sensation far more visceral than the body-quakes of rap or the mental aerobics of jazz. When Ike wants to elicit a particular emotion from a listener he can be as accurate as acupuncture. And that is why he's worth listening to today." On the other hand, Allmusic.com dismissed it as "one directionless vamp after another [like] a soundtrack in search of a movie." Robert Christgau, who gave *Branded* four out of five stars in his *Record Review* anthology, branded *R&R* as merely "tossoffs, too slight to really grab your attention."

For that purpose, Ike now made his first videos other than those of him on a stage, choosing "Thanks to the Fool" and "Fragile." Both were directed by Erick Ifergan, "Thanks" a parable of a young boxer in the grip of pimp-like handlers, with Ike in a long black *robe de chambre*, lounging on a red velvet brothel bed, lip-syncing the song. The "Fragile" video was also mock-arty, with Ike in a black caped turtle-neck cowl looking like a Pope Shaft, optically floating through city streets and ending encircled by The Watoto Children's Choir. The problem was that there was no soul music channel to play on—not even *Yo! MTV Raps*, which went off the air that very year. Ike did his part touring to support the albums. In July, he co-headlined the Beat Goes On benefit concert at New York's Beacon Theater to spread the word of safe sex in the AIDS era, opening with "Thanks to the Fool," which was progressively heard on the Black stations, as were "Hyper...," "Funky Junky," and "Funkalicious" on the dance floors. But *Branded* only reached number seventy-five on the soul album chart and *Raw & Refined* was shut out. The singles mainly gathered dust on the shelves.

It seemed to be one more noble attempt at self-preservation, with mixed results. Ike's foreseeable future again was undetectable, back on a treadmill, his next move unknown to him. He went through another personal low when Rushia Wade, in whose home Ike's Oscar was kept and polished daily after he had bought it back after its seizure by his creditors, died in 1997, taking from him the only real parental figure he ever had and causing more angst about life. But those uncertainties quickly fell into line when fate seemed to pay him back. Not in anything related to music but in the giggling guise of a cheaply made animated odyssey of brash adolescents and dim grownups in a fictional, always too-cold, always too-white Colorado town.

SOUTH PARK WAS not the first outlandish cartoon series Ike dipped into. In fact, passively, he became a considerable marker of *The Simpsons*'s growth spurt when Lisa (Yeardley Smith) sang the "Theme from Shaft" with perfect '70s lingo and inflections, in a 1991 episode—proving yet again Ike was very much part of a world rooted in nostalgic tribute and parody. He then agreed in 1996 to write and perform a song for the movie version of MTV's *Beavis and Butt-Head* series that made infantile idiocy cool by the two animated nitwits mocking clips of normally terrible rock 'n' roll videos. *Beavis and Butt-Head Do America* cost $13 million and made $68 million, with Ike's song "Two Cool Guys"—a *Shaft* gag about "a couple of guys with fire in their eyes [who] will blow your ass off...know what I'm sayin'?"—ran with the opening credits, spoofing a '70s cop show with cartoon boobs aplenty.

A year later, Trey Parker and Matt Stone, the young and bent producers of Viacom's fledgling Comedy Channel series (produced under the aegis of its subsidiary MTV Networks), were working on the debut episode of that prosaic and pin-headed Colorado town. They needed a voice for school cafeteria chef Jerome "Chef" McElroy, a former soul singer who served food and old soul lyrics at South Park Elementary School, counseling the prepubescents and banging about all of their mothers (and in the past, Kathie Lee Gifford) while never taking off his chef's hat. Parker and Stone, who voiced the adolescent pinheads with sped-up tapes, were going to have either of them do Chef, but a white guy imitating a Black guy was problematic even for them. They thought of Barry White, Lou Rawls, and Ike, putting out a call for the Soul Man, who at the time was hosting a morning music and talk show called "Isaac Hayes and Friends" on "classic soul" station WRKS in New York, known as "Kiss FM," his voice rumbling through the canyons of Manhattan. He had also written his soul food cookbook that eschewed red meat for a vegan regimen based on that of "Organic Soul" chef Elijah Joy.

When asked how they landed him, Parker mused, "We'd like to know that, too." Indeed, when the call came for Ike to consider the gig, he said, "My agent didn't quite tell me what it was about, he was a bit nebulous. So I said, 'What is it about then?' He said, 'Well, it's kinda on the edge. Why don't you come up to the studio and meet with the creators.'" Parker and Stone had flown into New York to do some early work on the series. As Parker related, "We were at Sony Studios and Ike walked in and [said]"—breaking into a deliberate, guttural Ike imitation—"'Hey guys, how ya doin'? What're we doin' here?' [I said] 'You mean you don't know?' He said, 'No.' I said, 'Oh shit.' I grabbed Matt and took him outside and said, 'Man, he's gonna kick our asses!'" Added Stone, "Because [we had to tell him] 'You're big and fat and you're the only black guy in this whole town and you're a total stereotype and you're a chef and you sing love songs all the time.'"

For Ike, who thought the offer was for a Disney movie, got something entirely different and dangerous. "When I read the script it was really funny," he recalled, adding, "I hope you guys got insurance because you're going to get sued." His son Isaac III, who was spending more time with him, remembers that "He was very reluctant to do it in the beginning because I don't think he understood it....He was a very respectful guy and really didn't curse [off-screen]and never really put his brand in jeopardy like this. But at that time he had younger people around him like his assistant, who really, really, really encouraged him to do it."

And so he came aboard, not sure he should. The biggest hurdle for Parker and Stone was Chef's first song, which they recorded that same day, called "I Wanna Make Love to You Woman." Said Parker, "Trey wrote it but he ran to the bathroom when it came time for Isaac to sing so I was sitting there with Isaac Hayes when he began singing. And he was singing it wrong. So here I was, in a sound studio in New York City teaching Isaac Hayes how to sing— 'No, Mr. Hayes, it's actually like this. With feeling! With feeling!'"

Those petrifying circumstances aside, Ike got it, and the show premiered on August 13, 1997 with the episode "Cartman Gets an Anal Probe," a good indicator of the intellectualism one could expect from *South Park*. Under-budgeted as it was, the characters were cardboard cutouts that were moved about by hand, vivifying them through stop-action photography and creating a "floating" look – with feet unused, none were drawn in, even when computer animation took over the process. For Ike, it was the easiest bread he ever made. Much of his dialogue being little else than "Hello, children" and moral lessons cloaked in understated punch lines: "Don't do drugs, kids. There is a time and place for everything. It's called college" and habit of calling white people, even the kids, "crackers." As he said, "The more I did it, the more fun I had. But at the beginning of *South Park* I thought that I'd ruined my career."

Instead, Chef's enigmatic life, his clipped aphorisms, bug eyes, and adorableness were a staple of the newest vehicle for the aging Baby-Boomer set, which both guffawed at the bad taste and socially unacceptable speech (in one episode, the word "shit" was spoken over a hundred times) not seen before on TV—not for nothing was Isaac Hayes hired to intone station ID material for Nickelodeon's Nick at Night nostalgic programming. Chef, then, was a key cultural note. In season two's episode "Chef Aid," he was the entire show. His old song "Stinky Britches," ripped off by Alanis Morissette, leads Chef to sue her record company, which hires Johnnie Cochran. Chef loses and is ordered to pay court costs. He then happily turns tricks around town, but the money is stolen and he's sent to jail. The "children" then stage a "Live Aid"-style benefit concert including the stars whose careers Chef had helped: Elton John, Ozzy Osbourne, Meat Loaf, Primus, Rick James, and DMX, all of whom lent their voices to the episode. In the end Chef prevails. His name is put on the record label, though his future was still in the kitchen. In adult cartoon land, nothing ever changes, including people's ages and their lot in life.

For Ike, the issues and pitfalls for Chef rang true to his own scattered life, and Parker and Stone would find out more about him that could be lampooned right along with broader third-rail subjects like religion, homosexuality, death, drugs, politics, terrorism, Ritalin, politicians, foreign dictators, and self-indulgent celebrities (one of whom, Michael Moore, was blown to cartoon bits). In one episode, Chef was revealed as a Muslim named "Abdul." But Parker and Stone were on safe ground since the message sometimes seemed right-wing, sometimes left-wing, sometimes wingless, and almost always brainless. A character was established who was a pile of poop. There were raves, protests, and high ratings. And along with his deadpan lines, Chef's spontaneous songs, written by Parker and Stone, were relevant not as novelties but as Ike's latest recorded songs, no small thing, as the producers well knew. The most renowned, "Chocolate Salty Balls (P.S. I Love You)," was also unveiled in season two, in an episode of the same name, with Chef singing with not a trace of irony, that if you need a quick pick-up, his delicacy was the answer: "They're big and salty and brown...Just stick my balls in your mouth." Parker and Stone originally wanted a song on every show but realized that would ruin a good thing. As it was, the music from the show footed an album in 1998 produced by Rick Rubin, *Chef Aid: The South Park Album* on the Columbia label, with twenty-two tracks including those sung by Elton John, Devo, Primus, Lil' Kim, and Master P. Ike sang three, one being "Chocolate Salty Balls." All would be issued on extended CD singles, which, like the album, sold like crazy in England and Australia but, oddly, not in America. A year later, the movie *South Park: Bigger, Longer and Uncut* rolled out, produced by the cable network's owners Paramount and Warner Brothers, the soundtrack poking fun at conventional musical forms, with Ike as Chef, singing "Good Love 6-9969" and leading the cast on "Mountain Town."

The film and soundtrack made astronomical profits; the picture, its extreme protest of censorship getting it an R-rating, was the first cartoon to wear that scarlet letter, not keeping it from making $83 million. As a shareholder in this unlikely bonanza, Ike had fallen into a professional hammock. As Isaac III put it, "It really gave him a huge second act as an artist, and he was very thankful and proud of that. That was huge for him. It gave him an opportunity to feel a little love and admiration that I think he might not have gotten throughout those years while he figured out the changes in music."

Needing no such further exhausting album projects, *Branded* and *Raw & Refined* would be the last serious work he needed to stress over. Moreover, as *South Park* took off, his classic Stax material would be released with increasing frequency in best-of anthologies and remastered albums, with four albums released by Fantasy on the Stax imprint, and another, *Isaac Hayes: The Best of the Polydor Years*, on the latter label. A 2002 documentary of the Stax rise and fall, *Only the Strong Survive*, co-directed by D.A. Pennebaker, showcased him and other survivors—one amusing moment cutting through the years, when the still-buff Ike called out to Sam Moore, "Break a leg!" and Sam, who'd just had a triple bypass, shouted back, "I'm trying!"

Ike was also back on the big screen in 1999, playing a gristly taxi dispatcher, anything but his classic image, in *Ninth Street*, the under-looked first movie written and produced by Kevin Wilmott, who later won an Oscar with Spike Lee for co-writing *BlacKkKlansman*. The small, superb "Black" movie, filmed in black and white, was a glimpse of life in Junction City, Kansas during the late '60s on the street where great jazz musicians once played but was now lined by strip clubs and bars frequented by Vietnam war-era soldiers. A year later, he vaulted onto the big-budget rung in a far inferior movie, taking a small part in director John Frankenheimer's last movie, the crime drama *Reindeer Games* starring Ben Affleck, which was so lame that it cost $42 million to make and earned $10 million less for the Disney-owned Miramax Films studio, whose executives probably did what Ike notably did in the movie as prison inmate Zook and puked up a bowl of Jell-O.

That same year, too, when the long-dormant *Shaft* franchise was dusted off with John Singleton's sort-of remake starring Samuel L. Jackson as John Shaft's similarly named nephew (Uncle John was played by Richard Roundtree), Ike performed and produced yet one more revival of the always apropos theme song, to which he now had finally been granted contemporary rights, with his new publishing company, ILH Music, collecting fresh proceeds from the soundtrack, but still not a dime from its halcyon. This *Shaft* had a $46 million budget and the soundtrack featured current soul stars like R. Kelley and Wycliffe Johnson; with its more bloody content and rawer sex scenes, the movie earned $70 million ($107 million worldwide), yet no sane critic placed it anywhere near the original, the cachet of which was still in that magical title song, which for all the postmodern electronic hawing Ike had to put into it didn't need any updating at all. *Shaft* was already fully formed, and it was forever his and his alone.

17

Midnight Train to Memphis

Not needing any reformation himself, in March 2002, when he turned sixty, Black Moses was bronzed when the sometimes myopic Politburo of the Rock & Roll Hall of Fame duly elected him to a class that also included Tom Petty and the Heartbreakers, the Ramones, the Talking Heads, Gene Pitney, Brenda Lee, Chet Atkins, and Jim Stewart. At the crowded ceremony held at New York's Waldorf Astoria, the show opened with a rousing rendition of "Theme from Shaft," Ike, in a floor-length black-and-white-trimmed robe and skull cap, conducted a full orchestra that included Skip Pitts doing his *wah-wah* thing, all involved having the time of their lives. Inducted by Alicia Keyes, who coyly asked, "You know what they call him, right? Black Moses," as Ike grinned offstage. She went on, "'Soul Man' wasn't a boast—it was a declaration of independence" for all Black artists. He then sauntered up to the stage and began his speech.

"I wanna thank my boss, Jim Stewart and Miss Estelle Axton, and the great disciple of our music, Mister Sam Moore," all of whom were there. Spreading his arms, Ike-style, he wailed, "Hello, Memphis!" He then turned serious, saying, "I wanna mention this, important," making some wonder if he was about to slather on a Scientology rap. Instead, he quietly continued, "To all the guys that are sitting on my royalties, I'm just asking you to practice some business ethics and a little humanity. Do the right thing by me and my contemporaries," to a burst of applause, though perhaps not from some of those same "guys" at the expensive tables. He also had a word up to the "rap and hip hop community"—"It's not all about the bling bling and all the gold and the Cristal. [Let] the music create an art flow. That's what it's all about. Know the business, learn the business. Own something. Don't slip into the traps, and don't forget about your 'hood, the kids in the 'hood." He finished with an emotional thanks to "my fans. Without your support through the years, it could've been rough. I might not have made it. I love all of you."

It was perhaps the best, most simple yet powerfully defined speech the Hall had or has ever heard, drawing upon the same sincerity he put into his music. Despite the incongruity of Isaac Hayes decrying bling and especially *gold*, he stood as a simple soul man, with no chains or golden vests, his face a bit lined but about as untouched by nature as was possible at sixty, and surely wizened by the sweet and sour of too much good and bad. The closing number that night was "When Something Is Wrong with My Baby," Ike at a piano stage front, Sam Moore at the mic and Steve Cropper among the band backing him. The place rocked again, and the ending sight was Ike and Sam walking off the stage arm in arm. It was the kind of breathless tribute he had earned, and a sign that time really did stand still for him.

Invited to play across the pond at the weekend Glastonbury Festival in June, he came on in leather pants and a denim jacket and roused 140,000 young British rock fans with an extended take of "Theme from Shaft," laying waste to other mainline acts like Coldplay, Manu Chao, Kosheen, and the old homeboys Rod Stewart and Roger Waters. His wallet again fat, Ike had ended his New York radio show and made the decision to end his alienated wanderlust and make Memphis the place where he would stay, until his final breath. A few weeks later, in May, he had dropped $1.1 million on a five-bedroom, six-bath, 7,205-square-foot house at 9280 Riveredge

Drive, on three woody acres in the Cordova section called The Bluffs, bringing to mind another Chuck Berry line in "Memphis, Tennessee" about a home high up on a ridge, half a mile from the Mississippi Bridge. He could afford this aerie with a big backyard swimming pool because a new and eager lender, Regions Bank, became his newest spigot for loans, mortgaging him the property for the full $1.1 million, a real ripoff given that today it is valued at only $737,000.

But he was home and working hard. In his basement studio he taped his Chef dialogue, with Parker and Stone on a long-distance computer phone line giving him his cues. He immersed himself finding ways to rebirth Black commerce in Memphis, opening a restaurant and nightclub in a Peabody Place office building downtown. Living in the mansion with Adjowa, they married in May 2005 and the following April she gave birth to Ike's fourth son by marriage, and eleventh overall, Nana Kwadjo Hayes. At the same time, he had gotten closer to the children he had mostly ignored all his adult life, pulling some strings for Isaac Hayes III, a now beefy man whom Ike had taken to the Hall of Fame shindig and called out from the stage as "big boy." Ike III was now going by the pseudonym Ike Dirty and had become a commercial voice actor in Atlanta and a hip-hop producer, his production company called IKE Father IKE Son Music. Ike's daughter Heather was fronting the Heather Hayes Experience in Atlanta, playing at weddings and company parties, and his older son Darius had also attempted a singing career.

All of which made for a feel-good ending. By the mid-'90s, in fact, it seemed the two main survivors, or victims, of the Stax collapse had made it all the way back. Al Bell, who had owned two other short-lived labels was hired by Berry Gordy to be president of Motown during its own corporate reshuffling. He then opened another label, Bellmark, striking lightning in 1993 with the hip-hop twosome Tag Team (the guys on the later insurance commercial scooping ice cream), who sold two million copies of the hip-hop novelty "Whoomp! (There It Is)"—the sort of thing Bell and the

Stax crowd used to crow about when a record went to number one—and Prince's "The Most Beautiful Girl in the World," the latter's last Top 10 hit. By 1997, however, Bell declared bankruptcy and had to fight in court again, when the company he sold Bellmark to in 2002 decreed it alone owned the rights to "Whoomp!" Bell, a very gifted courtroom performer, won his case and was awarded over $2.2 million in damages.

One of the most honored record executives in the world again, he reunited with Ike in their dual belief that they both had unfinished business in Memphis and guilt that they could not stem Stax's rollover. Issac Hayes and David Porter committed to reviving the grandeur and presence of Stax and with Bell—all three of whom were named to the Memphis Music Hall of Fame—helped establish the Stax Museum of American Soul Music, rebuilding the old theater as the museum's home and now-permanent landmark. The result was the faithful reproduction of the theater, right down to the "Soulsville USA" marquee and lettered "STAX" signage on top—the theater that would be the cover image of the 2017 *The Spirit of Memphis (1962-1976)*, the massive Ike-onography CD set. The original 850-pound "STAX" sign was visible, too, inside the museum and preserved as an exhibition piece with hundreds of photos, instruments, and other items, a human one being Jim Stewart to schmooze with tourists. The biggest drawing card in this everlasting soul milestone, however, was Ike's storied gold-engulfed El Dorado, which had gone down its own long road before being located.

Its mega-famous former owner, who had also been lost and then found, donated more memorabilia, including the Oscar he reclaimed when Rushia died and much of the old bling, and performed at fundraisers for new Memphis blues clubs and studios. What could not be redressed was the sad part of the Stax epitaph, that despite his emotional plea at the Hall of Fame, his royalties from his prime never did come home. Nearly all the music that had sprouted from the company still belonged to others, and the owner of the post-'68 song catalog, Fantasy Records, benefited from it, in 2004 selling its Stax holdings to Concord Records. As much as his fame was set in stone, Ike never learned to live with that hole in his life. It wasn't just the bread; it was that his life's best work was stolen from him. And deep in his gut, deeper in his soul, he felt violated.

STILL, HE WAS as good as gold, and well paid. There was a nice spike in royalties when the long-belated complete *Wattstax* album sets were released in the early millennium. In 2005, a movie was made of his mesmerizing July concert at Auditorium Stravinski in Montreux, which was released that year in England and later in 2007 in America. But 2005 was also when his world began to turn. On November 16, 2005, *South Park* aimed at his infatuation with Scientology in the episode "Trapped in the Closet," the title satirizing the song by R. Kelly, who is also mocked along with Scientology true believers John Travolta and Tom Cruise. The plot had it that Stan was induced to join the cult and would be hailed as the second coming of Hubbard, but turns on the flock, renouncing Scientology as "just a big fat global scam," daring the notoriously litigious church to sue him. The shots Parker and Stone took at them were dead-on and hilarious, such as when a cultist went over the crazy sci-fi tenets, a crawl on the bottom of the screen read "This is what Scientologists actually believe," and the clear premise of "Cruise" and "Travolta" hiding in a closet gave rise to a societal punch line about somebody having to "come out of the closet."

It was arguably the best and most important episode of the show—more so since Viacom was producing the costly impending blockbuster *Mission Impossible III* and Cruise, its star, was raising hell for being derided by a cartoon. Chef wasn't in the episode but Parker and Stone, who were nominated for an Emmy for the episode, had made sure to explain to Ike what they were doing. Parker said, "Isaac was the nicest guy, and we had a really great working relationship. And when we came up with the Scientology episode we just had to tell Isaac, 'Dude, we totally love working with you, and this is nothing personal, it's just we're *South Park*, and if we don't do this, we're belittling everything else we've ripped on.'"

Stone told it like this: "It was like a day or two after it had already gone on the air—and we didn't tell him about it before that because we didn't want him to be held accountable, we wanted plausible deniability about directly involving Isaac. But it was pretty obvious from the conversation that somebody had sent him to ask us to pull the episode [for future showings]."

If so, Ike stopped short. He told them, "Guys, you have it all wrong. We're not like that. I know that's your thing, but get your information correct, because somebody might believe that shit, you know?" Still, he let it fly, telling the press, "I understand what they're doing. I told them to take a couple of Scientology courses and understand what we do." However, the church didn't leave it at that, and the dynamic would worsen after Ike coincidentally had health problems. On January 17, 2006, his unbreakable body finally broke. Exhausted, he suffered a stroke that left him hospitalized and weak. He had trouble speaking at times and Parker and Stone put Chef on hold. Not as sharp or decisive as usual, his memory problematic, he may not have had the will to keep the church off his back. On March 13, he suddenly released a statement that he was quitting the show, ending his role after being in 136 episodes. It read, "There is a place in this world for satire, but there is a time when satire ends and intolerance and bigotry towards religious beliefs of others begins. Religious beliefs are sacred to people, and at all times should be respected and honored. As a civil rights activist of the past 40 years, I cannot support a show that disrespects those beliefs and practices."

Given the 180-degree turn, it was at once assumed he had been manipulated by the Scientology claque. "We sort of figured out the whole picture a bit later, but that's totally what happened," Stone said during a 2016 panel discussion with Parker and Isaac III. "It really sucked, the whole thing. This statement put out that he was quitting, it kind of called us bigots." Parker's view was that "we knew in our hearts there was something way more rotten going on." He and Stone had to come down on Ike to defend themselves, with Stone telling the media, "This is 100 percent having to do with his faith of Scientology. He has no problem—and he's cashed plenty of checks—with our show making fun of Christians. He wants a different standard for religions other than his own, and to me, that is where intolerance and bigotry begin. To bring the civil rights struggle into this is just a non sequitur. Of course we will release Isaac from his contract and we wish him well."

The media labored to run with the story as a scandal. A reporter for Fox News online, Roger Friedman, wrote, "I can tell you that Hayes is in no position to have quit anything. [It's] absolutely ridiculous to think that Hayes, who loved playing Chef on 'South Park,' would suddenly turn against the show because they were poking fun at Scientology.... It's hard to know anything since Hayes is constantly monitored by a Scientologist representative most of the time." It was further revealed that Ike's statement was not actually put out by him. But who? The church denied it was they as rumors ran that Viacom's movie distributor, Paramount, or Cruise himself, would sue the network for defamation, and, if not, Cruise would refuse to promote the movie—rumors that seemed to explain why the episode, scheduled to be rebroadcast in March, was pulled and replaced by "Chocolate Salty Balls."

Parker and Stone all but confirmed they had buckled, identifying themselves in jest as "servants of the dark lord Xenu"—not meaning Ike but a mythic Scientology figure. They bid an official farewell to Ike in a bizarre but truly sad episode in the season ten premiere "The Return of Chef," using old sound clips of Chef in a maelstrom of tears, violent images, and amended abuse on Scientology. Chef, having returned from a very thinly veiled Scientology retreat, is in peril and the boys try to save him, but he's mauled to death by a lion and a bear, tearing his face off, with Kyle blaming it all on "that fruity little club, for scrambling his brains." Cartman suggests that Chef is not really dead; to the "club," he lives on as Darth Chef, and in the end, he wears a Darth Vader outfit being levitated into the sky. During the final credits the screen read: "Dedicated to Isaac Hayes."

South Park fans, meanwhile, threatened to boycott the show if it didn't repeat the episode, and Parker and Stone put it on YouTube, the show's website—drawing tons of hits—and in a London theater. Finally, on July 19, the episode was replayed and again four days later. In September it was included in the season's DVD release. At the August Emmy Awards, host Conan O'Brien opened the show with an animated mini-sequel skit with the Stan character. Clearly, the controversy did much for both sides. For Ike, though, it continued to be an embarrassment. He didn't say more about it, and no one ever solved the mystery of who had issued the memo in his name, even years later.

in 2016, when Isaac Hayes III addressed it, he had no idea, but insisted his father would never have been "that hypocritical" to quit because of Scientology-bashing while the show "poked fun at African-American people, Jewish people, gay people." He also was sure Ike "did not quit *South Park*; someone quit *South Park* for him. He was in no position to resign under his own knowledge. At the time, everybody around my father was involved in Scientology— his assistants, the core group of people. So someone quit *South Park* on Isaac Hayes' behalf. We don't know who."

IKE SLOWLY RECOVERED, resuming his daily workouts in his basement gym and riding a stationary bike in his bedroom. He re-learned the piano and trained his voice all over again, and, like Chef, who was dropped into the show in bit parts spouting recycled dialogue, Ike was hardly unseen. He was the most obvious candidate to be in the 2008 movie called *Soul Men*, the Stax legacy all over the tale of two old-time soul men, Samuel L. Jackson and Bernie Mac, driving cross country for a tribute concert for the recently deceased lead singer of their once-prominent group. Along the way they run into Ike, who sends up himself in a delicious self-portrait. However, even sadder than the movie's failure after its release in November was that the fifty-year-old Bernie Mac was dying of sarcoidosis, making the film a tribute to *him*. What no one knew, however, was that it would actually be a postmortem tribute to Isaac Hayes as well.

He began 2007 with a bevy of concerts, starting in Brooklyn's Prospect Park, then at the Rams Head in Baltimore, Virginia State University, and a long way off in Piraeus, Greece. In March, he was at the KBLX Stone Soul Concert in Hayward, California. The results were mixed; at some gigs blowing the roof off the sucker and at others unable to hit some notes and sitting, the whole time obviously fatigued. Doing radio interviews, he would fumble his words and speak incoherently, generating whispers that he seemed to be high—one radio host even suggesting this to him, his frazzled denial only fueling the speculation more.

More painful than any lingering effects of his stroke, though, was the blow of having to close the restaurant and nightclub. He had done so temporarily in 2003 but remodeled the place with a bigger dance floor and expensive lighting, but crowds fell off and he was bleeding red ink. On April 22, he cut the cord with a statement that said, "It's disappointing that the restaurant didn't work out. However, I would like to personally thank all the patrons who have supported the restaurant over these past years." That letdown would send him back on the road on an itinerary his doctor could not have approved. In July he went back across the pond for the Festival Cognac Blues Passions in France, and in 2008 his schedule was heavy, including summertime treks back and forth across the country, from Highland Park, Illinois to Brooklyn to Pittsburgh, then on July 3 the Waterfront Blues Festival in Portland.

He was back home for the rest of summer, planning more gigs, spending hours on the exercise bike. There was no halfway life for him. As always, he looked and believed that he was at his peak. The roomy house was normally filled with his children, enjoying the bonds he had never given much effort to in his prime. On Sunday, August 10, Adjowa had taken Nana Kwadjo shopping with her. Ike repaired to the bedroom to ride the bike. After a few minutes, he suddenly collapsed, landing in a seated position against the still-running bike. He lay there for about an hour when Adjowa, having returned, called out to him. When there was no response she went to the bedroom and gasped seeing him lifeless on the floor. Unable to rouse him, she called Shelby County police. Deputies arrived and they too could not revive him and called an ambulance. He was taken to Baptist Memorial Hospital where at 2:08 p.m. he was pronounced dead, ten days before his sixty-sixth birthday and one day after Bernie Mac had died. The cause of death was a second stroke.

The Soul Man had gone down on his terms, believing that nothing either inside him or outside him could break his predestined endurance. Lord knows he had proved that enough. And, in death, he would be remembered just that way.

As THE NEWS bled across the showbiz meridians, the Soulsville Foundation put out a statement saying, "We are in state of shock. Isaac is one of the most beloved members of the Stax family and we all cherish him." Condolences came in from the Stax soul men and women, the district's congressman Steve Cohen, and standouts from the entertainment circle. There was almost literally no end to those who had spent some time or another with him and came out better for it.

A public funeral was announced for Monday, August 18, at Memphis's Hope Presbyterian Church on Walnut Grove Road, but laying Isaac Hayes to rest would not be so easy to accommodate. The problem, once more, was the Scientology connection. That crowd had streamed in and pulled rank on Adjowa, who was technically a member, to hold a "private" service a day early, on Sunday, so that the church itself could have its own service without having to share any with Ike's meddlesome music cohorts. The seats on that day were filled with the likes of Tom Cruise, John Travolta's wife Kelly Preston, actress Anne Archer, piano great Chick Corea, trumpeter Mark Isham, and aging rapper Doug E. Fresh, but also Scientologist leaders David Miscavige and Tom Davis (Archer's son), who had written out speeches praising Scientology and Ike—in that order.

However, they had to share space at the Hope Church with some upper-case arrivals who *weren't* in the cult but dropped in, including not only Dave Porter, Al Bell, Eddie Floyd, Marvell Thomas, and Mable John, but also Denzel Washington, Wesley Snipes, Jesse Jackson, Al Sharpton, Bootsy Collins, Chuck D, Maurice White, Richard Roundtree, and John Singleton; all of whom were aghast at the pseudo-religion being tossed around the Presbyterian church as if dropped from pickup trucks. Indeed, the church's administrators were so horrified about hosting a Scientology event that they insisted the service be presided over not by a Scientology quack but by Ike's old Stax confrere William Bell. Even so, the ceremony, which the local papers called a "secret," was all but taken out of Bell's hands. The Rev. Alfreddie Johnson rose to tell an endless story of how he had recruited Ike into the cult, and the name L. Ron Hubbard was heard from the podium at least as much as Ike's. Roving cameramen filmed the proceedings for another of those Scientology training movies. As reported in one news story:

> *[N]o one bothered to sing an Isaac Hayes song or talk much about his music. Most of the offerings were about the speakers, with little light shined on the man they were honoring. The exception was a Ghanian woman named Princess Asie Oscansey, who described in lengthy detail the charitable contribution Hayes had made to her village to support an 8,000-square-foot school that uses Scientology teaching methods.*

Not only were there no Hayes songs, there was little discus-
sion of his movie career, barely a whisper about his famous
"Theme from Shaft," and not even a suggestion of his long,
funny career as Chef on "South Park."

The Scientology speakers and performers—there were seven
in all—made little reference to Hayes' 11 grown children, just to
his wife of three years and their 2-year-old son. This prompted
Hayes' eldest daughter, Veronica, who didn't get to speak until
nearly two and a half hours had passed, to declare, "Just to clear
it up, there are 11 children." Ouch!"

The non-Scientologists left confused and bitter that Ike's musical life had been treated like a trespasser—one of the papers calling the vibe "surreal." The Monday service was when the world said goodbye. Booker T. Jones had to take three plane flights to get there on time. Emotional performances by Aretha Franklin, Stevie Wonder, Sam Moore, and Dionne Warwick laid on hands for a man they called their friend above all. Then he was taken to Memorial Park Cemetery, where his grandmother Rushia Wade was buried, and he was lowered into the empty plot beside hers, in an open area where their graves were alone on a gently rising hill, Ike preceding by twelve years his sister Willette, who died in July 2020 at eighty. Dave Porter, offering a few words at the grave marker, said that Ike "would do things and say, 'We don't want you to say anything to anybody.' That happened for many many years. I could tell you some things that would blow your mind that Isaac Hayes did for many people." Al Bell said, "What they said couldn't be done, Isaac Hayes did. For all of that and the good and caring spirit that lived in him, today we bring roses for 'Black Moses.'" Then Nana Kwadjo placed a rose next to the grave.

Eulogies continued from all over the globe, all echoing the music journalist Chris Roberts' paean that "Isaac [was] a man possessed, [who] made epic, cinematic, novelistic, symphonies." His farewell appearance was posthumous, when *Soul Men* hit the screens, with the director Malcolm Lee having re-edited some of the rougher edges to soften the demeanor of both Ike and Bernie Mac. In truth, Isaac Hayes probably would have been pissed off by that revision. As he had lived all through his life, he all but screamed, or purred, that when he had to go, it would be as the cat who wouldn't cop out with danger all about. Life was his danger, and he lived it hard. With a smile, but hard.

HE CHECKED OUT with all the honors he could have had: an Oscar, a Grammy, a berth in the Hall of Fame, five BMI R&B awards, two BMI Pop awards, two BMI Urban awards, and six million air plays. He was honored by the Virginia House of Representatives for "invaluable contributions to the American culture." After his death, a section of Tennessee's I-40 was renamed the Isaac Hayes Memorial Highway, the dedication held at his grave site with Jacqueline, Dave Porter, and Memphis Mayor A C Wharton giving speeches. His daughters would be photographed in a newspaper story proudly holding his Oscar trophy.

But, being Ike, he also left a scab of never-ending financial tribulations. His Cordova mansion was in default; the *Memphis Daily News* noting that "It was not immediately known if Hayes' estate was in default on the loan following his death, or if the default preceded his passing," and that "His name is listed on the notice of foreclosure sale as 'Isaac Hayes, a/k/a Isaac Lee Hayes, Jr., Unmarried,'" raising the question of whether his marriage to Adjowa was somehow not legal or if someone simply made a mistake on the notice, not changing the status after the marriage. The property, which had been refinanced in 2003, was put up for auction in March 2009, and after being sold soon degenerated and mysteriously burned to the ground. None of which remotely mattered. His legend has carried on, with no spoilage, though a story rolled out in 2014 that a man named Earl Hayes, who had killed actress Stephanie Moseley and then himself, was reported to be Ike's son—but only until Heather Hayes corrected the error, tweeting that "my father had 11 children. Earl Hayes is not one of them. Please retract."

Shaft, of course, has never died. *Another* redo was spawned, *Shaft (2019)*, with the newest Black private dick, a gun-loving FBI analyst and the original Shaft's *grandson*, played by baby-faced Jessie T. Usher, with a bald, bearded Richard Roundtree and an also-bald Samuel L. Jackson in supporting roles. While intended to be what *Rolling Stone* pegged as "shamelessly regressive," the only regressive part is the still refreshingly original "Theme from Shaft" sounding as the closing scene number put all three Shafts together in matching brown suede jackets strolling not through Times Square but midtown—although this crowd-pleasing moment likely came far too late to save the film, which with a $35 million budget and distribution by Warner Bros. and Netflix, took sharp jabs from reviewers and only made back $21 million. Indeed, it was another use of the song, over the opening credits, sampled by Quavo and Saweetie in an unfortunate rap that spun it forward half a century, that put it all in perspective. It was called "Too Much Shaft," as opposed to Too Much Isaac Hayes.

Unlike any other performer of the last sixty years, his life story can be heard in every one of his grooves. It can be permanently gleaned in the last lines of one that tells us more than what the ghetto was in 1971 but also Isaac Hayes's fixed belief that the place he lifted on his shoulders, and on which it still rests, was still capable of healing the human condition, and delivering the peace neither of them never found: promising that "deep in their souls" those who heard and felt his embrace would at last be able to cast off "all this misery that they have here in Soulsville, Soulsville, Soulsville, Soulsville."

About the Author

Mark Ribowsky is the acclaimed author of more than thirty books on music, sports, and pop culture, his definitive biographies including those of Phil Spector, the Supremes, the Temptations, Stevie Wonder, Otis Redding, Lynyrd Skynyrd, James Taylor, Hank Williams, and Little Richard. His biography of Otis Redding was a finalist for the prestigious Marfield Prize. Some of his sports subjects include Al Davis, Satchel Paige, Howard Cosell, Tom Landry, Don Shula, the football Manning family, and a complete history of the Negro baseball leagues. He co-authored Dale Berra's *My Dad, Yogi*. He has also written major articles for *Playboy*, *Penthouse*, and *Sport*, and has appeared on Dateline NBC, Primetime Live, The Tavis Smiley Show, and numerous radio and Internet programs and documentaries.